SHAKESPEAREAN MEANINGS

Shakespearean Meanings

BY SIGURD BURCKHARDT

PRINCETON UNIVERSITY PRESS

PRINCETON, NEW JERSEY

MCMLXVIII

Library of Congress Catalog Number: 68-15765
Printed in the United States of America
by Princeton University Press
Princeton, New Jersey

FOREWORD

SHORTLY before he died, 15 December 1966, Sigurd Burckhardt drafted a Preface and a Table of Contents for this book. Insofar as the state of his papers allows, we have prepared the book for publication exactly as he planned it.

For an unwritten "Discourse on Method," which was to have been the second chapter, we have substituted "The Poet as Fool and Priest," the earliest of Burckhardt's published essays on Shakespeare and the one in which he had most to say about his "method." (He indicates in a note that for the "Discourse on Method" he planned to adapt an essay of his in German, "Zur Theorie der Werkimmanenten Deutung," which he had contributed to a *Festschrift* for his teacher and colleague, Bernhard Blume. We have put a translation of that essay in the appendix.) All but the fourth and sixth of the essays were either in print or in press at the time of his death. The fourth, "Shakespeare, Peele, and the King of the Scots," was in a penultimate holograph draft; it is the only one of the essays which has required much editing. The sixth, " 'Swoll'n with some other grief': Shakespeare's Prince Hal Trilogy," was in final typescript. An essay on *Hamlet* and *Julius Caesar* was not developed to a stage where Burckhardt was ready to publish it; accordingly, we have omitted it. He planned to conclude the book—as the argument of the first essay, "How Not to Murder Caesar," would demand—with an essay on *The Tempest*; this he did not live long enough to begin.

For permission to reprint the published essays, usually in slightly different form, we are grateful to the editors of *ELH, The Antioch Review, The Minnesota Review,* and *Modern Language Quarterly,* and to the publishers of the Blume *Festschrift,* Vandenhoeck and Ruprecht.

We wish to thank our colleague Thomas Dunseath for his editorial work on "Shakespeare, Peele, and the King of the Scots"; Anne Hohenemser for her translation of "Zur Theorie der Werkimmanenten Deutung" and E. D. Hirsch, Egon Schwarz, and Bernhard Blume for their help in putting it into a final version; and Alice Birney, Fredrick Dean Altizer, David Clayton, and Diane Darrow for their help in checking the text. Quotations from Shakespeare follow, according to Burckhardt's practice, the New Cambridge Edition, ed. W. T. Neilson and C. J. Hill (Boston 1942).

November 1967

ROBERT C. ELLIOTT
ROY HARVEY PEARCE

PREFACE

Almost nothing, these days, can justify the writing of a book about Shakespeare. Only what follows—both the pages and the (not impossible) reader's response—will tell whether I have slipped through the needle's eye of that "almost."

The title is intended as a warning: This book is concerned with what Shakespeare *meant.* I believe that Shakespeare's plays, to put it bluntly, have messages and that these messages are discoverable, in fact statable. I believe that when we read Shakespeare, we are—ultimately—reading his mind; the question is only how well or badly, how scrupulously or wilfully we go about reading it. Shakespeare not only abides our questions, he tells us what questions to ask; he took infinite pains to be precisely understood. I am convinced that he can be understood much more truly than he has been so far.

I am also convinced that to be understood he must be *read*—with attention to sometimes minute detail. There is an odd superstition abroad that nothing can be part of Shakespeare's intention that cannot be communicated directly across the footlights. First and foremost, we are told, he was a "man of the theatre"; the implication is that what we see when we see a play of his acted is the unmediated thing itself. Of course this is nonsense; what we see is an interpretation, derived (it is to be hoped) from a very careful reading of the text by the director and the actors. A large part of such an interpretation is subliminal; the stage action expresses it only by indirection. Unfortunately, this subliminal interpretation is often also undisciplined and irresponsible, dictated by vanity, desire for effect or novelty, misunderstanding, or even sheer ignorance. I have heard a respectable actor read Macbeth's "tomorrow" speech as though the first line—"She should have died hereafter"—meant: "I wish she had not died quite so soon." The interpretation was disastrous, but the point is that it *was* an interpretation—as is every inflection, every gesture, every choice of costume or scenery. Actors and directors have compelling reason to call on the advice of those who have the time and the patience to *read* Shakespeare, down to the minutest detail. (I am assuming, of course, that the aim is to present Shakespeare, not to use him as a vehicle.) The interpreters have nothing to be apologetic about, provided they have learned to read with care.

Which is not to say that *I* have nothing to be apologetic about. My reading of Shakespeare scholarship and criticism has been far from systematic; I cannot claim to be a professional. Shakespeare commentary has grown so vast that, in order to get on at all, I found I had to focus sharply on the text and be rather haphazard in my explorations of the secondary literature. It is more than probable that I have missed things I should have looked at; but I hope I have seen enough to make sure that the substance of what I say has not been said before.

Though generally my interpretations follow the chronology of Shakespeare's works, I have placed first an essay on *Julius Caesar,* because it illustrates the method of interpretation which I believe Shakespeare demands of us. I have placed next a theoretical account of that method, even though there are few things I find more fruitless than methodological discussions. A method can, and should, be justified solely by its results; but my unhappy experience is that purely methodological objections are often considered more important than substantive questions of interpretation. I have no intention of "justifying" my method; but I hope I can anticipate some *a priori* objections to it and prevent some misunderstandings of it. Readers who find themselves persuaded by the *Julius Caesar* essay may well wish to skip the next one.

I am conscious of many debts, and no doubt unaware of many more which I should be conscious of. Most of them remain unacknowledged; perhaps the paucity of footnotes and the absence of "apparatus" will be counted as compensating for this lack. I discovered that the effort to "bring in the scholarly literature" (even within the rather narrow limits of my knowledge of it) distorted my style in a way I thought unacceptable; hence I have, by and large, treated prior criticism as though it were public property. I shall be content to see my own criticism treated in the same way; I enter no proprietary claims. The true and sole owner, after all, is Shakespeare.

Debts of a more personal sort, however, do demand mention. I will not specify the debts but rather mention the creditors and thus pay myself under the guise of giving them their due: my wife Peggy; many colleagues, students, and friends, particularly Dieter Cunz, Bernhard Blume, Oskar Seidlin, George P. Elliott, Robert C. Elliott, Harry G. Frankfurt, Leonard Newmark, Roy Harvey Pearce, Earl Wasserman, and Andrew Wright; the Guggenheim Foundation, the Ohio State University, and the University of California; and Miriam Brokaw of the Princeton University Press.

SIGURD BURCKHARDT

TABLE OF CONTENTS

SHAKESPEAREAN MEANINGS

I

HOW NOT TO MURDER CÆSAR

I

IT HAS been true of Shakespeare critics—as it has been of others supposedly in pursuit of knowledge—that they have felt pretty free to speculate about what Shakespeare "was really like" or "really believed"—or even whether he was real at all—and then to interpret the plays to fit their speculations. As regards *Julius Caesar,* they have argued for better than a century and a half about its political meaning. There are what we may call the republican critics, who believe that Shakespeare's political sympathies are with Brutus, the republican idealist, who is defeated by the very nobility of his ideals. There are, on the other side, the monarchist critics, who cite authorities from Dante to Hooker to prove that Shakespeare's age considered Caesar the founder of the monarchical order in Rome, and Brutus, for all his fine speeches, as no better than a regicide, who is justly punished for his terrible crime. Still other critics try to find a compromise solution; and finally there are those—usually gentlemen of the theatre, with a no-nonsense attitude toward ideas—who are sure that Shakespeare didn't care one way or the other, as long as he came up with a play that filled the house and the cash box.

Another preconception about Shakespeare took root even in his own lifetime and grew so sturdy that today it is still hard to eradicate. I mean the notion that Shakespeare was a "natural genius," somehow directly in touch with the Muse, without the intervening benefit of a solid education. Hence, he wrote splendid poetry, to be sure, and had an unerring instinct for what goes on in men's souls, but he also, alas! committed some sad boners. Not that anyone is pedant enough to hold these boners against him. But still, there they are; and since a critic of this persuasion, though he may be a little short on genius, has at least got a degree from an institution of higher learning, he does note the boners and treats himself to a few moments of complacent condescension.

The striking clock in *Julius Caesar* is Shakespeare's most notorious boner. Everyone knew it for an anachronism—everyone, that is, except Shakespeare, who was out poaching and seducing Anne Hathaway when he should have been at school parsing his Latin. So it is that all annotated editions of the play carry a note to Act II, Scene I, line 192, duly explaining that Shakespeare erred at this point. What I propose to do is simply this: I shall assume that Shakespeare did know that he was committing an anachronism—and see what follows from this assumption.

One thing follows immediately: if he did know, he must have intended his readers—and most particularly his learned critics, i.e. those most certain to notice the anachronism—to be struck by it. And beyond that he must have expected his learned critics to divide into two groups: those who would promptly, in the assurance of their prior learning, charge him with an error, and those who would submit to the facts as given by him and say: "How odd! Let's see if we can discover what Shakespeare may have had in mind."

The latter group, instead of writing a condescending note, will start looking carefully, not just at the line in question, but for other instances of time-telling in the play. And they won't have far to look: the scene itself is rich in such instances. It is the so-called "Orchard

Scene." It opens with Brutus alone in his garden, late at night, talking to himself about his decision to join the conspiracy. A little later the conspirators enter, led by Cassius, and confer with Brutus on the details of the murder plan. But, throughout, the scene is punctuated with time references. In the very first line Brutus lets us know that he is unsure of the time of *day*:

> I cannot by the progress of the stars
> Give guess how near to day.
>
> (II, i, 2-3)

Forty lines later he shows himself equally unsure of the time of *month*:

> Is not tomorrow, boy, the first of March?[1]

and his servant boy has to inform him that he is off by a full fourteen days. Another forty lines, and Cassius enters with the conspirators. And now something odd happens: while Brutus and Cassius withdraw immediately to the background and confer in inaudible whispers, the secondary conspirators take the center of the stage and engage in a seemingly pointless dispute over the points of the compass, the point of the sun's rising, and the time of *year*. Only after some ten lines of this do Brutus and Cassius come forward, and the main business of planning the assassination is taken up. As soon as the plan is agreed on, the clock strikes three times and is carefully taken note of.

The mere facts of the matter prove design; clearly Shakespeare had something in mind. The time references progress from time of day to time of month to time of year; they are thrust into the foreground when much more important business is relegated to the background; and they all testify to confusion and uncertainty—until

[1] I have here restored the First Folio reading—thus amending the text I regularly follow.

the fateful decision has been made, when suddenly these groping guesses yield to the countable precision of a novel chronometric device. So the first result of my assumption has been the discovery of a design; the obvious next question—much more difficult, of course—is: what does the design signify?

Here we need to recall two historical circumstances, which Shakespeare and his audience had reason to be very concretely aware of. One is that Caesar's fame rested in good part on his institution of the Julian calendar. Plutarch—Shakespeare's source—praises this great reform and mentions it as one of the reasons why Caesar was hated: the Roman conservatives felt it to be an arbitrary and tyrannical interference with the course of nature. The second circumstance is that in 1582 Pope Gregory had decreed the reform of the Julian—that is to say, of the traditional Christian— calendar, which in the meantime had drifted almost ten days out of phase. This reform had immediately become an issue in the bitter politico-religious struggles of the age; the Catholic countries accepted it and so adopted the so-called "New Style," while the Protestant countries rejected it and clung to the "Old Style." Thus at the turn of the century—Shakespeare wrote *Julius Caesar* in 1599—a situation existed in Europe exactly analogous to that of Rome in 44 B.C. It was a time of confusion and uncertainty, when the most basic category by which men order their experience seemed to have become unstable and untrustworthy, subject to arbitrary political manipulation.

With these facts in mind, we return to the Orchard Scene. The scene's core is the planning of the conspiracy. Three proposals are made and, on Brutus' insistence, rejected; the third of these is to kill Mark Antony along with Caesar. The rejection—which, of course, soon proves to be a fatal mistake—is based, not so much on grounds of expediency or even morality, but on grounds of *style*. Indeed, under Brutus' influence the planning generally becomes a stylistic question. The plot as such is already decided on, the actors are chosen, the parts in the main assigned; but what still needs to be determined, at least in Brutus' view, is the style in which the action is to be carried out. And on this he has firm opinions; Antony must be spared because otherwise

> Our course will seem too bloody, Caius Cassius,
> To cut the head off and then hack the limbs,
> Like wrath in death and envy afterwards . . .
> Let's be sacrificers, but not butchers, Caius . . .
> Let's kill him boldly, but not wrathfully;
> Let's carve him as a dish fit for the gods,
> Not hew him as a carcass fit for hounds . . .
> This shall make
> Our purpose necessary and not envious;
> Which so appearing to the common eyes,
> We shall be call'd purgers, not murderers.
> (II, i, 162-80)

And later, when it is a question of whether or not to let Antony speak, Brutus repeats:

> Though now we must appear bloody and cruel,
> As by our hands and this our present act
> You see we do, yet see you but our hands
> And this the bleeding business they have done.
> Our hearts you see not; they are pitiful;
> And pity to the general wrong of Rome—
> As fire drives out fire, so pity pity—
> Hath done this deed on Caesar.
> (III, i, 165-72)

In speaking of the conspiracy I have slipped into the metaphor of the drama: I have talked of plot, action, actors, and style. There is ample warrant for the use of this metaphor in the play itself; Brutus and Cassius employ it repeatedly—most explicitly right after the murder, when in fact it ceases to be a metaphor:

> How many ages hence
> Shall this our lofty scene be acted over
> In states unborn and accents yet unknown!
> (III, i, 111-13)

Let us think of Cassius and Brutus as manifestly they think of themselves: plotters in the dramatic sense, men who have decided to author and produce a tragedy entitled "Julius Caesar." Really it is Cassius who has had the idea for the plot; but he feels the need of a co-author —Brutus—to give the production the kind of prestige and styling that will make it a hit with the audience, the Roman populace. Somewhat to Cassius' distress, Brutus takes his function very seriously and overrules his partner on a number of points which later turn out to be crucial. Evidently we must look a little more closely at the style Brutus has in mind.

What he wants is not a bare assassination, but a tragedy of classical, almost Aristotelian, purity. There is to be no wholesale slaughter, with the curtain coming down, as in *Hamlet*, on a heap of corpses. Only the tragic hero is to be killed, and the killing itself is to be a ritual, a sacrifice, formal and even beautiful. Nor is there to be any unseemly vilification: the victim is to be presented, not as a villain like Claudius of Denmark, but as a great and noble man, who falls because he has one tragic flaw: ambition. And his killers, the authors, must not act from personal motives; they must be as priests and physicians, performing their solemn duty of purging the commonwealth. Everything Brutus says and does—most particularly his permitting Antony to speak and his own speech in justification of his act—is informed by this determination to make the tragedy a classical one: noble, purgative, impersonal, inevitable.

He is only too successful. The classical style has disastrous consequences, because Brutus is utterly mistaken about the audience for whom the tragedy is intended. He is thinking of an audience of noble, sturdy republicans, capable of the moral discrimination and public spirit which classical tragedy demands. But *we* know from the opening scenes that the actual audience is very different: eager to be led, easily tricked, crude in their responses. The people insist on having their good guy and their bad guy; they are perfectly ready to accept Brutus as their good guy, provided he lets them have Caesar for their bad guy. But this, Brutus' ideal of style forbids. Brutus is most irretrievably damned, not when the mob is ready to stone him, but when it acclaims him: "Let him be Caesar!" Nothing shows so clearly as this shout of applause how totally the audience has missed Brutus' point, and how totally Brutus has misjudged his audience.

That is why Shakespeare makes the clock strike at the very moment when Brutus has persuaded the conspirators to adopt the classical style for their performance. The political point of the play is not that the monarchical principle is superior to the republican—nor the reverse—but that the form of government, the style of politics, must take account of the time and the temper of the people, just as the dramatist's style must. Brutus is not guilty of treachery, nor of having embraced an inherently wrong political philosophy; he is guilty of an anachronism. The clock, striking as soon as he has irrevocably committed himself to the Old Style, signifies to us—though not to him—that time is now reckoned in a new, Caesarean style.

There were in Shakespeare's day, as there are always, those who retreated from a confused and turbulent present to older forms, older certainties. In literature they preached the return to the great classical models, on their knowledge of which they naturally prided themselves, and in the name of which they felt confident they could judge their own day. Ben Jonson, Shakespeare's contemporary and competitor, was of this faction. With an irony so gentle that it is almost a salute, Shakespeare shows not only the fate of such retreats but the way to diagnose them. The striking clock is not only a metaphor; it is a touchstone. Proud classicists, sure of their learning, will mark it as evidence that Shakespeare had, in Ben Jonson's words, "small Latin and less Greek." But in the very act of doing so they betray their blindness, their refusal fully to surrender to the actually *given*—in this case to the carefully wrought pattern of time references by which Shakespeare defines the precise meaning of his anachronism. Instead of first submitting to the present, the given, and trying to discover its inner structure and meaning, they judge and condemn it by preestablished standards. And so they are blind not only to the present but even to the past they know so well.

Very few of us have read Ben Jonson's Roman tragedies. And probably none of us has seen them performed; they have long since vanished from the stage and into the stacks. On the other hand, most of us have read *Julius Caesar*; most of us have seen it—or at least had the opportunity to see it; and all of us have, at some time or other, quoted phrases from it. If we ever have occasion to look at an edition of Ben Jonson's *Catiline* or *Sejanus*, we find the margins covered with references—supplied by Jonson himself—to his classical sources. Every line is buttressed with classical authority; one would have to be very learned indeed to catch Jonson in an anachronism. The only trouble is that the plays in their entirety are anachronisms—while Shakespeare's work is as alive as ever. Why? Not because Jonson was the lesser "creative genius," in the vague, inspirational sense in which that term is commonly understood; but because, though he knew very well that no clock ever struck in ancient Rome, he did not know what the clock had struck in his own day. Hence, while *Sejanus* gathers dust on library shelves, Caesar's death and Brutus' fall, as Shakespeare has taught us to see them, and as he confidently predicted, are acted over in states unborn and accents yet unknown.

That is the point of his anachronism—precisely defined, exactly calculated, and placed with shrewd irony so that it would serve as an acid test for his critics. It proves, not his ignorance, but his incredible capacity for laying himself open to the tumultuous realities of his age and situation and experience—and his extraordinary ability to penetrate them and embody them in metaphors so true, so carefully wrought, that they have remained valid ever since. We often hear it said that Shakespeare still lives because he had the genius to penetrate beneath the temporary and superficial to what is permanently and immutably true. But this, though perhaps not wrong, is a dangerously misleading way of stating the case. It is the classicists, the Brutuses, who believe they are in possession of the eternal verities; and we have seen what happens to them. Shakespeare knew that the truths that last are painfully purchased by those who without reserve expose themselves to reality in all its confusion and still preserve within it the will to order, the will to form.

It's not so difficult to kill Caesar, to kill the ruler; once you get close enough, a bare bodkin will serve.

Like Hamlet, one could do it pat. What *is* difficult is to discover how to kill him. For however corrupt, however tyrannical the ruler may be, he does, as of that moment, represent what order there is; do away with him, and you do away with order. That is why the style of killing Caesar is of such importance; the style must embody the vision of order—presumably better, truer, stabler—that will take the place of the order embodied in Caesar. And because that style is necessarily an embodiment, an incarnation of vision in the flesh-and-blood realities and corporealities of the moment, it stands under the judgment of those realities and of that moment.

II

There is a line by Emily Dickinson which catches, better than anything else I know, the essence of what we loosely call the "creative experience," which I take to mean the experience of anyone—artist, scientist, scholar, statesman, philosopher—who tries to create shapes truer than those existing. The line reads: "After great pain a formal feeling comes." What sets the great creators apart from ordinary men is not so much the capacity for inspiration, for vision—though of course these too play a part—as the ability to sustain, often for a long time and without letup, the pain of disorder. Aware of the inadequacy, the falsity, the injustice of the existing orders, the creator must wish to demolish them—that is what it means to murder Caesar—without as yet knowing what orders will take their place; he must suffer the confrontation with an unstructured reality—a reality that refuses, in its chaotic multiplicity, to yield to man's need of form, of intelligible shape. Modern critics often speak of creative tension; in the last analysis, I believe, this is the tension between the surrender to the raw substance of experience, the given, and the will to order. Brutus is aware of this tension and has felt this pain:

> Since Cassius first did whet me against Caesar,
> I have not slept.
> Between the acting of a dreadful thing
> And the first motion, all the interim is
> Like a phantasma or a hideous dream.
>
> (II, i, 61-65)

But he cannot sustain the pain long enough to forge a new style, a new mode of order. To gain the blessed release of the "formal feeling," he flees to an old style. Judged in terms of beauty, of purity and nobility, there is no fault to be found with this style. Listen to Brutus rejecting the proposal that the conspirators bind themselves by an oath:

> No, not an oath! . . .
> What need we any spur but our own cause
> To prick us to redress? What other bond
> Than secret Romans, that have spoke the word
> And will not palter? and what other oath
> Than honesty to honesty engag'd
> That this shall be, or we will fall for it? . . .
> Do not stain
> The even virtue of our enterprise . . .
> To think that or our cause or our performance
> Did need an oath; when every drop of blood
> That every Roman bears, and nobly bears,
> Is guilty of a several bastardy
> If he do break the smallest particle
> Of any promise that hath pass'd from him.
>
> (II, i, 114-40)

Even in Shakespeare's own work we will search a long time before we find another speech of such purity: so free of all verbal and metaphorical trickery, so simple, and yet so nobly eloquent. And if we compare these lines to those of Hamlet when the Prince makes his comrades swear—not just once but three times over—not to divulge what they have seen, we have some measure of the sheer beauty of the form Brutus retreats to.

But it is a retreat all the same; the pain has not been great enough, nor deep enough. This is the pain Hamlet suffers and breaks under and finally hands on to his friend Horatio as his bitter legacy:

> Absent thee from felicity a while
> And in this harsh world draw thy breath in pain
> To tell my story. (v, ii, 358-60)

In fact, Hamlet is the exact counterpart to Brutus. Like Brutus he accepts the task to kill the ruler, to fashion a tragedy; and like Brutus he botches the job. But he botches it for the opposite reason; instead of settling too quickly for a ready-made form, he despairs of the very possibility of form. The corruption of the world he is supposed to purge enters into his very soul, so that he spends his energy probing the infection, in himself as well as in everyone about him. He is so overwhelmed by his discovery of monstrous disorder that his great enterprise loses, in his words, "the name of action," and the initiative passes to the king. Unlike Brutus, he knows only too well that the clock has struck upon the old style:

> The time is out of joint;—O cursed spite
> That ever I was born to set it right!
> (I, v, 189-90)

But he sees, from the depth of his loathing and self-loathing, no possibility of forging a new style, of passing through the great pain to a formal feeling, a truer, more valid shaping of reality. In the end he settles for a stoic resignation which is moving and impressive, but which nevertheless signifies an abdication from his task to discover a new order:

> If it be now, 'tis not to come; if it be not to come, it will be now; if it be not now, yet it will come: the readiness is all. (v, ii, 31-34)

For in the meantime there are corpses lying about of people—most tragically Ophelia—who might have lived but for his inability to rise above his pain.

A tragedy—to define it very simply—is a *killing poem*; it is designed toward the end of bringing a man to some sort of destruction. And the killer is, quite literally, the poet; it is he, and no one else, who devises the deadly plot; it is he, therefore, who must in some sense accept responsibility for it. Even if the events of the plot are drawn from history—as with *Julius Caesar* they obviously are—what is the poet's purpose in reenacting them and shaping them as he does, at that particular time and place? Why does he not leave history to the historians? Why, and how, does he represent as a living reality what is, or seems to be, a dead past? In other words, what is he, the plotter, *doing* when he has Caesar killed?

These questions are not simply speculative. It is always true that a poem—especially a dramatic poem—is an act, not just a report; but this truth used to be felt more concretely in Shakespeare's day than it is in ours. When the Essex faction was preparing an armed uprising in 1601, they induced Shakespeare's company to put on a performance of *Richard II*, to serve as a prelude to the revolt. And after the uprising had collapsed, Shakespeare and his colleagues were summoned by the authorities to be questioned about their possible implication in the plot. Queen Elizabeth knew very well that the plotting of playwrights and that of rebels may have more in common than merely the name: "I am Richard II, know ye not that?" I am not suggesting that anyone producing a play by Bertolt Brecht should be subpoenaed to testify before the Un-American Activities Committee. But I am suggesting that Shakespeare had pressingly concrete reasons to know that when he was plotting a tragedy—even a historical tragedy—he was not just retelling a story in dramatic form; he was committing an act—the action of his play—in the full moral and social sense of the word "act."

Not that he needed the reminder; he was poet enough—proud poet enough—to claim the responsibility he incurred by this kind of action. That is why, in so many of his plays, he has a part for himself as *deviser of the plot*, and why again and again he probes the problem: what am I doing when I invent, or reinvent, a mechanism designed to bring about a man's destruction? In the name of what, for the sake of what, do I do this? And even assuming the necessity of doing it, how well do I do it? Is my aim so sure that there is no unnecessary killing, or is it so uncertain that all Italy is plunged into civil war, or that Ophelia and Gertrude, Polonius and Laertes, Rosencrantz and Guildenstern, must die along with the king?

III

It may be, of course, that the tragic poet does not worry about this kind of accountability, but takes the position that after all he is only the poet, trying to write as perfect a tragedy as he knows how. This role also Shakespeare watched himself playing and wrote into a play. His "perfect tragedy," in this sense of the term, is *Othello*, by general agreement the most flawlessly structured of all his tragedies. In it he devises a plot so beautifully tooled, so accurately deadly, that, once set going, it seems of its own momentum to bring about the destruction for which it is designed. But into it he writes his own part as the deviser of a perfect tragedy—and the part is Iago's. Iago it is who composes the tragedy called "Othello"; he stands at the footlights and tells us, step by step, how he shapes it, from the first most general idea through the overall scheme down to the specific devices of plotting. And beyond that he lets us share the keen joy of mastery, of subtle skill and power, that he derives from this enterprise. If Othello is a great tragedy and not just a perfect one, this self-portrait of the "pure" tragic poet is the reason. The play shows what manner of man he is who creates art for art's sake, or at least tragedy for tragedy's sake.

This kind of tragedy was real enough for Shakespeare to have done it once, in full awareness of what he was doing; but it was not, on the whole, his kind. He admits, in Iago, to the sense of triumph which every craftsman is bound to feel when he fashions a perfect instrument, no matter what the ultimate end. But the triumph is sterile. None of Shakespeare's plotters—not even the well-intentioned ones—are presented as fathers; Brutus and Hamlet as well as Macbeth and Richard III are childless. But the most childless of all, if so illogical a superlative is permitted—the man whom we cannot even imagine as being a father, the way we *can* imagine Brutus and do imagine Macbeth—is Iago. There is, as it were, no blood in him—hardly even that which boils with hatred or is fired by ambition. He is a perfect craftsman.

Permit me, at this point, a brief parenthetical digression. I cannot think of any more devastating revelation of how we today feel and see reality than the fact that we accept—without revulsion and even without a sense of incongruity—a metaphor such as "father of the H-bomb." It is not the H-bomb as such that I have in mind, terrifying though it is. Mankind has always invested a good part of its ingenuity in devising more perfect engines of destruction. But I doubt that any previous age has called the devisers of such engines by the name of "father." "Father of poison gas," "father of the machine gun," "father of the electric chair"—these, it seems to me, would have been impossible. The mere phrase "father of the H-bomb" betrays more of what we truly are than a thousand pages of the Congressional Record can conceal. For we speak the truth about ourselves, not in our pious sentiments, but in the metaphors we find for them.

It was not, I am convinced, Shakespeare's ambition to write perfect tragedies; my guess is that the very term would have made him shudder, as Iago makes us shudder. It is no mere paradox to say that Shakespeare wrote great tragedies because he thought it monstrous to think of them as perfect. Murder is, at best, a bleeding or strangling business; we are dangerously deceived if we believe that it can be styled into beauty. That is Brutus' illusion. True, he does not enjoy his work, as Iago does; he feels driven to it in the service of a higher cause. So, for that matter, does Othello, another sacrificial killer who thinks he must and can purge the world and goes about his work with noble pity. But Othello is never so deluded as when he is most priestly; and Brutus, after his fine words about not being a butcher and not hewing Caesar as a carcass fit for hounds, stands on the stage, his arms bloody to the elbows and at his feet Caesar's pitifully mangled carcass.

The eighteenth century felt squeamish about Shakespeare's tragedies and preferred to pretty them up a little —especially *King Lear*, the end of which was rewritten so that Cordelia was saved to marry Edgar and live happily ever after. Today we smile condescendingly at such prettifying; we pride ourselves on being able to take our Shakespeare straight. But I am not at all sure that this pride is in Shakespeare's spirit. I think he meant the end of *King Lear* to be as Samuel Johnson found it: unbearable.

We take our Shakespeare straight; but our critics supply us with chasers. There are various comforting theories about the nature of tragedy—theories which sound disconcertingly like those of Brutus and Othello. A tragedy, we are told, is a kind of sacrifice brought to purge the world of some disorder and restore it to its natural harmony. To be sure, we pity the victim; we feel terror at the price that has to be paid for the restoring of order. But in the end we feel rather as Brutus does:

> And pity for the general wrong of Rome
> As fire drives out fire, so pity pity—
> Hath done this deed on Caesar.

It is this comforting theory that the clock tolls into an irrecoverable past. For it rests on a no longer tenable faith in an underlying universal order—an order that may be temporarily disturbed but can, by the proper purgatives properly administered, be reestablished. This faith Shakespeare felt compelled to abandon. Measured by Caesar's time, the Caesarean system is not a general wrong but a true order, however it may look measured by another time. The natural order cannot be known, or at least not be known certainly enough to legitimize the murder of Caesar in the classical style. Once the time is out of joint, sacrificial tragedy is no longer possible—or rather, it is an illusion by which we deceive ourselves, if not about our motives, at least about the consequences of our action.

All this is not to say that Shakespeare gave up the

quest for order and subsided into a flaccid relativism. Rather, he found that he had to accept undiminished responsibility for his failures to create order—for his tragedies, in other words. Order, for him, was not something that needed only to be restored; it had to be continually created. And the great metaphor for his vision of order is not something grand and cosmic like the harmony of the spheres or the chain of being; it is something modest, earthly, human—marriage. He does see his function as that of a priest—only not the sacrificial priest who protests that the victim must have, like Caesar, "all true rites and lawful ceremonies," but the priest performing the sacrament of marriage. What he has to learn is the true rite of this sacrament—the words which will make the marriage of true minds truly binding, stable and fruitful. There are fearful impediments to this kind of marriage; and once Shakespeare can no longer refuse to admit these—as he still does in his famous sonnet—he engages in a series of fierce attempts to remove them. These attempts are his tragedies, ending in separation, death—failure. But they are all directed toward the same ultimate end: the creation of new order, new unions. And being that, they are redeemed, in retrospect, as necessary steps, necessary failures. In *The Tempest,* Shakespeare as Prospero shows us how all the chaos and turbulence, the separation and loss and grief and madness, were but means to the one true end: the joining of two young people who would, except for the tempest, have remained apart. When all is said and done, the poet's job has been to learn, as Shakespeare puts it in his twenty-third sonnet, "the perfect ceremony of love's rite"—not of murder, not of sacrifice, but of marriage:

> As an unperfect actor on the stage
> Who with his fear is put besides his part,

Or some fierce thing replete with too much rage,
Whose strength's abundance weakens his own heart,
So I, for fear of trust, forget to say
The perfect ceremony of love's rite,
And in mine own love's strength seem to decay,
O'ercharg'd with burden of mine own love's might.
O, let my books be then the eloquence
And dumb presagers of my speaking breast,
Who plead for love and look for recompense
More than that tongue that more hath more express'd.
O, learn to read what silent love hath writ:
To hear with eyes belongs to love's fine wit.

II

THE POET AS FOOL AND PRIEST

A DISCOURSE ON METHOD

> FESTE: But, indeed, words are very rascals since bonds disgraced them.
> VIOLA: Thy reason, man?
> FESTE: Troth, sir, I can yield you none without words; and words are grown so false, I am loath to prove reason with them.
> (*Twelfth Night*, III, 1, 23-29)

WE KNOW of Goethe that he was prompted to resume work on his "tragedy of the poet"—*Torquato Tasso*—while he was modeling a foot in a sculptor's studio in Rome. Following this evidently potent impulse, he recast the unfinished play into blank verse and painfully completed it, with what he called "scarcely justifiable transfusions of my own blood." What the connection was between modeling and the decision to take up again a long abandoned and extraordinarily difficult project, he did not say; but perhaps one may speculate. While his hands shaped the formless, malleable clay, may he not have wondered about the radical and dismaying difference between the sculptor's medium and his own: between clay—or marble, pigment, tones—and words?

For the difference is radical. All other artists have for their medium what Aristotle called a material cause: more or less shapeless, always meaningless, matter, upon which they can imprint form and meaning. Their media become media proper only under their hands; through shaping they communicate. As artists they are uniquely sovereign, minting unminted bullion into currency, stamping their image upon it. The poet is denied this creative sovereignty. His "material cause" is a medium before he starts to fashion it; he must deal in an already current and largely defaced coinage. In fact it is not even a coinage, but rather a paper currency. Words, as the poet finds them, are tokens for "real" things, which they are supposed to signify—drafts upon a hoard of reality which it would be too cumbersome to put into circulation. Not merely is the poet denied the creative privilege of coining his own medium; his medium lacks all corporeality, is a system of signs which have only a secondary, referential substance.

A painter paints a tree or a triangle—and there it is. He may be representational, but he need not; whether he paints trees or triangles, they are corporeally there for us to respond to. There can be no nonrepresentational poetry; the very medium forbids. MacLeish's "A poem should not mean but be" points to an important truth; but as it stands it is nonsense, because the medium of poetry is unlike any other. Words must mean; if they don't they are gibberish. The painter's tree *is* an image; but if the poet writes "tree," he does not create an image. He *uses* one; the poetic "image" is one only in a metaphorical sense. Actually it is something that evokes an image, a sign pointing to a certain preestablished configuration in our visual memory. The man who first "imagined" a unicorn could paint it; the poet could use the word only after the image had been created and seen (or else he would have had to describe it, i.e., to establish it as a composite of other preexistent images). The so-called poetic image achieves its effect only by denying its essence; it *is* a word, but it functions by making us aware of something other than it is. If many key terms of literary analysis—"color," "texture," and "image," for example—are in fact metaphors borrowed from the other arts, this is the reason: poetry has no material cause. Words already have what the artist first wants to give them—meaning—and fatally lack what he needs in order to shape them—body.

I propose that the nature and primary function of the most important poetic devices—especially rhyme, meter, and metaphor—is to release words in some measure from their bondage to meaning, their purely referential role, and to give or restore to them the corporeality which a true medium needs. To attain the position of creative sovereignty over matter, the poet must first of all reduce language to something resembling a material. He can never do so completely, only proximately. But he can—and that is his first task—drive a wedge between words and their meanings, lessen as much as possible their designatory force and thereby inhibit our all too ready flight from them to the things they point to. Briefly put, the function of poetic devices is dissociative, or divestive.

The pun is one—I would say the second most primitive—way of divesting a word of its meaning. Where writers find so primitive a method especially appealing, we may suspect that they feel the need to create a true medium, and so to rebel against a token language, with particular intensity. When Shakespeare concludes his 138th sonnet, which explores the very complicated inversions of truth and falsehood between him and his mistress, with the couplet:

> Therefore I lie with her and she with me,
> And in our faults by lies we flattered be,

the pun is more than a joke, however bitter. It is the creation of a semantic identity between words whose phonetic identity is, for ordinary language, the merest coincidence. That is to say, it is an act of verbal violence, designed to tear the close bond between a word and its meaning. It asserts that mere phonetic—i.e., material, corporeal—likeness establishes likeness of meaning. The pun gives the word as entity primacy over the word as sign.

In doing so it gives the lie direct to the social convention that is language. Punning fell into disrepute in the eighteenth century and has only recently recovered its poetic respectability. Is not perhaps the reason that it is, by its very directness, revolutionary and anarchic? It denies the meaningfulness of words and so calls into question the genuineness of the linguistic currency on which the social order depends. It makes us aware that words may be counterfeits. When Adam asked Eve why she called that huge, flap-eared, trunk-nosed beast an elephant, she is said to have answered: "Because it *looks* like one." Somehow, insofar as we are good, law-abiding linguistic citizens, we all share this feeling of our common mother: that there is an inherent propriety in the sounds we make, a preestablished harmony between them and the things they designate. The pun shatters it. In an age which was determined to create and affirm a purely human order, to awaken and strengthen in men a sense of the fitness of things here and now—in such an age it was scarcely an accident that the no-nonsense critic Dennis classed punsters with pickpockets, and the gentle Addison was "desirous to get out of [their] world of magic, which had almost turned my brain" (*Spectator* 63). The covertly rebellious Pope was partial to the pun's tamer brother, the zeugma; and Swift, anarchic idealist *malgré soi,* remained a privately passionate practitioner of this kind of subversion.

But the dilemma which the pun seeks to solve by violence confronts all poets; in a sense all poetic devices are more civilized forms of punning. That rhymes are partial puns is obvious. It is not often that they do their dissociative business as perfectly as at times with Pope:

> Receive, great Empress! thy accomplished Son:
> Thine from the birth, and sacred from the rod,
> A dauntless infant! never scared with God.
>
> (*Dunciad* IV)

where, interacting with "Son" and "sacred" (and its impious anagram "scared"), the words "rod" and "God" create the blasphemous identity schoolmaster's birchrod = Holy Cross. But at least rhymes do one thing: they call attention to the purely sonant nature of words. Though they rarely shatter the unity of sound and meaning, as the pun does, they aid the poet in weighting the balance on the side of sound and thus giving the words body, which simply as signs they lack. To the degree that rhyme becomes a virtually mandatory convention of poetry, it necessarily loses a great deal of this force; the poet may then—as G. M. Hopkins does almost systematically—revitalize it by using it where it is not conventionally expected and so discounted: internally. But even in its faded form it serves its purpose.

Metaphors act analogously. When Octavius Caesar says of Antony and Cleopatra: "No grave upon the earth shall clip in it a pair so famous," he is doing more than comparing two disparate things. By saying "clip" he makes of the grave a nuptial bed and beyond that of the bed one of the partners to the nuptials. As the bridegroom clips the bride, so the grave will embrace the now finally united and inseparable pair. In this way analysis transforms the metaphor into a conceptual simile, but the word "clip" does not invite comparison; rather it fuses separate and distinct meanings into a new verbal identity, a trinity. And thereby it does something also to language. A grave which is likewise a bed and a bridegroom is, in fact, no longer a grave; neither are a pair of bodies corpses, who are at the same time a bride. The metaphor does not only fuse, it dissociates words from their meanings.

Ideally the language of social intercourse should be as windowglass; we should not notice that it stands between us and the meanings "behind" it. But when chemists recently developed a plastic coating which made the glass it was spread on fully invisible, the results were far from satisfactory: people bumped into the glass. If there were a language pure enough to transmit all human experience without distortion, there would be no need for poetry. But such a language not only does not, it cannot, exist. Language can no more do justice to all human truth than law can to all human wishes. In its very nature as a social instrument it must be a convention, must arbitrarily order the chaos of experiences, allowing expression to some, denying it to others. It must provide common denominators, and so it necessarily falsifies, just as the law necessarily inflicts injustice. And these falsifications will be the more dangerous, the more "transparent" language seems to become, the more unquestioningly it is accepted as an undistorting medium. It is not windowglass, but rather a system of lenses which focus and refract the rays of an hypothetical unmediated vision. The first purpose of poetic language, and of metaphors in particular, is the very opposite of making language more transparent. Metaphors increase our awareness of the distortions of language by increasing the thickness and curvature of the lenses and so exaggerating the angles of refraction. They shake us loose from the comfortable conviction that a grave is a grave is a grave. They are semantic puns, just as puns are phonetic metaphors; though they leave words as sounds intact, they break their semantic identity.

Metaphors, then, like puns and rhyme, corporealize language, because any device which interposes itself between words and their supposedly simple meanings calls attention to the words as things. Meter has the same function; it is most like rhyme in that it also is a conventional means of stressing the purely phonetic matter which words without meanings are. It does not merely establish a mood; that can be done in thousands of other ways. If it serves to channel the chaotic emotions of the poet into a manageable flow, that has nothing to do with us as readers or listeners. Insofar as it becomes, like rhyme, a binding convention of poetry, it loses its dissociative force; and so it is used by poets like, again, Hopkins in a special way. What internal rhyme does in a conventionally rhyming poetry, syncopated rhythms do in a prosody which conventionally demands a regular beat; Hopkins' "sprung rhythm" is the exact metrical analogue to his internal rhyme. But even in less systematically syncopated poetry the counterpoint of metrical and speech rhythms results in a dissociation. Since the words of a poem function simultaneously in two rhythmic systems, they belong fully to neither, just as the metaphorical word and the pun belong fully to neither of the two semantic systems they fuse.

Primarily all these devices do what the sea does in the song from *The Tempest*:

> Full fathom five thy father lies;
> Of his bones are corals made;
> Those are pearls that were his eyes:
> Nothing of him that doth fade
> But doth suffer a sea-change
> Into something rich and strange.

Sea-nymphs hourly ring his knell:
Burthen: ding dong
Hear! now I hear them,—ding-dong bell.

These lines state so perfectly what poetry does to ordinary language that one can hardly resist reading them allegorically; as the play is the poet-magician's testament to the world, so this song is the glance he grants us into his "bag of tricks." The word, which in prose fades into a sign, yielding its original invocative power to the thing which, by having named, it has in a manner created—the word is transformed into something rich and strange by poetry. But to become rich it must first become strange. Bones and eyes—purely functional things in the living organism—no sooner are divorced from it than they become macabre and grotesque. Yet if the poet allows his words no more than their functional identity in the body of the "living language," he surrenders his sovereignty as an artist; he creates nothing, says nothing that is true beyond the partial and distorted truths this language has seen fit to grant us. He must tear the words out of their living matrix, so that they may not merely mean, but be. Perhaps I did Gertrude Stein an injustice just now when I paraphrased her to instance the comfortable conviction that words are of course what they mean, neither more nor less. For an even more primitive way than punning to strip words of their meanings is repetition. Say "a rose is a rose is a rose" a few more times, and what you have is a meaningless sound, because you have torn the word out of its living linguistic matrix and so are left with nothing but a vile phonetic jelly. This first step toward becoming poets we all can take, even if we are not clever enough to think of puns. And again it is often the greatest poets who avail themselves of repetition:

They that have power to hurt and will do none,
That do not do the thing they most do show.

So Shakespeare opens his 94th sonnet. The fourfold repetition of *do* is of course not clumsiness; Shakespeare takes this seemingly most transparent, most purely functional, of words and makes it gain body by repetition. A word we have been accustomed to look through as a mere auxiliary and expletive, having not even the referential substantiality of a proper verb or noun, becomes something in its own right, a dimension of existence, by repetition; so that when we read at the end: "For sweetest things turn sourest by their *deeds*," we are prepared for the frightening force of the act merely as act. And if here repetition is used to give a "meaningless" word meaning, the fact nowise invalidates my argument, but rather enforces it; it is precisely the initial meaninglessness which makes this kind of change possible. Where there is a meaning already, as in:

So shalt thou feed on death, that feeds on men,
And death once dead, there's no more dying then.
(*Sonnet* 146)

the effect is, initially at least, the opposite (though basically the same): the word "death" and its derivatives come close to losing their signatory force. Repetition—and it would be easy to cite instances from other poets, especially those of the seventeenth century and of our time—makes the word malleable, ready to take the imprint the poet wants to give it. It might not be bad pedagogy, in a course devoted to the teaching of poetry, to make the student repeat a poem's key words over and over, until they lose all semblance of meaning. He may then get a sense of what is the essence of poetry: the making such a vile jelly into a pearl.

What I have said of words holds true also of their combinations and relations: phrases and syntactical patterns. Empson has called attention to the frequency and efficacy of syntactical ambiguities; I need only to add that through them the meanings of syntactical relations are again called into question. A word which can function simultaneously as two or more different parts of speech, a phrase which can be parsed in two or more ways—to the despair of all teachers of grammar—simply extends the pervasive incertitude of poetry from words to their connections into statements. And inversions and similar poetic "licenses" are after all not merely allowances made to compensate for the self-imposed handicaps of rhyme and meter—as though the poet were a golfer who engages to use only one hand if we allow him two extra strokes on every hole. They tend to become that, it is true; but it is just this tendency of theirs which causes the periodic rebellions against them and everything that bears the stigma of "poetic diction." For poetic words and phrasings are not exempt from the fading process which bleaches ordinary language; they soon come to be felt as having an inherent "poeticalness," which relieves the poet of the responsibility to make them strange. They too acquire a designatory function; only instead of meaning a thing or relation of things they mean: "This is poetry." It is not surprising, therefore, that poets often feel impelled to do the very opposite of what, by my analysis, they ought to be doing—that they use the phrasings of the most ordinary speech and reject the built-in dissociations of "elevated" language. Once a generally accepted "poetic" idiom has developed, it is precisely by the return to the "Hurry up, please; it's time" kind of diction that the effect of dissociation may be achieved and we are made to attend once more to words *as* words. As the "pastoral" sentimentality of certain people's poets shows, a return to common speech which is motivated by the will to "regain contact with the common man" yields poetry of a very low order. The true poetic meaning of such a return is almost the opposite: when the common reader has learned to accept the "unnatural" as natural—"because it's poetry, you know"—the poet may take to the "natural." The real motive remains the same: to wrest from a functionalized idiom the material which the artist needs for a true medium.

Under the headings pun, rhyme, metaphor, and meter I have in fact already been discussing an aspect of poetic language which, since Empson, no treatment of poetics can afford to ignore: ambiguity. For Empson, ambiguity became all but synonymous with the essential quality of poetry; it meant complexity, associative and connotative richness, texture, and the possibility of irony. The ambiguous word proliferated like a vine, wove or revealed hidden strands between the most various and distinct spheres of our prosaically ordered world. By exploiting the ambiguity of words the poet could ironically undercut the surface meanings of his statements, could avail himself fully of the entire field of meanings which a word has and is. I want to shift the stress of Empson's analysis a little. He made us aware that one word can—and in great poetry commonly does—have *many meanings*; I would rather insist on the converse, that many meanings can have *one word.* For the poet, the ambiguous word is the crux of the problem of creating a medium for him to work in. If meanings are primary and words only their signs, then ambiguous words are false; each meaning should have its word, as each sound should have its letter. But if the reverse is true and words are primary—if, that is, they are the corporeal entities the poet requires—then ambiguity is something quite different: it is the fracturing of a pristine unity by the analytic conceptualizations of prose. The poet must assume that where there is one word there must, in some sense, be unity of meaning, no matter what prose usage may have done to break it. The pun is the extreme form of this assumption, positing unity of meaning even for purely accidental homophones, such as the sound shifts of a language will happen to produce.

Ambiguity, then, becomes a test case for the poet; insofar as he can vanquish it—not by splitting the word, but by fusing its meanings—he has succeeded in making language into a true medium; insofar as it vanquishes him, he must abdicate his position as a "maker." I would say, therefore, that he does not primarily exploit the plurisignations of words, as though they were a fortunate accident; rather he accepts, even seeks out, their challenge, because he knows that in his encounter with them the issue of his claim is finally joined and decided. A pun may be a mere play, a rhyme a mere jingle, even a metaphor only an invitation to conceptual comparisons; true ambiguities are another matter. With them it is not a question of taking two words or meanings and showing how, in some sense, they are one, but rather of taking one word and showing that it is more than a potpourri of the meanings we have a mind to attach to it. Since the poet's credo must be the opening of St. John: "In the beginning was the Word," he meets the temptation of meaning ultimately in ambiguity.

Empson takes ambiguity in the widest sense; of his seven types it is the last which is of special interest here. In it the ambiguity of contradiction, or to take it more narrowly, of negation. If the preceding argument is valid, negation poses for the poet a crucial problem: it denies the existence of something which, simply by mentioning, it affirms, almost creates. The problem is not, of course, confined to poetry; if I say, "There is no God," I am caught in something of a contradiction. But in prose I have a way out; I can interpret my statement to mean: "The word 'God' refers to nothing that exists and therefore has no true meaning"; or more cautiously: " 'God' is only a notion in the heads of some unenlightened people and cannot be said to 'be.' " This way out is not available to the poet, since even the negated word is corporeally there and so demonstrates its reality. Nietzsche said: "God is dead."

There is a passage in the *Aeneid* in which Jupiter foretells the future achievements of Rome and the Julian family; it ends thus: "Then shall war cease, and the iron ages soften. . . . The dreadful steel-clenched gates of War shall be shut fast; inhuman Fury, his hands bound behind him with an hundred rivets of brass, shall sit within on murderous weapons, shrieking with ghastly blood-stained lips." This is rather like the allegorical sculptures in which a triumphant main figure has its foot firmly planted on the neck of a now impotent, teeth-gnashing figure of War (or perhaps Disease, or Hunger). It is evident that the sculptor—or painter, or musician—cannot negate; he cannot express "There is no War," since War, even to be negated, must be physically there. In prose, a negative particle or pronoun is a sign that what follows is to be ignored or discounted; if I say "Nothing pleases him," I expect my listener to discount the word "pleases." But it can, and in poetry often must, be taken differently, as "He is pleased by nothingness." The classical instance of this ambiguity is the story of Ulysses and Polyphemos; Ulysses exploits it by giving his name as "Nobody." Polyphemos, having visible proof of the corporeality of this "nobody," accepts the word in its poetic sense; his fellows later, lacking such proof, take the word in its prose sense; it is through this split in human discourse that crafty Ulysses escapes. But the poet's purpose is to tell truths—truths which escape the confines of discursive speech. And to do so, he is committed to the word, even the negative, as in some sense physically present. How, then can he express negations?

I believe that one of the more puzzling of Shakespeare's sonnets poses this problem sharply and so may yield an answer—the 116th:

Let me not to the marriage of true minds
Admit impediments. Love is not love
Which alters when it alteration finds,
Or bends with the remover to remove.
O, no! It is an ever-fixèd mark
That looks on tempests and is never shaken;
It is the star to every wand'ring bark,
Whose worth's unknown, although his height be taken.
Love's not Time's fool, though rosy lips and cheeks
Within his bending sickle's compass come;
Love alters not with his brief hours and weeks,
But bears it out even to the edge of doom.
If this be error and upon me proved,
I never writ, nor no man ever loved.

Shakespeare here tries to define the core word of the entire sonnet sequence in a series of negative and positive equations. The rhetorical structure implies a debate; the disputatious dare of the couplet is almost strident. We can do no less than accept the challenge.

There is no arguing about definitions; but this one of love is more than commonly wilful. Shakespeare is more of a "high-flyer" even than Plato; where Plato wisely excepted Eros from his Ideas so that he might have some means of bridging the chasm between them and the world of appearances, Shakespeare Platonizes this very force. The definition he proposes removes love completely from the sphere of human feeling, even puts it into explicit contrast with the sole plainly human element in the sonnet: "rosy lips and cheeks." Love is the Pole Star, fixed in timeless immobility infinitely far above the sublunary world of change and decay; it is incommensurable to human understanding, let alone attainable by human striving. A word which in ordinary usage is warm, intimate, and caressing, Shakespeare makes cold, hard, and precise. Not even Dante managed to live up to standards as rigorous as the sonnet prescribes; ordinary men could claim to have loved only if the definition were lowered a good deal. What we should expect Shakespeare to say at the end is the opposite of what he does say: not "If this be error," but rather "If this be *true*, no man ever loved." (I am leaving aside, for the moment, the equally startling other conclusion: "I never writ.") We may not be able to dispute his definition, but his conclusion is another matter. On the face of it, it seems nonsense.

There are two ways out of the dilemma; or, to put it differently, the dilemma results from the sonnet's being read partly as if it were prose, partly as if it were poetry. If I read the second line ("Love is not love") as a discursive proposition—"Love is not a feeling which . . ." or "That love is not true love which . . ."—I must read the double negative of the last line in the same way, "so that [as Feste says], conclusions to be as kisses, if your [two] negatives make your [one] affirmative, why then" —everyone has always loved. Unless, that is, the poet's definition is the true one, anyone's claim to the feeling is as good as anyone else's; brutal lust and sophomoric sentimentality, sordid calculation and disguised hatred

—whatever feeling man has seen fit to baptize "love" is then entitled to the name. If we read "love" as we do in prose—as a sign for a feeling—the first negation must be in some manner rephrased in order to make sense at all; the simplest way is to rewrite it so that within a larger genus of feelings love is the species which has immutability as its differentia. This logical rewording—which I think we do almost without being conscious of it—compels us to a logical reading of the double negative, so that the sonnet concludes: If this definition is erroneous, if the differentia is not applicable, then love is not a separate species but returns into the chaos of meanings which men, deceiving or self-deceived, have called "love"; that is, every man who ever said he loved did so.

But in poetry two negatives do not make an affirmative. To the poetic reading of the last line—in which one negative reinforces the other—corresponds a poetic reading also of the earlier negation. Then, since it is the word *itself* which is negated, the word is annulled, struck from the language. "On any terms less than mine," so Shakespeare says, "the word 'love' is expunged." The corporeal entity he put there was cancelable by nothing less than an absolute negation, the negation of the word itself. He could not say: "Love which alters is only lust (or some other feeling)," because one real entity does not cancel another. He could not say: "Love which alters is not real love," because entities are real simply by being there. He could not equate negatively in the ordinary way, because a negative equation always implies that the word is used differently on the two sides. If I say: "Your love is no love," I mean: "You are using the wrong word for the thing (feeling) in question." One of the two loves stands in quotation marks, or else the statement is nonsense. But the poet does not have this out, since his universe is a verbal one; every one of his words has quotation marks around it. His negations therefore are absolute—they are destructions. Love which alters is not love, its own negation; it cancels itself into nonexistence. This reading likewise makes sense: with the word "love" struck out—as it is if the poet is in error—no man can ever have loved.

Now the first conclusion ("I never writ") reveals itself as no mere hyperbolic reaffirmation, but an equally rigorous consequence. Shakespeare defines love as a superhuman, transcendent constancy and offers, as the only alternative to his definition, not any change or reduction of criteria, but the annulment of the word, and with it of whatever it may stand for. It is as though one were to define light and then claim that if one's definition were proved false, light did not exist. The claim is as arrogant as it is, for the poet, necessary; it can, in fact, be justified by nothing less than his staking his existence as poet on it. If the word has not the absolute constancy assigned it by the poet, it is nothing; and then the words he has been writing are meaningless doodles. If the word is a sign drawing for its substance upon the multifarious and ever shifting meanings given it in the intercourse of men, the poet's business is at an end—and really also that of ordinary language, which rests on the faith that words are fixed and determinable. If "love" receives its semantic content from what I happen to be feeling at the moment I say it, it is not a word any longer but an emotional grunt. Or, to put the matter again in terms of the other reading of the ambiguous double negative: If everyone has true title to saying "love" when he feels like it—to coin the word without regard to what it "means" by itself—everyone is in effect a poet, using words with creative sovereignty. Every fleeting utterance is then poetry, and the claim to more than momentary validity which the poet "proper" has entered and symbolized by the act of writing is a vain pretension. It all comes to the same thing: there is no real difference between All and Nothing, since both deny the possibility of differentiation. If all speech is poetry, no speech is; if we all have always loved, none of us has ever loved.

What I have done amounts to substituting the term "word" for "love" in the sonnet; I believe we are meant to. I would even propose as a working hypothesis that a great many puzzles—and not only in Shakespeare—might be solved by such a substitution. To stay with the 116th sonnet: what is the marriage of true minds? How is it to be consecrated and consummated? In the already quoted 138th sonnet the mere sexual act is equated with lying; the marriage of true minds must be its polar opposite. I do not see how it can be consummated except verbally; *speech* is the marriage of true minds. And the impediments to it are the infinite possibilities of deception which words, in their ambiguity, contain. Unless words are constant, union of minds is impossible, even if these minds can be assumed to be individually and severally true.

But insofar as words are signs for meanings, they cannot be constant, for meanings are necessarily private and may shift from moment to moment, from person to person. The problem does not become acute in the crude approximations of everyday life, to be sure; as the laws of Newton are still very adequate to describe the behavior of the gross physical bodies about us, so ordinary language will serve for the gross needs of social intercourse. But none of us need rack his memory long for instances where it did not serve—where one cannot be sure that the meanings one clothes in words are also the meanings these words will convey to the person addressed. Occasions of saying "love" will be the most signal examples. The laws of verbal gravitation are operative as long as we can rely on an absolute frame of social reference; but when it comes to determining the relationship of two bodies in absolute isolation and no longer referable to a system of social coordinates which posits a pre-established harmony—when, in other words, the need of communion becomes most insistent, the problem of language most acute—precisely then these laws break down and we are cast into a time-space continuum of verbal relativity which seems to deny all possibility of relation, because none of our terms are meaningful except as we arbitrarily assume a reference point —which can be only ourselves.

The syntax of the sonnet does not determine whether "love" is to be considered as synonymous with "marriage of true minds" or as an instance of a possible impediment to such a marriage. But I do not think this ambiguity matters. Unlike ordinary marriage, that of true minds can be consecrated and consummated only verbally; it has no sacrament, nor ring, nor ritual cohabitation to give it body. The impediments people are invited to bring forth when the banns are published are therefore not impediments to this kind of marriage; there is no physical fact, such as consanguinity, which could invalidate it, since it is of minds. The only possible impediment lies in the danger that the words by which the marriage is consecrated and consummated are not valid—as, for example, the words "I now pronounce you . . ." would not be, if the speaker were not a true priest. It is the absence of this third party to the sacrament—this bodily representative of both the social and the divine coordinates—which makes the question of the validity of the words themselves so extraordinarily urgent.

The Oxford philosophers have recently called attention to a class of statements called "operative," which do not describe but rather perform by statement. The sacramental statements are the readiest instances. But what makes them possible, or "operative," is the entire order and authority, human and divine, which the speaker represents, the sanctions and penalties it commands. A marriage of true minds is without benefit of clergy and consequently has no other sanction and sanctity than what is contained in the words themselves which seal it. If words are ambiguous, such a marriage is a farce.

It can, therefore, be challenged simply by the question: "What do you mean by love?" (Indeed, what do you mean by anything you say to another person?) It is this challenge, and the implied impediment, which the sonnet is written to meet. But it cannot meet it by saying: "By love I mean. . . ." Feelings, and consequently meanings, can never be enough here; what is wanted is an *operative* word, not a meaning—a sacramental word, which carries its sacramental force within it, as an immanent meaning. And that means: a word no longer a sign; a word removed from the mutability of things, the infinitely greater mutability of feelings, of which ordinary words are the signs. This kind of word does not *have* meanings, but rather *gives* them.

Of course there is a paradox here: such a word is empty sound. In order to rescue it from the tempestuous chaos of meaning, the poet, so it seems, has had to remove it to a height so great, to reduce it to a point so without area, that its "worth's unknown." The gyrating planets and signs of the zodiac have a known worth—i.e., determinable astrological meaning; but they have it only, the language of the Heavens is intelligible only, because their gyrations are referable to the Pole Star, which could not give meaning if it had any itself. Words are infinitely "meaningful"; they are man's cry for union and the answering cry. But more than a cry is required, if a word is to be more than mere animal sound; in order that a marriage of minds may be celebrated, not only the pathetic, inarticulate "bark" of the dog baying at the stars is needed, but likewise the sacramental sign—the "mark." Both sign and sound are meaningless, taken by themselves; hence the syntactic ambiguity of "whose" in line 8, which has for possible antecedents both "star" and "bark." (The ambiguity of "bark" itself, as drifting ship and aimless animal sound is a relatively simple one.)

What Shakespeare is saying, then, is something like this: "You have raised an impediment, challenged the possibility of human communion, called into question the legitimacy and sanctity of speech, where its meaning is not authorized by church and state. This challenge I will not—as poet cannot—admit. If you ask: 'What do you mean by . . . ?' I answer: 'I *mean* what I *say*.' As poet I pledge myself to use words with a constancy so inhuman and remote from the chaotic meanings you attach to them that they would, taken by themselves, be empty signs. You may rely on it that when I say 'love' or any other word, I do not mean by it whatever vaporous feelings or notions may be agitating my viscera or brain. I shall be the priest to this marriage; that is, I shall forego human love so that your love may be sanctified. I will be celibate and renounce self-expression, so that you may speak truly or, what is the same thing, truly speak. But there is meaning in what I say, because without me you are merely making emotional grunts. The meanings of your words can never be just what you have in mind when you say them; to have anything like meaning they must have an external pole. Meaning is the product of what you 'mean' and of the word as an absolute constant independent of your private thoughts, just as marriage is the product of your human intentions and the sacramental act. Where there is no social and religious authority to guarantee and compel validity and constancy, there I am and speak. If I am heretical in making this claim, then I have done nothing but made doodles on a sheet of paper; but likewise no man has ever talked meaningfully, except where he spoke for or answered to authority."

It is tempting to trace, in its minute precision, the sonnet's verbal structure and thereby to show how Shakespeare, in this reply, also refutes the traditional, common-sense method of fixing meanings by definitions. From line 2 through line 11 he ironically demonstrates that definitions, instead of fixing words, split them. In the first quatrain, identity is denied—"love is not love"—but denied through a monotonous sequence of verbal identities: love-love, alter-alteration, remover-remove. In the second quatrain identity is affirmed—love is something—but affirmed through equations with two terms completely different from the term to be defined. Lines 9-11 involve in their negation not only man, the fool of time, nor only the terms "alter" and "bend" of the first quatrain, but also—through "bending sickle" (= moon) and "compass"—the hitherto positive celestial-navigation metaphor of the second. In other words, as long as Shakespeare tries to define by the traditional method of predication, he gets only into a muddle of self-contradictions: the word is not what it is; it is what it is not; it is not what it is not. When Sir Toby Belch greets the disguised Feste as "Master Parson," Feste accepts the honor thus: "As the old hermit of Prague, that never saw pen and ink, very wittily said to a niece of King Gorboduc, 'That that is is'; so I, being master Parson, am master Parson; for what is 'that' but 'that,' and 'is' but 'is'?" The point is, of course, that he is *not* a parson, but Feste the Fool, the "corrupter of words." As soon as a real word is set for the hermit's pronoun, the most unchallengeable of all tautologies—the principle of identity—turns into a falsehood. (Not a complete one, however; in taking on a parson's appearance, Feste in a sense becomes one.) The poet must always be half fool, the corrupter of words; but he has seen pen and ink, has written, and must therefore be a parson in a much more serious sense than Feste; else he "never writ."

All these paradoxes and contradictions are resolved—insofar as words can ever resolve them—in line 12. Already in line 11 an *action* has been predicated of 'love,' but only a negated one; now finally, after all the contradictory attempts to say what love *is,* we are told that it does something. "But bears it out" is the poet's final and unequivocal answer to the challenge. The word ("love") is not an entity, but rather an act; this is the first time in the sonnet that the subject is not directly followed by its predicate, but stands removed from it by a whole line. Moreover, whereas action necessarily involves change, *this* action is duration, the opposite of change. Yet it is not passive and intransitive, as duration normally would be; it has no subject in a sense, but it does have an object: "it," which hitherto has always stood for "love," but now stands not really for anything. The word is an act which is neither subject to time nor transcends it, but is time's coequal. But beyond all this the word is pregnant and fruitful, it "bears" and so serves the true purpose of all marriages.

These few notes must do to show how aware Shakespeare is of the ironies of his enterprise, the paradoxes of his medium, and with what almost desperate precision he seeks to overcome them. As a poet he cannot negate, though that must again and again be his impulse toward false words; the limitation upon omnipotence is that it cannot say "no"; it can only destroy. The poet's negations are destructions; "love is not love." But he cannot affirm either; that is, he cannot predicate by equations; for to say of a word that it is something other than itself is to lie. The definitions of logic are monstrous confusions if we hold words sacred, as the poet must. Indeed, the poet hardly dare write words; ambiguity always threatens. The poet's undertaking—to make words into a material cause—draws with it such formidable dangers that he is constantly teetering on the edge between the lie and silence: between tyranny and abdication. (Shakespeare's repeated treatment of this theme —*King Lear, Measure for Measure,* and *The Tempest* are not the only instances—suggests that it is a besetting and lasting problem for him, demanding again and again to be solved.)

What sustains him in this perilous balance is the love of the Word in its absolute integrity. As *Othello* demonstrates, that is no easy matter; the most sacred thing is also the most vulnerable. The poet would be much safer if he did not commit himself to the Word, but in ironic detachment exploited the infinite ambiguities of speech. Or he could retreat to the safety of a socio-religious order, give up his claim to verbal priesthood, and turn "mouthpiece." Both roads have been taken; but they lead to self-abnegation. The poet as a fool must be a corrupter of words, a punster, rhymster, verbal trickster, for there is no other way to break the disgraceful bonds into which words have fallen. But if he is not also, and ultimately, priest—if he is not a parson disguised as a fool rather than a fool disguised as a parson—speech will be "wanton" rather than sacramental: "Why, sir, her name's a word; and to dally with that word might make my sister wanton."

Our Empsonian delight in the poet's play with ambiguities, our Richardsian mistrust of a critical mystique, ought not to dissolve our awareness that, when all is "said and done," the poet *acts* by *speaking*. The bawdy of his fools is necessary; poetic devices must be dissociative, for the common-law marriage between meaning and sound—ordinary language—is a denial both of sanctity and freedom. But lust is not the last word; it is an expense of spirit in a waste of shame. In the end the poet must commit himself unequivocally; the last word is love. It is the poet's minimum indefinable (in Russell's sense) ; the word without which not only all other words, but the very act of speech, the very attempt to enter into a marriage of minds, would be meaningless. When Shakespeare equates it with the star, the equation is not reductive, as in logic, but transformative: "love" is both itself and the star, both the inarticulate sound and the empty sign. Where the philosopher seeks certitude in the sign—the "p" of propositional calculus—and the mystic in the ineffable—the "OM" of the Hindus—the poet takes upon himself the paradox of the human word, which is both and neither and which he creatively transforms in his "powerful rhyme." This rhyme is his deed; it dissociates, dissolves the word into its components—mark and bark—but simultaneously fuses it into a new and now sacramental union.

III

"I AM BUT SHADOW OF MYSELF": CEREMONY AND DESIGN IN *1 HENRY VI*

IT IS difficult, perhaps impossible, to say anything about *1 Henry VI* without raising the still vexed question of authorship. I too shall have to raise it, but I do not want to attack it frontally. I would rather state my position as a *working* assumption and hope that what follows will prove sound enough to bear me out. Here, then, is what I shall assume: *1 Henry VI* was written or thoroughly reworked—possibly both—by Shakespeare himself. As we have it in the Folio, it represents his effort to shape the chronicle accounts—whether directly from Hall, Holinshed, and Fabyan, or mediately from a play now lost—into a coherent dramatic whole within the still larger whole of the first tetralogy. In short, in the following interpretation I shall treat *1 Henry VI* as the Folio editors treated it: as part of the Shakespeare canon.

The scholars who have argued for this assumption have properly made it one of their tasks to show that most of the incidents in the play are by no means simply episodes but have a clear dramatic function.[1] In this they have, I think, been generally successful—especially where the incidents are not traceable to any source and so are

[1] For the most complete and thorough statement of the "integralist" case, literary as well as textual, see A. S. Cairncross' introduction to his edition of *1 Henry VI* (Arden Shakespeare, London, 1962), which refers abundantly to other recent criticism. For the "disintegrationist" position, see J. D. Wilson's introduction to the play, Cambridge edition (Cambridge, 1952).

likely to be Shakespeare's own, considered additions. The rose-plucking scene in the temple garden, the Mortimer-Richard scene right afterward, and the final scenes between Suffolk and Margaret of Anjou are all manifestly intended to knit the play more tightly into the larger design. Similarly, the great theme of dissension as the cause of English misfortunes—and of the disturbed succession as a cause of dissension—is more fully worked out in the play than it is in the sources. The hand of the dramatic strategist disposing events according to a master plan is clearly discernible.

Still it seems to me that the "integralists" have not given due weight to one obvious fact: that their arguments were needed. What Samuel Johnson said about the supposed benefits of poverty is not altogether inapplicable here; no one labors to persuade us that, say, *Richard II* is of one cast, just as no one labors to convince us that it is possible to live happily upon a plentiful fortune. Can the disintegrationist heresy—if such it is—be accounted for by no more than the obstinate longevity of Malone's error? Doesn't it feed upon some qualities in the play itself? That is the question to which, in a very indirect manner, I mean to address myself.

I

I shall do so by looking closely at the scene between Talbot and the Countess of Auvergne (II, iii). The scene is brief: right after the conquest of Orleans, Talbot is invited to visit the Countess at her castle. When he presents himself, she first taunts him with his smallness of stature; when he turns to leave, she reveals that she has lured him into a trap and means to hold him prisoner. But Talbot has anticipated her plot; he has placed soldiers in readiness to occupy the castle. The scene ends amicably, with apologies offered and accepted and a joint feast.

For an integralist, the scene presents a difficult problem; it seems irretrievably episodic. It grows out of no prior event, leads to no subsequent one; the Countess appears in no other scene and is never again heard of. No major theme seems to be illustrated, no moral pointed. Moreover, there is no hint of the incident in any of the play's sources. Oddly, Shakespeare appears to have composed, with full deliberation, a scene that is purely episodic. The very oddity demands attention.

Here is the opening exchange between the Countess and Talbot:

> Countess: Is this the scourge of France?
> Is this the Talbot, so much feared abroad
> That with his name the mothers still their babes?
> I see report is fabulous and false.
> I thought I should have seen some Hercules,
> A second Hector, for his grim aspect,
> And large proportion of his strong-knit limbs.
> Alas, this is a child, a silly dwarf!
> It cannot be this weak and writhled shrimp
> Should strike such terror to his enemies.
> Talbot: Madam, I have been bold to trouble you;
> But since your ladyship is not at leisure,
> I'll sort some other time to visit you (15-27)

What happens here is that a *ceremony* is startlingly interrupted. The ceremony is that of the taunt, and the Countess' language is properly ceremonial, in the true Marlovian cadence: "Is this the face that launched a thousand ships?" Her lines call for a counter-taunt or defiance, a reply in the manner at least of Gloucester defying Winchester:

> Presumptuous priest! this place commands my
> patience,
> Or thou shouldst find thou hast dishonored me.
> (III, i, 8-9)

Substitute "lady" for "priest" and "thy sex" for "this place," and the reply should serve quite nicely. Talbot himself knows, elsewhere in the play, what the ceremony calls for:

> Foul fiend of France, and hag of all despite,
> Encompassed with thy lustful paramours!
> Becomes it thee to taunt his [Bedford's] valiant age,
> And twit with cowardice a man half dead?
> (III, ii, 52-55)

But here he refuses to play his part, to pick up the verbal gauntlet. With ironic urbanity, he implies that he has broken in upon the Countess as she was rehearsing a set-piece; his apology leaves her in the silly posture of someone striking a mighty blow at a vanished target.

It is the Countess, not Talbot, who in this scene speaks the language of the play. About *her* style there is nothing unusual; it is of a piece with the play's world. That world is one of vaunt and taunt, of "high terms" ceremonially put forward and ceremonially responded to—usually with the explicit or implicit invocation of force as the final arbiter:

> Thou hast astonished me with thy high terms.
> Only this proof I'll of thy valour make,
> In single combat thou shalt buckle with me,
> And if thou vanquishest, thy words are true;
> Otherwise I renounce all confidence. (I, ii, 93-97)

"Single combat" or multiple—the sword is always at least half unsheathed to make good the words. Gloucester or Winchester, Red Rose or White, England or France, it is all the same; as the Mayor of London says: "Good God, these nobles should such stomachs bear!"

My point is not that the language is appropriate to the world, but rather that it allows of no other. Every major actor is compelled—not necessarily by pride and pugnacity but by the language available to him—to step onto the stage, assume the proper posture, and rehearse his piece. The burden of the piece need not always be self-assertion or defiance, though most often it is. The mode lends itself equally well to grief:

> Hung be the heavens with black, yield day to night!
> (I, i, 1)

or to praise:

> And all the priests and friars in my realm
> Shall in procession sing her endless praise.
> A statelier pyramis to her I'll rear
> Than Rhodope's of Memphis ever was (I, vi, 19-22)

or even to submission:

> In sign whereof, this arm, that hath reclaimed
> To your obedience fifty fortresses,
> Twelve cities, and seven wallèd towns of strength,
> Beside five hundred prisoners of esteem,
> Lets fall his sword before your Highness' feet,
> And with submissive loyalty of heart
> Ascribes the glory of his conquest got
> First to my God and next unto your Grace.
> (III, iv, 5-12)

Self-assertion and praise (or submission) are difficult to tell apart. The ceremonial mode lends itself to every occasion, but what matters is that it makes an "occasion" of whatever it lends itself to. It is like Concord grapes: no matter what it is made into, the residual taste is always the same.

Prosodically, the mode engenders the end-stopped line. The lines of verse behave like the characters, each striving to stand in self-sufficient and self-assertive orotundity. A speech is like a recital of titles and honors (or dishonors, it makes no real difference):

> But where's the great Alcides of the field,
> Valiant Lord Talbot, Earl of Shrewsbury,
> Created, for his rare success in arms,
> Great Earl of Washford, Waterford and Valence;
> Lord Talbot of Goodrig and Urchinfield,
> Lord Strange of Blackmore, Lord Verdun of
> Alton . . .

etc., etc., for six more lines. Joan's response is predictable:

> Here's a silly stately style indeed! . . .
> Him that thou magnifi'st with all these titles
> Stinking and fly-blown lies here at our feet.
> (IV, vii, 60-76)

But even in ridiculing the stately style, Joan pays unwilling homage to it by obediently falling into the vaunt-taunt pattern. The speakers may think they master and use the style, but in fact it masters and uses them. Margaret of Anjou becomes a kind of embodiment of it:

> Henry: Your wondrous rare description, noble
> earl,
> Of beauteous Margaret hath astonished
> me.
> Her virtues graced with external gifts

Do breed love's settled passions in my
    heart;
And like as rigour of tempestuous gusts
Provokes the mightiest hulk against the
    tide,
So am I driven by breath of her renown
Either to suffer shipwreck or arrive
Where I may have fruition of her love.
Suffolk: Tush, my good lord, this superficial tale
Is but a preface to her worthy praise.
The chief perfections of that lovely dame,
Had I sufficient skill to utter them,
Would make a volume of enticing lines,
Able to ravish any dull conceit;
And, which is more, she is not so divine,
So full-replete with choice of all delights,
But with as humble lowliness of mind
She is content to be at your command.
(V, V, 1-19)

Is she indeed? This "volume of enticing lines" will presently become Queen of England: contentious rather than content, overbearing rather than humble. She will have a major share in the ensuing shipwreck. As she is here talked about, she furnishes as neat an illustration as we can hope for of a style which, seeming to do its master's bidding, drives him toward a disastrous conclusion.

Rhetorically, the mode engenders hyperbole—a relentless reaching for the superlative which, in the effort to outdo what has gone before, is sure to end in collapse. We are warned at the outset:

England ne'er had a king until his [Henry V's] time.
Virtue he had, deserving to command.
His brandished sword did blind men with his beams;

His arms spread wider than a dragon's wings;
His sparkling eyes, replete with wrathful fire,
More dazzled and drove back his enemies
Than mid-day sun fierce bent against their faces.
What should I say? his deeds exceed all speech.
(I, i, 8-15)

Here the mortal contention, closing with a feeble gasp, is between the similes of one speaker; elsewhere it is between those of two. In either case it is a "jarring discord of nobility":

But howsoe'er, no simple man that sees
This jarring discord of nobility,
This should'ring of each other in the court . . .
But that [he] doth presage some ill event.
(IV, i, 187-191)

Where every line, every trope, every man strives for preeminence, what can come of it but "intestine broils"?

The mode of *1 Henry VI* seeks, in fact compels the seeking of, the fullest self-assertion at every moment; it is impatient of indirection, refuses to sacrifice immediate effects for long-range gains. It permits strategic retreats as little as litotes, genuine negotiation as little as genuine dialogue; it always "goes for broke." It has no sense of the implicit; whatever is not asserted does not exist. Its "order," except where it is kept in check by external, higher authority, is that of combat; by inner necessity it escalates toward more and more violent confrontations. The duel, single or multiple, is its most adequate metaphor, until finally it drives even duelling into "mere oppugnancy," sheer, vengeful slaughter (as it has in *3 Henry VI*).

My intention has not been to point up once again the obvious faults of Shakespeare's "immature" style, but rather to suggest that he *himself* was fully aware of them.

Even in this supposedly early play he has mastered the trick of making the style he employs comment upon itself; is a better description of it imaginable than "rigour of tempestuous gusts," a phrase which catches precisely both its rigid compulsiveness and its destructive, blowhard yet short-winded unrestraint? But more important: Shakespeare has discovered that there is a perfect analogy between the verbal and the social order—an analogy that is almost an identity. Both the *modus loquendi* and the *modus agendi* of a society are governed by the same inner law or laws. For the dramatist who grasps this law, the stage *is* the world.

II

At this point I should like to construct a speculative little playlet of my own. I do not intend to claim historical validity for it, though I shall try to show that it is plausible, congruent with what we know. The playlet will serve me, I hope, to explain more easily and clearly the nature and implications of Shakespeare's discovery; but it is meant to be no more than a model, an interpretive device.

What little we do know about the textual history of the Henry VI plays indicates that they were involved in, were very possible the object of, a "war of the playwrights." There is, first of all, Greene's famous attack on Shakespeare in *A Groats-worth of Wit*, with its allusion to *3 Henry VI*. There is Chettle's subsequent apology, apparently at the instance of "diverse of worship," for having published the attack. There is the fact that the theatre in question was the *Rose*; Shakespeare would hardly have been Shakespeare if he had not been aware of the strangely significant coincidence that the *Rose* should furnish the stage for a "War of the Roses" which at the same time figured importantly in a war of playwrights. (Witness his later awareness of the dramatic significance of the *Globe.*) There is, finally, the fact that plays often were written in collaboration—a practice which must have encouraged each playwright to try to be the best "Shake-scene," to outdo his colleagues and competitors in the writing of theatrically effective scenes and let the play as a whole shift for itself.

Greene's attack has been variously interpreted and endlessly debated. The disintegrationists have naturally made the most of it, while the integralists have tended to explain it as the spiteful outburst of a bitter and destitute writer who saw himself neglected for a highly successful young rival. The integralist argument has been that where *Henry VI* sounds more like Greene or Nashe or Marlowe than like Shakespeare, we have evidence of a young poet's inevitable and natural tendency to imitate his elders, and that Greene's charge of plagiarism refers to this kind of imitation. But that can hardly be a correct reading of the passage. For Greene distinguishes explicitly between "past excellence" ("Let those apes imitate your past excellence") and "inventions" ("and never more acquaint them with your admired inventions").[2] *He* at least believed that the "feathers" with which Shakespeare had "beautified" himself were something a good deal more substantial than the imitation of past excellence; and his belief must have had sufficient basis in fact for his fellow playwrights to understand the allusion.

The question to ask, therefore, is: What did Greene mean by "admired inventions"? Let us imagine that several collaborating playwrights, Shakespeare and Greene among them, have met to block out a play or sequence of plays they have undertaken to do. Ideas are

[2] A. B. Grossart, *Life and Complete Works in Prose and Verse of Robert Greene* (New York, 1964), vol. xii, p. 144.

pooled, a division of labor is arranged. It becomes evident that each collaborator means to out-bombast the others as best he can; whereupon one of them, unwilling to see the whole torn apart by this contentious striving for short-range effects and personal glory, withdraws from the partnership and writes his own version of the play.

How are the others likely to react? Greene's attack, not only in general but in its actual wording, would be a very natural reaction. The others are almost certain to believe that their "admired inventions" were stolen by the defector, who, having picked their brains, then arrogantly set himself up as the "*only* Shake-scene" (i.e., demanding to write *all* the scenes), as an "absolute *Iohannes fac totum*." And they are almost certain to have some plausible grounds for this belief; for, with the basic story given by the chronicles and the natural give-and-take of a planning session, there is bound to be considerable overlap between the ideas proposed and the defector's final product.

Greene's admonition to his fellow playwrights is most naturally read, I think, as a warning against any future collaboration with players, more especially with Shakespeare. Never, he enjoins, let the players see anything but your finished (and paid-for) products. Those they will imitate; let them. But beware of sitting down with them to plan a new play, for they will first steal your ideas and then (with a fine show of artistic integrity yet!) your credit. This reading would also explain the next sentence: "For it is pity men of such rare wits should be subject to the pleasures of such rude grooms." Is not Greene here alluding to attempts by Shakespeare to curb the self-seeking and self-will of the other writers, or (as naturally Greene saw it) to lord it (a mere player!) over these rare University Wits?

The scene, then, of my model shows Shakespeare sitting with other playwrights, arguing for a coherent and organic scheme for the Henry VI plays and more and more unhappily watching his collaborators tear the whole apart in a compulsive contention for the "finest" scenes and "noblest" speeches—in a "jarring discord of nobility." And suddenly the thought strikes him: Why shouldn't they? How could it be otherwise? Is not this exactly what the whole story is about? Are we not here *enacting* what we mean to represent? Would my idea of an integral dramatic whole not falsify the essence of the story we are supposed to tell? Is not the play we are here cutting into segments a perfect analogue of its true subject—England torn by civil war—and am I not in the position of Henry VI, a child, a mere beginner in the art of governing this play-world, surrounded by powerful and headstrong nobles, pleading helplessly for peace and amity, for subordination to the common purpose?

And then a further thought strikes him: Do we not also enact, act in, the very style in which, as dramatists, we speak? Is not this scene the inevitable result of the concept of ceremonial "order" implicit in that style, and is that concept of order not exactly analogous to the larger image of order, the "world picture" we have been taught to accept? Is there not a grim and self-destructive necessity governing a world, a kingdom, a body of playwrights, a play, or a speech which is constructed on this model? And if so, where is the remedy? Exit Shakespeare, pursued by troublesome doubts.

III

Where was the remedy? The first need would seem to be the discovery of what was wrong with the "picture." What were its essential qualities? One was that it was static; it existed in space but not in time. It allowed for a limited amount of internal motion (though even that seemed rather an unhappy violation of its spirit, commotion rather than motion); but it did not allow for general progressive change. It valued stability to the point of rigidity; what occurred in it was not so much an ordered sequence of events leading from the past into a different future as a succession of *exempla*, episodes meant to point the same permanent morals. Enthroned at its apex sat God, the fount of honor, the source of all authority, more unmoved than mover, more substance than energy, a figure encrusted with the symbols of macrocosmic sovereignty. Below Him, step by step, stood the hierarchical "orders": the angels in their various "degrees," and then men: kings, nobles, burghers, peasants, and, near the very bottom, even vagrant comedians.

A second essential quality of the picture was that it was rigorously analogical. Differences were of degree; unity was assured by analogical identity. A king was "God in little," while God was the "King of kings." A kingdom was to Christendom what a dukedom was to the kingdom. There were also, of course, innumerable "collateral" analogies, whose force was symbolic rather than legal: to the animal kingdom, the vegetable kingdom, the "little kingdom" man, the kingdom of the heavens. For the explaining of actual events, these analogies were heavily drawn upon: "distempers" or "perturbations" at one level were mirrored by disturbances at other levels; a king who did not control his subjects was like a man who did not control his appetites. Everything was like everything else; beneath the diversity in degree there was a remarkable likeness in kind.

Third, harmony at any level depended on both the acknowledgment and the effective exercise of the authority vested in the next higher level. Order was not implicit but always external to what was being "kept in order"—and consequently explicit. Of course, the picture as a whole was supposed, ideally, to rest in beautiful and total harmony; if every inferior acted in unfailing obedience and every superior in unfailing wisdom and justice, there was no reason why authority had to become explicit. But obviously this was a mere ideal, not the observable reality; and since the picture was in fact used as a tool of government, as a means to inculcate obedience and to discourage "rebellion," what was emphasized was the danger and wickedness of conflict and the duty, whenever conflict did arise, to submit to authority. The picture militated against any distinction between political and religious duty, between unlawful acts and sinful acts. Disobedience was the root and prototype of all evil, private as well as public; to it all sins were reducible. God was the King of kings much more than the Father, while the father was a "king in little," as the king was "God in little." At every level—since every level had *some* authority, i.e., some beings inferior to it over which it was appointed to rule—there was need for constant and explicit assertion of that authority. (I am speaking, of course, not of sociological realities in Elizabethan England, but of its world picture and what it implied.) The very logic which demanded submission in one direction demanded self-assertion, jealous insistence on one's place, titles, and prerogatives, in all others. Answerability was always vertical, never horizontal; always public, never private. When a man spoke on matters of importance, he spoke ceremonially, as belonging to a certain order, occupying a certain degree in the picture.

These, then, were the essential qualities of the picture; how well did it explain the actual events to be accounted for, the Wars of the Roses? At first glance, all seemed easy: England, under the rule of an ineffectual king, had fallen into dissension; her nobles had become rebellious and self-willed; and God had grievously punished her for these sins and failings. First she had lost her French possessions and then she had turned upon herself, falling into chaos and tyranny, until finally God had mercifully sent a redeemer, Henry VII.

But upon a closer look the picture proved to have some very disturbing consequences. Its structure of analogies contained the equation king=God; Tudor doctrine never tired of making that equation emphatically explicit, seemed in fact designed for no other purpose. But if under a king's ineffectual rule England suffered the horrors of the Barons' War, what followed about the King of kings and the horrors of, say, the Hundred Years' War?

A question not to be asked; and scholars and critics are virtually unanimous that Shakespeare, at least the Shakespeare of the histories, did not ask it. He would never have thought of drawing the analogy between the civil wars in England and the English wars against the "arch-enemy" France, however imperatively the God-king/Christendom-kingdom analogy seemed to demand it; his patriotism was logic-proof. But was it? Let us listen:

See, see the pining malady of ____________!
Behold the wounds, the most unnatural wounds,
Which thou thyself hast given her woeful breast.
O, turn thy edgéd sword another way;
Strike those that hurt, and hurt not those that help.
One drop of blood drawn from thy country's bosom
Should grieve thee more than streams of foreign
gore. (III, iii, 49-55)

This is not Henry or good Duke Humphrey pleading with one of the English barons; it is the witch Joan persuading Burgundy to break off his English alliance and return to his true allegiance. To be sure, as soon as Burgundy yields, she comments cynically: "Done like a Frenchman! Turn and turn again!" But that is precisely the point: this fine patriotic rhetoric is as available to her as to the sincerest Englishman—and more effective. The rhetoric is quite independent of the speaker's motives; it belongs to the nation. Which nation? We are at liberty to fill in the blank. Shakespeare gives it to France; and it strains credulity to believe that he did not know what he was doing. If Elizabethan attitudes argue otherwise, what—apart from the picture's logic, apart from Shakespeare's composing such a speech and then giving it to Joan—about medieval attitudes? The time lay not so far back when Christian kingdoms were considered provinces of Christendom and wars between Christian kings civil wars (so that the only pious war a king could wage was a crusade against the infidel). But if they were, what kind of sovereign was the King of kings?

There is, in *1 Henry VI*, at least one clear sign that Shakespeare did ask this forbidden question. At the end of IV.i, Henry, claiming to "be umpire in this doubtful strife" between Lancaster and York, puts on a red rose and explains this gesture, seemingly so contrary to the impartiality he has just professed, by saying:

> I see no reason, if I wear this rose,
> That anyone should therefore be suspicious
> I more incline to Somerset [Lancaster] than York.
> Both are my kinsmen, and I love them both.
> As well they may upbraid me with my crown,
> Because, forsooth, the King of Scots is crowned.
>
> (IV, i, 152-157)

I have not seen the last two lines glossed, though surely they are puzzling. Henry's argument makes sense only on the assumption that he happens to be King of England (and of France; he has just been crowned in Paris) *in exactly the same sense* as he happens to be of the house of Lancaster. Both are accidents of birth; they have no bearing on his function as umpire, which thus must rest on another quality altogether. That quality can only be his pious and loving Christian spirit, which is independent of his royal degree and both commands and entitles him to "instruct and teach" men to "continue peace and love." This view of himself is perfectly in keeping with his bearing throughout the trilogy; but of course it is this same view which makes him so disastrously ineffectual as a king. Christian precept and example are not enough to keep the ceremonial world in order; what is required is the full exercise of higher *authority*. His claim to impartiality even while putting on the symbol of partisanship can mean only that he refuses to exercise that authority.

An impartiality truly divine; how many divisions has God? Suppose there is a war between England and Scotland (there had been so many that Scotland was almost as much an "arch-enemy" as France, was in fact usually in league with France against England); what then? Is not Henry here saying that a king of England warring against a king of Scotland or any other Christian king is, from the divine purview, doing exactly the same thing as Somerset quarreling with York? And in saying this, is he not faithfully obeying the "ana-logic" of the Elizabethan world picture? If, therefore, Christendom is continually ravaged by wars—

Henry: I always thought
It was both impious and unnatural

That such immanity and bloody strife
Should reign among professors of one faith
(v, i, 11-14) —

what blasphemous inference inescapably arises about the governance of the world and the fitness of its supreme head? Given the manifest facts of history, does not the world picture that is devised to give them meaning positively compel an impious conclusion?

IV

At this point—if I may briefly resume my little dramatic fancy—it may well have occurred to Shakespeare that there was a mode of ruling other than the picture provided for, a form of authority other than that of ceremony backed by force. He did not even have to invent it; it was embedded in the story itself but so overlaid with the ceremonial pomp of the picture that it was easily overlooked. As told by Hall and others, the story was, after all, *not* just one of discord, a succession of more and more savage spectacles; it did have a unifying design: beginning, middle, and end. It began with Richard II and ended with Henry VII; it told how the English monarchy, once having fallen from the happy state of unbroken succession and unquestioned legitimacy, sank into ever deeper confusion (except for one brief and glorious reign) and had to suffer all the horrors of civil war and tyranny before order was restored through the happy "Union of the two noble and illustre famelies of Lancastre and Yorke" in the persons of Henry Tudor and Elizabeth of York. That was the overall plot within which the events of the story had meaning; that was the design which created order out of the apparent chaos.

"Plot"? "Design"? What words were these? The effort to grasp the unity of the story seemed to call forth the vocabulary of sedition. In the picture designs and plots were proscribed; they were the work of "designing, crafty knaves," sinister and ill-meaning men whose "policy" (another word of evil) could not stand the light of the sun. The world, unless it was disordered, was a "goodly frame," essentially stationary, a palace that was like a statuesque body, or a body that was like a palace:

> And all her body, like a palace fair,
> Ascending up with many a stately stair. (Spenser)

Men who had grievances expected, and men who had done evil were summoned, to appear before the throne of justice to have their cases adjudicated—openly, explicitly, in due form. Sovereign decrees were solemnly promulgated and proclaimed by heralds or angels; every occasion was an occasion "of state," provided with the appropriate ceremony. Even war and combat, though temporary breaches of order, were ritualized; "stratagems" were wicked and dishonorable, devil's work. Indeed, all that was indirect and hidden belonged to the ignoble sphere of Satan; God's world had no room for it.

Strange: the God of Tudor history turned out to be a being altogether different from what the picture called for. The range and complexity of His plots—not to mention of the Master Plot from Fall to Resurrection—were the envy and despair of any merely human plotter. History, more particularly English history from Richard II to Henry VII, was anything but an orderly succession of events in the ceremonial mode of Henry VI's pastoral dreaming:

> So many hours must I tend my flock,
> So many hours must I take my rest.
> So many hours must I contemplate,
> So many hours must I sport myself.
> (*3 Henry VI*, II, v, 31)

"How sweet! how lovely" the world would be in which the Lord could be our shepherd. Evidently He couldn't; at least He wasn't. But neither was He the stern and prepotent judge and lord who in the fulness of His power and glory summoned evildoers directly and openly before His seat to receive their punishment and correction, or in righteous anger led His hosts against the rebellious. If He had heavenly hosts at His command, they must be committed elsewhere; at least they were not deployed in Christendom to check the wicked. The King of kings, it appeared, was altogether unlike His ideal earthly image, altogether unlike what the analogy to Henry V would lead one to expect.

What *was* He like, then? Surprisingly, He was like a dramatist. He planned, designed, plotted, employed stratagems; He worked by indirection and implication. Unable or unwilling to exert open authority and force, He nevertheless did not retreat into the pastoral mode, writing wistful Third, Fourth, and Fifth Shepherds' Plays and appealing to the still, small voice in men's hearts to do the rest. He wrote *histories* which, though on the surface they might look like savage spectacles, moved in truth by careful plotting toward an ordered conclusion. His purposes were hidden, wholly implicit in the design; while the action was still in progress, they could at most be guessed at. To the careless spectator as to the vain actor they were invisible: the actor would imagine that the play existed only to give him a chance to strut and rant and upstage his rivals, while the spectator would see it as a string of exciting episodes intended to entertain him, to confirm his nationalist self-esteem, and here and there (no pleasure is unalloyed) to point an obvious moral. But the divine dramatist knew better; in the end, and only then, His design would be manifest. And it might well be that the seemingly most episodic would, in retrospect, prove the most calculated and revealing.

With respect to kings and men of power, God evidently resembled the bad more than the good. Poor Henry VI, bullied by ambitious subjects, spoke his pitiful pieces and was discarded; but Richard III had an almost divine talent for long-range plotting. Generally, the more a king relied on the ceremonial mode and on the "picture" behind it, the surer was he to come to grief; witness Richard II. True, in the end even the plotters were only actors; the prouder they were of their subtle designs, the more harshly were they shown that they themselves had only played parts in a master plot. Their self-seeking vanity betrayed them; they could never resist the temptation to become explicit, to brag at least to the audience of their clever schemes. They fell short of the master dramatist's ultimate achievement: total self-effacement, complete immersion in the design. They wanted the glory as well as the power; even when, like Warwick, they were satisfied with being king-makers rather than kings, they wanted the world and the kings to *know* them as such. By their soliloquies they reimbursed themselves for the self-denial of plotting; they had not grasped the secret of divine dramaturgy: never to speak in the first person. Still, they had grasped enough of it to be temporarily successful. It was as though God, like men, judged less by virtue than by likeness to Himself and by pleasure received—as though He were bored by the arrangers of ritual and ceremonial tableaus and inclined to reward even wicked plotters for pleasing Him with genuine drama.

V

I seem to have moved far away from the Talbot-Countess episode, to have plunged headlong into the

Intentional Fallacy, and constructed a playlet of my own under the presumptuous title "Shakespeare Thinking about *Henry VI.*" Let me repeat, therefore, that I claim no factuality for my drama, either in the setting or in the thought. I have tried to construct a model to account for observable facts, and I have chosen the narrative form simply because that seemed the best expository strategy. Like any other model, mine must be judged by the problems it solves—which brings me back to Talbot and the Countess, whom I hope I have kept in mind throughout.

Briefly to recapitulate: I began by pointing out that the scene shows every sign of being *deliberately* episodic and called attention to the programmatic contrast between the Countess' mode of speech and that of Talbot's reply. I identified the Countess' mode—which is that of the play as a whole—as ceremonial and argued that it is inherently combative and episodic. I then presented my model and tried to show not only that it satisfied the details of Greene's attack but, more importantly that it suggests how Shakespeare may have discovered some disquieting analogies between the problems he encountered in writing the play and problems at the heart of the Elizabethan world picture. The solution to these problems I described in terms of plotting.

Both Talbot and the Countess are plotters; but their plots are as different in quality as they are in final success. The Countess cannot resist telling us about hers:

> The plot is laid: if all things fall out right,
> I shall as famous be by this exploit
> As Scythian Tomyris by Cyrus' death. . . .
>
> (II, iii, 4-6)

Contrast Talbot upon accepting the Countess' invitation:

Come hither, captain. [*whispers*] You perceive my
mind? (II, ii, 59)

It is a contrast between a design announced, made explicit, and a design barely hinted at. It is at the same time a contrast between a less and a more encompassing plot, as well as between one that aims at personal glory and one that has no such aim. The parallel to, respectively, the Countess' mode of speech and Talbot's is evident.

What does the parallel signify? This question leads to the second part of the scene, in which the reason for the Countess' ill success is explained:

Countess: Long time thy shadow hath been thrall
to me,
For in my gallery thy picture hangs;
But now the substance shall endure the
like. . . .
Talbot: Ha, ha, ha! . . .
I laugh to see your ladyship so fond
To think that you have aught but Talbot's
shadow. . . .
No, no, I am but shadow of myself.
You are deceived, my substance is not here;
For what you see is but the smallest part
And least proportion of humanity. . . .
Countess: How can these contrarieties agree?
Talbot: That will I show you presently.
[*winds his horn: drums strike up: a peal of ordnance: enter soldiers*]
How say you, madam? are you now
persuaded
That Talbot is but shadow of himself?
These are his substance, sinews, arms and
strength. (II, iii, 36-63)

Talbot is the more successful plotter because he does not naively and vainly assert himself as a "first person," a substantial being in and of himself. He is not what he is—to cite Shakespeare's favorite paradox for describing effective plotters. His strength lies precisely in his "negative capability," his having learned the secret of self-effacement, of assertion only through the larger design.

We must be clear that this is the Talbot of the episode, not that of the rest of the play. The "character" Talbot does not essentially differ from the other characters. He is, to be sure, loyal to his king and country; he puts the common cause above personal gain if not always above glory. But his *style* is ceremonial, and it is style that determines likeness. The first time we see Talbot, he shows himself as concerned about his dignity as the proudest baron. When he was a prisoner of the French:

> With a baser man of arms by far
> Once in contempt they would have bartered me;
> Which I disdaining scorned and cravéd death
> Rather than I would be so vile esteemed.
> In fine, redeemed I was as I desired. (I, iv, 30-34)

The French offer a remarkable bargain: the foremost English general for some nondescript soldier of their own. But ceremony is so much more important than function that Talbot refuses the bargain and, at risk of total loss, insists on a much worse one.

Talbot's notion of warfare is literally medieval, strictly ceremonial. When Joan takes Rouen by stratagem, he shouts "treason" and "hellish mischief" and challenges the French to come out and fight "like soldiers":

> Talbot: Dare ye come forth and meet us in the
> field?

Joan: Belike your lordship takes us then for fools,
To try if that our own be ours or no.
Talbot: I speak not to that railing Hecate,
But unto thee, Alençon, and the rest.
Will ye, like soldiers, come and fight it out?
Alençon: Signior, no.
Talbot: Signior, hang! base muleteers of France!
Like peasant foot-boys do they keep the walls
And dare not take up arms like gentlemen. (III, ii, 61-70)

Railing Hecate! There is no need to multiply instances; Talbot never opens his mouth but to pay tribute to ceremony. In the end it is not he who captures Joan, but the wily plotter Richard of York. Talbot, unsuccoured by his contentious countrymen, is "tangled" in French "snares" and dies in glorious rhymed combat with his son over who should flee to fight again and who should die for the honor of the Talbot name. He makes a splendid exit:

Then follow thou thy desperate sire of Crete,
Thou Icarus; thy life to me is sweet.
If thou wilt fight, fight by thy father's side;
And, commendable proved, let's die in pride.
(IV, vi, 54-57)

Just as a reminder of what he sounded like when he did *not* get tangled in French snares, here is his reply to the Countess once more:

Madam, I have been bold to trouble you;
But since your ladyship is not at leisure,
I'll sort some other time to visit you.

Which of these two men, so strangely yoked by one name, is the "real" Talbot? It is the Countess' question. Relying on "great rumour" and "rare report" as well as on his picture in her gallery, she thinks to trap the man's substance, "writhled shrimp" though he suddenly turns out to be. His laughter makes her ask: "Why, art not thou the man?" It develops that where before she had but the shadow of his shadow, she still has no more than his shadow; substantiality is inversely proportional to illustriousness and "presence." The substance escapes her; but in that one little scene she and we come as close as we ever shall to actually *seeing* the real Talbot. For only in that scene is he gifted, for a moment, with the style of speech and action which must be learned if his true purpose, the cause of England, is to be served. Sincerity of intention is not enough; valor and nobility do not ensure success—rather the contrary. His one brief moment, not of glory—of those he has only too many—but of genuinely dramatic effectiveness comes when he realizes that his substance is in the "sinews, arms and strength" of common, anonymous Englishmen *and* in the plot, the design in which they are made to act.

I believe that we can and must expand the question: "Who is the real Talbot?" into the broader one, "What is the real play, the real *1 Henry VI*?" Some critics, usually disintegrationists, have called it a "Talbot-play," taking their lead from Nashe's *Pierce Penniless*:

> How would it have joyed brave Talbot (the terror of the French) to think that after he had lain two hundred years in his tomb, he should triumph again on the stage, and have his bones new embalmed with the tears of ten thousand spectators at least (at several times), who, in the tragedian that repre-

sents his person, imagine they behold him fresh bleeding.[3]

(There is the Countess' "picture" again!) The integralists, on the other hand, have argued that the real heroine of this as of the other histories is England, and that even Talbot is no more than a servant in her cause. I should say that the integralists are *demonstrably* in the right—but mostly on the strength of the Auvergne episode. For it is there, and there only, that Talbot clearly eliminates himself as "hero"; everywhere else he plays the part to the hilt.

This suggests that this most episodic of episodes is the "real" play, just as the Talbot in it is the "real" Talbot. How can that be? I am afraid the explanation will sound rather paradoxical, because in answer to the question: "How can these contrarieties agree?" I am unhappily not in the position to "wind my horn" and enact the answer physically. I shall try, however, to find help in my model. I suggested that Shakespeare saw the Wars of the Roses as a function and necessary product of the ceremonial style. This meant that, on the one hand, his immediate subject, if it was to be truly represented, required that style; while on the other hand his larger subject—the divine plot in which all the disorders and episodic contentions were but steps toward a new kind of unity and order—required a style altogether different. His way out of this dilemma was this: he *plotted*, on the whole, according to the new, functional style: looking ahead, condensing, eliminating episodic matter, adding and elaborating anticipatory scenes, strengthening the themes most important to the general design. But he *wrote* according to the old, ceremonial style—in part, quite possibly, because it was still the only style

[3] R. B. McKerrow, *Works of Thomas Nashe* (London, 1910), vol. i, p. 212.

he fully controlled. But being Shakespeare, he could hardly be happy with these unresolved "contrarieties"—even though they were implicit in Tudor doctrine. So he plotted a scene which, looked at casually, seems purely episodic. But into the scene he wrote an utterly unexpected speech of three lines, which should startle us into looking closely. If we do, we discover that here the contrarieties, *both* in speech *and* in plotting, are made to confront each other, and that the victory goes to the new style—again both in speech and plotting. Drama wins over ceremony, self-effacement over self-assertion, the implicit over the explicit.

The expression "wins over" contains an ambiguity useful for my purpose; it can be read with the stress either on the first word or on the second. This brings me to the last part of the scene, which contains a final surprise. Of the "brave" Talbot, the "terror of the French," we would surely expect that he would take the Countess' treachery in very ill part. How is a man who is outraged by a ruse of war (employed by a declared enemy) likely to react to the discovery that he was to be trapped by feigned hospitality? Given the general level of rage and vengefulness in the play, a clean killing—after fearful verbal abuse—would seem a mild form of retaliation. But no; apology is sufficient to win grace:

Countess: For I am sorry that with reverence
I did not entertain thee as thou art.
Talbot: Be not dismayed, fair lady; nor misconster
The mind of Talbot, as you did mistake
The outward composition of his body.
What you have done hath not offended me;

No other satisfaction do I crave,
But only, with your patience, that we may
Taste of your wine and see what cates
    you have;
For soldiers' stomachs always serve them
    well.

Countess: With all my heart, and think me
    honourèd
To feast so great a warrior in my house.
(II, iii, 71-82)

End of our scene. Having *won* over the Countess, Talbot now wins her over. Not with words or postures of ceremonial forgiveness; there is no kneeling and lifting up, no begging for mercy and magnanimous, magniloquent granting of it. The reconciliation is managed with unassertive kindness and wholly implicit generosity: "What you have done hath not offended me." It has not offended him because this is the real Talbot, whose mind we misconstrue if we interpret it by his "outward composition" in the rest of the play. This is the sovereign plotter, who has learned from his divine counterpart both the style and the responsibilities that go with such plotting and such sovereignty.

Shakespeare's *ultimate* purpose is not to unite the English by whipping and stirring them with self-assertive nationalist bombast into once again being "the terror of the French," by directing their vainglory and ceremonial combativeness outward. That style is outdated, undramatic; worse, it is self-defeating. Not only do the French master the same style (in fact, *Henry V* suggests that originally it *was* a French style, which the English adopted to their sorrow) ; the style is too readily importable for domestic use. Having learned to employ it against the French, the Yorks and Lancasters, the

Suffolks and Cliffords (as well as the Raleighs and Essexes?) are only too ready to use it upon each other. The disorder in the world of *Henry VI* is not so much a rupture, a break in the chain of ordered being; it is a disease, an infection endemic in the all-too-pure, all-too-ceremonial lily that makes the noble flower smell far worse than weeds.

Shakespeare's ultimate purpose is greater, more encompassing, dictated by the new analogy (God-dramatist) he has discovered and by the old analogy (Christendom-kingdom) he has rediscovered beneath the rhetoric of nationalism. His immediate responsibility is to his nation; he does speak English, he is not God. But that responsibility is to teach his nation a *new style*: of grace, of easy self-confidence, of implicit courtesy and generosity, of function rather than ceremony. United by and in this style, England would deserve to "win over" other nations and to play a leading part in the divine masterplot. After the "Union of the two noble and illustre famelies of Lancastre and Yorke" there is promise of a still greater union, no longer "noble and illustre" but for that very reason likely to prove finer and truer, more lasting and closer to men's real needs:

> No other satisfaction do I crave,
> But only, with your patience, that we may
> Taste of your wine and see what cates you have.

But that final feast is still far off—many wars off. The action is still in progress; the design can only be guessed at. Meanwhile—a brief interlude of ease and grace in a spectacle of bloody stridency—the glimpse of it must suffice to keep up the soldier's energy and spirit:

> For soldiers' stomachs always serve them well.

A concluding comment on the textual question seems

in order. If the foregoing interpretation is valid—by which I mean, necessary to solve the problems posed by *1 Henry VI* as a *work of literature*—it is a plausible guess that the play as we have it was reworked by Shakespeare. The shape of the original version, and hence the degree of Shakespeare's revisions, we can only surmise. It may be that the original play was indeed a "Talbot-play," a collaborative effort; that might account for Nashe's suspiciously generous praise of it. In that case my "model" would have to be adjusted— for instance, by assuming that it was Greene who bitterly withdrew (because he had been overruled by Shakespeare and his colleagues had failed to support him?), while the others stayed and did the job. Greene's attack would then be a plea for solidarity among playwrights against players—a very possible reading of it. Shakespeare's experiences would still be essentially what I suppose them to have been; in fact, the necessity of taking a hand in the making of an unsatisfactory play may have made them still more pointed. If so, it would be this play which he reworked, rather than a version that he could call fully his own. As for the date of the revision, I would propose one close to *King John* (1595?), which Shakespeare reworked from *The Troublesome Reign of King John* in a spirit and manner quite similar to that of *1 Henry VI*.[4] But these are all surmises; they are secondary, to be accommodated to what I am convinced is the primary evidence: the Folio play as an integral whole and the meanings implicit in its design and style.

4 Cf. the following essay on *King John*.

IV

SHAKESPEARE, PEELE, AND THE KING OF SCOTS

I

In Act IV, Scene i of *1 Henry IV*, the boy-king, having just been crowned King of France, must settle the first open quarrel between the Red Rose and the White. Retainers of the dukes of Somerset (Lancaster) and York, wearing their party emblems, demand a duel and are supported by their masters. The king forbids it and admonishes them to preserve concord:

O, think upon the conquest of my father,
My tender years, and let us not forgo
That for a trifle that was bought with blood!
Let me be umpire in this doubtful strife.
I see no reason, if I wear this rose, *putting on a red rose*
That any one should therefore be suspicious
I more incline to Somerset than York.
Both are my kinsmen, and I love them both.
As well they may upbraid me with my crown,
Because, forsooth, the King of Scots is crown'd.
(148-157)

There are two puzzles here. One is the very act of Henry's putting on a red rose while claiming to be an impartial umpire. To call the act "frivolous" or "thoughtless," as some critics have done, is entirely unjustified; Henry acts with full deliberation and is pleading most earnestly with his factious nobles. Obviously he is trying to make an important point; the question is: what can it be?

Even more puzzling than the act is the explanation, or more precisely, the analogy by which it is accounted for:

> As well they may upbraid me with my crown,
> Because, forsooth, the King of Scots is crown'd.

The analogy itself is clear: Red Rose: White Rose= English ("My") Crown: Scotch crown. (The analogy is somewhat complicated by the fact that the crown Henry is wearing at this moment is the French one, and that Burgundy has just sent a message announcing that he has "forsaken Henry's pernicious faction/And join'd with Charles, the rightful King of France." But since Henry does not doubt the legitimacy of his title, we may disregard this complication, at least for the present.) Henry is saying, in effect, that in a quarrel between England and Scotland, his wearing the English crown would no more disqualify him as an umpire than his wearing the Red Rose of Lancaster disqualifies him in a quarrel between Lancaster and York.

The claim is astonishing, in fact paradoxical. For though we might be willing to grant him impartiality in the last *by virtue of his wearing the crown* (as a symbol of authority transcending the ducal authority of the rose), his analogy seems to undercut the very claim he is making. What authority transcends that of the king? Does he claim to be not just King of England but also the King of kings? In view of his general meekness, that seems improbable. The only explanation is that he means to include crowns (and by extension all symbols of authority) among the "trifles," the "toys," and "things of no regard." His authority as an umpire must be derived from a source that is beyond all such symbols. We may well ask what source that could be.

II

But there is a more immediate question: what is the King of Scots doing here? And why that oddly scornful "forsooth," so out of keeping with Henry's normal mode of speech? By way of answer, I suggest that Shakespeare is here replying to a passage from George Peele's *Edward I*:

> Now brave JohnUblioll Lord of Gallaway,
> And king of Scots shine with thy goulden head,
> *Shake* thy *speres* in honour of his name,
> Under whose roialtie thou wearst the same.[1]

The lines are the first of a long speech by Queen Eleanor; their occasion is the scene (no. 3 in Hook's edition) in which the nine lords of Scotland ask King Edward—"to whom the Scottish kings/Owe homage as their lorde and soveraigne"—to select a new king from among them, so that Scotland may be spared the ravages of civil war. Edward grants the crown to their spokesman, John Balliol; and Eleanor, before she launches into an extravagant glorification of Edward, here stresses once more that John, though now a king, owes fealty to the King of England. Later in the play Balliol breaks his allegiance, is taken prisoner by the English, once again swears allegiance but once again rebels. At play's end Edward sets out with an army to punish "false Balioll" and "beat these braving Scots from out our bounds."

In his edition of *Edward I*, Hook shows—conclusively, I believe—that the quarto text abounds with evidence of having been substantially revised. (The play was entered in the *Stationers Register* on October 8, 1593; the original version may date back as far as 1590.) The

[1] *The Dramatic Works of George Peele,* ed. by F. S. Hook and J. Yoklavitch (New Haven, 1961). The lines are numbered 697-700 in this edition. Italics are mine.

Queen's speech figures importantly in Hook's demonstration. It is broken up by the odd stage direction "Queene Elinors speeche" at a point where she has already been speaking for four lines (those quoted above); moreover, there is so little connection between these lines and the "speeche" which follows that Hook finds it necessary to transpose three lines from earlier in the scene (where they make no sense at all) and to insert them before the "speeche." His entirely convincing explanation is that the confusions in the quarto text stem from Peele's having added to the printer's copy: the "speeche" was written on an insert leaf and bore a heading which became the stage direction, while the misplaced three lines—needed to provide a transition between the opening lines and the "speeche"—were written on the margin in such a way that the compositor mistook the place where they were to be inserted. Thus there is clear evidence of revision at the point directly following the "shake-spere" passage.

The passage itself contains at least one verbal oddity; spears are not normally *worn*. Nor is their mention particularly meaningful in this context. What is required is some symbol of royal authority, and the preceding lines leave no doubt what the symbol is. As soon as the Scottish lords have agreed to accept whomever Edward shall choose as their king, Edward says:

> Deliver me the golden Diadem.
> Loe here I holde the goale for which ye strived . . .
> Baliol behold I give thee the Scottish crowne,
> Weare it with heart and with thankfulnesse.
>
> (671-80)

We are witnessing an act of feudal investiture: with these words Edward places the crown on the kneeling Balliol's head. And while spears are not normally "worn," crowns are; while the shaking of spears is no very apposite symbol of royal sway, the wearing of a crown is. The internal evidence strongly suggests that the words "Shake thy speres" constitute a minor revision, made at the time of, and probably in line with, the other major revisions of the whole episode.

If this is granted, there can be, I think, no reasonable doubt that F. G. Fleay was right.[2] Peele's alluding in this way to Shakespeare fits perfectly with what we know from other sources about the "biography of the English Drama" in the years 1592-1593. A year before the publication of *Edward I*, Greene's "Groats-worth of Witte" had appeared, with its admonitions to Marlowe, Nashe, and Peele, its bitterly abusive warning against "Shake-scene," and its allusion to *3 Henry VI*. Early in 1593 Chettle had found it advisable to apologize for having published Greene's attack—possibly because "divers of worship" had informed him of Shakespeare's "uprightness of dealing" forcefully enough to prompt him to placate a man with such influential patrons. Whether or not Peele had any personal grievance against Shakespeare, clearly he was among those who by Greene's account had reason to feel threatened by the "upstart crow's" success.

If we admit "Shake thy speres" as an allusion, the im-

2 Seventy-five years ago F. G. Fleay proposed these lines as a Shakepeare allusion (*A Biographical Chronicle of the English Drama, 1559-1642* [London, 1891], II, p. 157). W. W. Greg called the suggestion "rather doubtful" [*Henslowe's Diary* [London, 1904-1908], II, p. 176]. Since then, as Hook somewhat understates the matter, "few have seen fit to take [it] seriously" (*The Dramatic Works of George Peele*, p. 183, note to line 600). What the original wording may have been is, of course, a matter of conjecture. But a natural reading can be obtained by two very small changes. The kneeling Balliol is bidden by the Queen to rise:

> Now brave John Balioll Lord of Gallaway,
> And king of Scots, [lift up] thy goulden head,
> [Shine with thy crown] in honour of his name,
> Under whose roialtie thou wearst the same.

plication would seem to be twofold. Peele softens the line Greene had so sharply drawn between poets and players; in crowning "Shake-speare" Balliol, he admits him to the crowned ranks of the poets and distances himself from Greene's, calling him and his kind "puppets" and "apes." But at the same time Peele wants it understood that Shakespeare's dignity is of a subordinate kind—granted by and to be borne under a higher authority. I do not know if we can or should go so far as to ascribe a "Shakespearean" meaning to Balliol's later rebellion and defeat, either in the sense that Shakespeare's actual conduct was so interpreted by Peele, or in the sense of a warning that, should Shakespeare refuse to acknowledge the authority of his betters, he would fare as badly as Balliol does. I do not believe that such an extension of the allusion into a full allegory is necessary; Peele does not strike me as the kind of writer who would have felt bound in this way by a bit of name-play. Probably the allusion was worked into the text simply as a pointed jest—and perhaps as a calculated move in a "war" in which Greene's attack and Chettle's apology had been prior moves. Peele meant to put Shakespeare in his proper place: more elevated certainly than the one Greene had assigned him but not as high as Shakespeare might think himself entitled to.

III

In suggesting that the "King of Scots" analogy in *1 Henry IV* is a retort to Peele's "Shake-spere" allusion, I realize that I am getting into the troubled waters of textual scholarship and controversy. My hope is that they will prove to be not nearly so deep as they are troubled; but, obviously, before proceeding with my arguments, I must try to cross those waters.

There can be no reasonable doubt that the Henry VI

plays must have existed, in some form, by mid-1592 at the latest. As to the form, most scholars at present believe that it must have been essentially that of the Folio text, and that *The Contention* and *The True Tragedy* are a "bad quarto" version of that text, heavily cut, much corrupted by memorial reproduction, but here and there preserving portions of true copy.[3] A certain, very limited amount, of revision is allowed for to account for some differences between Q and F; but "revisionist" theories in general—theories, that is, which would explain F as derived from Q and altered and expanded by revision—are in disfavor. For any specific difference, the burden of proof is considered to be on the revisionist rather than the reportorialist.

By way of proof, then, I offer a few lines spoken by Clifford over his father's body (2 *Henry VI, V,* ii):

O, let the vile world end,
And the premised flames of the last day
Knit earth and heaven together!
Now let the general trumpet blow his blast,
Particularities and petty sounds
To cease! Wast thou ordained, dear father,
To lose thy youth in peace, and to achieve
The silver livery of advised age,
And, in thy reverence and thy chair-days, thus
To die in ruffian battle? Even at this sight
My heart is turned to stone, and while 'tis mine,
It shall be stony. (40-51)

These lines, I submit, are *prima facie* proof that Shakespeare himself revised the text of at least the second part

[3] No Q version of *1 Henry VI* is extant, but Nashe's mention of a "Talbot" play justifies the inference that whatever holds for 2 and *3 Henry VI* and the corresponding quartos applies equally to *1 Henry VI*. In what follows, therefore, I shall use "Q" to stand not only for *The Contention* and *The True Tragedy* but also for the Talbot play.

of the *Henry VI* trilogy well after 1592. Unless we are prepared to abandon all our beliefs about Shakespeare's development as a dramatic poet—to level all distinctions between his early and his mature style—we have no choice but to assume that these lines got into the F text much later than the date now commonly assigned to it. There is no need of minute metrical or rhetorical analysis; if we have not been deafened by the clamor of the "textual" controversy, our ears immediately instruct us that no Elizabethan poet, not even Shakespeare, was capable of writing such blank verse in 1592.[4]

But the lines prove something more: that the present predisposition to explain differences between Q and F by cutting and reportorial reconstruction is in the highest degree questionable. In Q, Clifford's speech is not only less than half as long as in F; it is a different speech altogether:

O! dismall sight, see where he breathlesse lies,
All smeared and weltred in his luke-warme blood,
Ah, aged pillar of all Comberlands true house,
Sweete father, to thy murthred ghoast I sweare,

[4] Unhappily, many eminent scholars *have* allowed themselves to become deafened. J. Dover Wilson (Cambridge edition, notes) glosses, with what I can only call disingenuous caution: "And how mature this diction and metre are!" Similarly Tillyard (*Shakespeare's History Plays*, p. 215): ". . . gets beyond youthful rhetoric to verse that would not discredit Shakespeare in his maturity." A. S. Cairncross, on the other hand, appears to be genuinely deaf; for him (Arden edition, p. liii) Clifford's lines are simply "high poetry," of the same order as other "high poetry" in the play, such as:

The gaudy, blabbing, and remorseful day
Is crept into the bosom of the sea;
And now loud-howling wolves arouse the jades
That drag the tragic melancholy night.
(IV, i, 1-4)

At least E. K. Chambers, when he decided to endorse the memorial-reconstruction theory, did not simultaneously surrender his critical judgment but stuck to the conviction that Clifford's speech, at least, must be a later revision (*William Shakespeare*, I, p. 286).

Immortall hate unto the house of Yorke,
Nor never shall I sleepe secure one night,
Till I have furiously revengde thy death,
And left not one of them to breath on earth.[5]

Nothing in these lines justifies the supposition that they are not "true copy"—i.e., that they do not accurately represent the text of "2 Henry VI" as it stood in 1592. We have, on the contrary, compelling reasons to infer that at some later time, Shakespeare substituted another and much longer (as well as much better) speech for that of Q.

The force of this inference extends far beyond Clifford's speech; it extends to every passage in Q which, though different from F, is, by contemporary standards of play-book printing, not extraordinarily corrupt. The radical fallacy of the reportorial argument is that it begs the question: again and again it judges Q readings deficient not because they are in themselves manifestly corrupt or incoherent but because they compare unfavorably with F. Clearly, to make their case, the reportorialists must be able to show that Q is significantly inferior to quartos of other contemporary plays which we have no reason to suspect of being memorial reconstructions (such as, e.g., Peele's *Edward I* or *The Troublesome Reign of King John*). They must, in fact, exclude F entirely from their initial argument; in principle, though not in every detail, the reportorial character of Q must be established independently of any "evidence" derived from F. As far as I know, the reportorialists have not even tried to do so.

Take the argument of Madeleine Doran.[6] Miss Doran sets up five categories of evidence for memorial recon-

[5] *The Cambridge Shakespeare*, ed. by William Aldis Wright (London and New York), 1891-1893, vol. IX, p. 567.

[6] *Henry VI, Parts II and III*, University of Iowa Studies, 1928.

struction: corrupt verse, nonsense passages, anticipations and recollections, transpositions, and omissions. A moment's thought should make it clear that none of these categories has probative value except the second: nonsense passages. Transpositions—from where to where? Unless the text of Q *itself* compels us to assume that passages must have got misplaced—because as it stands, the text makes no sense—the F arrangement may just as easily be the result of a revision of Q as the Q arrangement a garbling of F. Omissions—or additions? Unless the Q text *itself* is incoherent to the point of making no sense, one explanation is as good as the other. Anticipations and recollections? Playwrights do repeat themselves; again, unless an "anticipation" or "recollection" makes nonsense of the passage in which it occurs, it proves nothing. Finally, corrupt verse (by which Miss Doran means prose printed as verse, verse printed as prose, mislineation, hypermetrical or hypometrical lines) ? Unless it can be shown that the corruption is much greater and more pervasive than the (possibly quite foul) condition of the copy and the compositor's lack of care can account for, there is no reason to suspect memorial reconstruction. The fact is that there is one and only one kind of valid evidence: a text which, *as a whole* and *in itself*, is so garbled, incoherent, and corrupt that, allowing for foul copy and careless printing, it could not have been written in that form by the dramatist. A mere straight reading of Q is sufficient to show that Q is very far from being such a text.

There are, to be sure, passages in Q sufficiently doubtful to invite a reportorial explanation; and the reportorialists have, naturally enough, made the most of these (especially of York's confused genealogical speech in II, ii) . But the number of such passages is very small, is indeed no larger than we find in unsuspected texts. If, to account for them, we label Q "bad quarto," the inevitable consequence is that we immediately have to erect a whole scaffolding of *ad hoc* hypotheses to explain how astonishingly accurate and coherent Q in fact is! Judged by the most elementary standards of acceptable explanation, the reportorial hypothesis stands condemned. It is much more plausible—and economical—to explain, case by case, the relatively few instances of manifest garbling in Q than to explain how, though reported, it is for the most part coherent, carefully and even effectively written, and no worse printed than comparable quartos of the time.

All this would be true even if there were no clear evidence of later revision by Shakespeare; *with* such evidence, it becomes not only true but necessary. But how, if the reportorial theory is manifestly untenable, has it won the assent of so many and eminent scholars, some of whom had previously been revisionist? One reason, I believe, is that Q had usually been read with the unconscious acceptance of F as the "norm." Another and probably more important one is that the case was not considered in itself but as an element of the "authorship" controversy. To be a revisionist was, and still is, virtually tantamount to denying Shakespeare's authorship of Q; conversely, affirming Shakespeare's authorship of *Henry VI* seems almost to entail an acceptance of the reportorial theory of Q. I think it unlikely that the theory would have been taken very seriously if there had never been any doubt of Shakespeare's authorship; it might have been proposed—as what theory is not, when it comes to Shakespeare?—but I should guess that it would have met just about the same reception as the analogous theory concerning *The Troublesome Reign of King John*. The fact is that it was not proposed because Q, considered by itself, compelled it;

it arose because it promised to clinch another and quite unrelated argument. From the outset it was *ad hoc.*

Both the reportorialists and (with few exceptions) the revisionists seem to accept an initial assumption which is greatly in need of critical scrutiny: namely that Shakespeare could not have written Q pretty much as it stands. I am unaware of any compelling argument in support of that assumption; I see no difficulty in crediting him with the kind of verse and dramaturgy found in Q. I am convinced of his authorship of *Henry VI,* without in the least feeling the need to discredit *The Whole Contention.* I would, in fact, claim it *for* Shakespeare—and challenge my opponents of the Malone persuasion to point to a single history play written prior to 1592 which is of comparable quality. With the exception of *The Troublesome Reign* (which proves little or nothing, since it also may well be an early, unrevised form of *King John*), I doubt if they can point to any. (Historical romances such as Greene's and Peele's hardly belong to the same genre; Marlowe's *Edward II* appears to postdate Q.) It goes without saying that Q is inferior to what we "expect" from Shakespeare from the retrospect of the Folio; but as a beginning dramatist's pioneering effort in what was virtually a new kind of drama—the pure and serious English history play—it stands in little need of apology.

In short, I believe that both Shakespeare scholarship and Shakespeare criticism should return to the position Courthope took fifty years ago. Untroubled by any suspicions that *The Contention* and *The True Tragedy* might be "bad" quartos, Courthope read them as plays in their own right and concluded not only that they must be by Shakespeare but that, for all their obvious shortcomings, they testify to his superiority: "These plays are the work of a single mind. That was not the mind of

Greene, Peele, or Marlowe. . . . Shakespeare was the one dramatist alive capable of imagining the vast conflict of powerful wills, selfish purposes, and struggling ambitions . . . the only one who had sufficient grasp of mind to imagine that historic drama as a consistent whole."[7] This is, to repeat, is Courthope's verdict on the *quartos.* To arrive at a similar one, very little is needed beyond a reading—after a suitable dose of other "histories" of the day—of the quartos by and for themselves rather than in constant, squint-eyed comparison with the folio texts. Whoever, after that, wants to determine, quarto line by quarto line, exactly what "feathers" Shakespeare stole from Greene, Nashe, Marlowe, and others is free to do so. He will contribute to Shakespeare scholarship an inventory of the kind of debts (some of which may of course be parodistic) that any young poet is likely to incur. The inventory will be a good thing to have, but it will hardly have bearing on the major point: that somewhere around 1590 Shakespeare wrote a series of history plays; that these plays somehow got into print as (entirely respectable) quartos; that Shakespeare later subjected them to substantial (and quite possibly, repeated) revisions; and that the end results of this process are the folio versions of these plays. This, I believe, is the true kind of "revisionism"—a theory which will account for the evidence more adequately, and economically, than any of those now fashionable.

IV

I have put my argument far more generally than my immediate case requires. It is enough to show that F contains revisions of a date later than 1593. For if Shakespeare worked on the text of *Henry VI* after the publication of Peele's *Edward I,* textual chronology does

[7] *A History of English Poetry* (New York, 1962), IV, 462-63.

not forbid the surmise that Peele's "Shake-spere" lines and Shakespeare's "king of Scots" lines are related as allusion and reply. But to give substance to the surmise, I must show, first, *what* the reply means and, second, that it is meaningful *as* a reply.

Shakespeare has no name-play, no obvious counter-allusions; the meaning, if any, is entirely implicit, entirely in the occasion. It may not be illegitimate to guess that precisely this implicitness is an essential part of the answer; but, however that may be, the occasion is the genesis of the Wars of the Roses. How did they start?

We know where they started: in the Temple Garden. But—much critical commentary to the contrary notwithstanding—we do not know how they started; Shakespeare takes considerable pains to leave us in the dark. Somerset and York do *not* quarrel over York's rights to reinstatement or to the crown; in the following scene York professes complete ignorance of his descent and status and begs the dying Mortimer for instruction:

> Discover more at large what cause that was,
> For I am ignorant and cannot guess. (II, v, 59-60)

Whereupon Mortimer enters into a long and detailed account of Richard's family history. The "truth" over which Richard and Somerset have their initial falling-out remains completely unspecified; all we are told of it is that it is a point of law.[8]

The quarrel, in other words, has no cause worth men-

[8] The ways of commentators are sometimes mysterious. Cairncross glosses as follows: "While this is . . . left undefined, it is clear that the question at issue was one affecting Plantagenet's reinstatement or the succession to the crown, or both combined. Such questions were best left undefined in that period, in view of the powers of the censor." The next scene—in which the question *is* defined with the utmost precision and circumstantiality—Cairncross glosses: "The scene continues and develops Plantagenet's claim to the crown." He offers no hint as to why the powers of the censor, so threatening in II, iv, need no longer be feared in II, v.

tioning; like many others in *Henry VI,* it springs from the sheer combativeness of "high-stomached" noblemen jealous of their "honor" and determined to back their unremitting self-assertion with their swords. Except for that, the quarrel has no cause; it *is* the cause. Once started, of course, it generates abundance of "causes"; the taunts—"peevish boy," "yeoman," etc.—promptly start the process of escalation. Shakespeare even arranges his scenes in such a way that the quarrel of the roses appears as the cause, rather than the effect, of Richard's discovery of his lineal claim; he demands to know from Mortimer why Somerset was in the position to call him a yeoman. The play's dramatic logic is quite different from what we would "naturally" expect.

Nor are the roses the symbols of Lancaster and York; in the play they *become* these symbols, again because they were first, and arbitrarily, chosen as "dumb significants" in a causeless quarrel:

> Since you are tongue-tied and so loath to speak,
> In dumb significants proclaim your thoughts.
>
> (II, iv, 25-26)

And dumb significants they remain—badges of party and partisanship for which no one troubles to offer a first cause or justification. What Henry later achieves by his strange analogy is to number crowns likewise among these dumb significants—symbols which, far from having any meaning at the outset, gather that meaning only as they become the emblems of ever bloodier quarrels.

The "where" of the quarrel is not without interest. The Rose Theatre—to quote from E. K. Chambers' *The Elizabethan Stage*—"owed its name to the fact that it stood in what had been, as recently as 1547-1548, a rose garden."[9] Plays which dealt with the Wars of the Roses

[9] *The Elizabethan Stage* (Oxford, 1961), p. 405.

and were involved in (if indeed they did not precipitate) a war of playwrights and actors were being performed at the Rose. Coincidence? Of course—exactly as the choice of roses in the Temple Garden is "coincidence." It pleases our rationalist vanity to think that "meanings" must be prior to the symbols in which they are "clothed." But meanings may well be—and often demonstrably are—*ex post facto*. It is the mark of Shakespeare—I am tempted almost to call it the secret of his genius—that he accepted such coincidences as somehow binding and revelatory, as belonging to the realm of dumb significants which, though initially and in themselves they seemed to mean nothing, had the most extraordinary way of acquiring meaning. Again and again, the stage turned out to *be* the world; the playwright's task was not to represent or mirror an outside "reality," but to discover within the realities of his craft and circumstances the truth of world and stage alike.

It is unlikely that we will discover the "real" cause of Greene's attack on Shakespeare and the players; but we may discover what Shakespeare "made of it." On the assumption that the Rose Garden scene is meant to represent the beginning of the theatrical quarrel as well as of that between York and Lancaster, we can infer that the precipitating cause was a minor dispute, insignificant in itself. It grew violent because of the intense, self-assertive pride of the parties to it. In the absence of a single strong "monarch," the quarrel grew until it brought a formerly strong and united "common-wealth" close to ruin.[10]

[10] We should recall here that the years preceding the closing of the theatres in June 1592 seem to have been singularly successful and prosperous for the Admiral-Lord Strange combination. Still there were troubles, principally the quarrel with the elder Burbadge and the company's move to the Rose. In the fall of 1592 (and coincident with Greene's attack) troubles seem to have piled up into a major crisis.

The wording not only of Greene's attack but also of Chettle's apology and (if it is admitted) of Peele's "Shake-spere" lines suggests that the true cause of the quarrel, as distinct from its immediate and probably insignificant occasion, was one of status, of "degree." It is not altogether clear whether and in what sense Greene was charging Shakespeare with plagiarism (though I believe with Dover Wilson that *some* sort of "theft" was implied); what is very clear is his rage that a mere player, a "rude groom," should consider himself the equal if not the superior of the "rare wits," gentlemen with university degrees and the learning requisite for the writing of true drama. For Greene and his friends the theatre is not a republic but a monarchy: "Yet let subjects ['a rabble of counterfeits'] for all their insolence, dedicate a *De profundis* every morning to the preservation of their *Caesar,* lest their increasing indignities return them ere long to their juggling to mediocrity, and they bewail in weeping blanks, the wane of their Monarchy."[11] Again and again he insists that acting is a "mechanical labor," worthy in its way, provided the rude mechanicals do not "waxe proud."

The thrust of Greene's complaint is directed, after all, not so much at "Shake-scene" as at playwrights so "base-minded" that they would acknowledge players as their equals or even "masters." Implicit in his words, it seems to me, is bitterness that—in some dispute with a player "conceited" enough to imagine he can write plays by himself—his colleagues did not side with him (Greene), at least as forcefully and unequivocally as they should

[11] Nash's preface to Greene's *Menaphon,* as quoted by T. W. Baldwin, *On the Literary Genetics of Shakespeare's Plays* (Urbana, 1959), p. 36. Baldwin shows that references to "crows" very often, especially for Greene and his group, implied not only the Aesopian fable but also the story of the Roman cobbler who taught his crow to say *Ave Caesar.* Marlowe being a cobbler's son, there is rich ground here for latent allusions.

have. What he urges is a common front, indeed a boycott: "never more acquaint them with your admired inventions" and let them discover where their reliance on their own abilities will take them. If they refuse to acknowledge the natural superiority of their betters, they will soon enough find themselves vagrant jugglers again.

Even Chettle's apology is cast in the language of "degree": "The quality he professes," "divers of worship," even "honesty"—call up hierarchical associations. Peele's lines in *Edward I,* of course, are explicitly feudal. "Order," in this world, means not only stability and harmony but *ordo,* each man's acceptance of his God-given place. Peele admits Shake-spere among the crowned heads, but not as an equal. The passage is stiff with the symbolism of "majesty," both political and poetic. The inserted "speeche" by Queen Eleanor celebrates in the most extravagant figures Edward's famous "suit of glass"—a noted and expensive piece of stage finery. Here is a sample:

> Thy [Edward's mirror-suited] person's garded with
> a troope of Queenes,
> And every Queene as brave as Elinor,
> Gives glorie to these Glorious chrystall quarries,
> Where every orbe an object entertaines,
> Of riche device and princelie majestie.
> Thus like Narcissus diving in the deepe,
> I die in honour and in Englands armes:
> And if I drowne, it is in my delight,
> Whose companie is cheefest life in death,
> From foorth whose currall [coral] lips I suck the
> sweete,
> Wherewith are daintie Cupids candles made.[12]

[12] Apparently baffled by this line—and, as I will argue, appropriately so—Hook and Yoklavich follow the practice of earlier editors in supplying the emendation "caudles" (a kind of warm drink). Nevertheless,

Then live or die brave Ned, or sinke or swim,
An earthlie blisse it is to looke on him.
On thee sweete Ned, it shall become thy Nell,
Bounteous to be unto the beauteous,
Ore prie the palmes sweete fountaines of my blisse,
And I will stand on tiptoe for a kisse. (708-24)

This, Peele seems to say, is a piece of truly *sovereign* writing—the kind that lesser men may try to ape but can never equal. The players may supply the physical finery (the suit of glass figures as a major item in Henslowe's accounts) ; but it takes a true poet to give it its full splendor. If Shake-spere wants to "imitate" such "excellence," let him; but let him always remember "under whose roialtie he wears the same."

V

Shakespeare, I believe, did "remember"—in his own way. In 2 *Henry VI* there is a scene (III, ii) in which Queen Margaret, to quell Henry's well-grounded suspicion that Suffolk is implicated in Duke Humphrey's murder, launches into an elaborately rhetorical counterattack upon the king. Her speech is a long set-piece on her crossing to England.

Was I for this nigh wreck'd upon the sea.
And twice by awkward wind from England's bank
Drove back again unto my native clime? . . .
What did I then, but cursed the gentle gusts
And he that loosed them forth their brazen caves;
And bid them blow towards England's blessed shore,
Or turn our stern upon a dreadful rock?
Yet Aeolus would not be a murderer,

both the copy text (Q1 of 1593) and Q2 of 1599 (the latter of which H and Y recognize to be "a superior piece of printing" and to be edited with respect to spelling) attest "candles."

But left that hateful office unto thee.
The pretty-vaulting sea refus'd to drown me,
Knowing that thou wouldst have me drown'd on
shore
With tears as salt as sea, through thy unkindness.
The splitting rocks cower'd in the sinking sands
And would not dash me with their ragged sides,
Because thy flinty heart, more hard than they,
Might in thy palace perish Elinor.[13]
As far as I could ken thy chalky cliffs, . . .
I stood upon the hatches in the storm;
And when the dusky sky began to rob
My earnest-gaping sight of thy land's view,
I took a costly jewel from my neck,
A heart it was, bound in with diamonds,
And threw it towards thy land. The sea receiv'd it,
And so I wish'd thy body might my heart. . . .
How often have I tempted Suffolk's tongue. . . .
To sit and witch me, as Ascanius did
When he to madding Dido would unfold
His father's acts, commenc'd in burning Troy!
Am I not witch'd like her? or thou not false like
him?
Ay me, I can no more! Die, Elinor!
For Henry weeps that thou dost live so long.

(82-121)

Nothing is more predictable than the editorial glosses on the odd fact that three times in this speech Margaret refers to herself as "Elinor" (and that Henry, a few lines before, calls her "Nell") : Shakespeare has forgotten that the queen's name was Margaret, not Eleanor. If so, it would be an extraordinary lapse of memory, unparal-

[13] Here, of course, and in line 120, I restore the Folio's "Elinor," for which the text I cite retains the standard emendation, "Margaret."

leled elsewhere in Shakespeare (and, I should guess, in all dramatic literature). Throughout four plays—the entire tetralogy, in which she plays a large and decisive role—Shakespeare remembers her real name, but in this one scene he forgets. Nothing, again, is more predictable than that J. D. Wilson, being a disintegrationist, should find his views confirmed by this slip: since Shakespeare was merely revising a play already substantially written by others, he had no very firm hold of the names of the characters, so that here he confused the rarely named "Margaret" with the often named "Elinor (Nell)," wife of Duke Humphrey. (Whereas Cairncross, an integralist, argues that the confusion is a mere "slip, which must have been corrected on the stage" and which consequently he corrects in his edition.) Since the assumption of error on Shakespeare's part relieves us of the burden of discovering what he may have *meant* by such oddities, both the memory and the knowledge of the greatest English poet turn out to be remarkably limited.

For there is also, of course, his ignorance, especially of the classics. Wilson finds in Margaret's speech further evidence for his position; he argues that it furnishes telling instances of a more general disparity between, on the one hand, an ostentatious display of classical learning and, on the other, an at times astonishing ignorance of classical sources. Had Shakespeare known his Virgil, he could not possibly have written of *Ascanius* as bewitching Dido, since of course in the *Aeneid* it is Cupid, in the appearance of Ascanius, who charms the queen. At the same time, Shakespeare could not have had Ascanius unfold, "his father's acts, commenced in burning Troy," since Aeneas himself tells his own story. Wilson believes Shakespeare's source must have been a passage from Chaucer's *Legend of Good Women.* Cairncross grants the mistakes but feels they could have arisen as easily from a misreading of Virgil as from a reading of Chaucer.

But were they mistakes? Wilson's notion that Shakespeare had to rely on Chaucer for his knowledge of Virgil may be regarded as thoroughly demolished—especially by T. W. Baldwin, who has shown that Shakespeare must have read, and intimately known, at least the first six books of the *Aeneid* in Latin.[14] If further proof were needed, it will be found in this very speech. For the mention of Aeolus, Ascanius, and Dido is not just classical window dressing. Margaret's entire account of her tempest-tossed crossing is patterned after Virgil's treatment in Book I of the storm by which Juno seeks to destroy Aeneas.

Thus, "the splitting rocks cower'd in the sinking sands" effectively combines the hidden rocks (*saxa latentia*) on which three of Aeneas' ships split and the shallows and quicksands (*brevia et Syrtis*) on which another three founder. The seventh and last is struck astern (*in puppim*) by a huge wave—which incidentally disposes of Cairncross' emendation "Or turn our *stem*" in line 90. The dusky sky which "robs" Margaret's "sight" of the view of England is much like the clouds which rob the heavens and daylight from the Trojans' eyes (*eripiunt subito nubes caelumque diemque/ Teucrorum ex oculis*). The "chalky cliffs" are of course those of Dover; they also happily coincide with the huge cliffs (*vastae rupes*) guarding the sheltering bay in which Aeneas finds refuge. Considering these and other distinct assonances to the *Aeneid* in the details of the "Nell" speech which argue convincingly for Shakespeare's intimate knowledge of Virgil, I find it diffi-

14 *William Shakspere's "Small latine & lesse Greeke"* (Urbana, 1944). But cf. especially, for the passage in question, Baldwin's *On the Compositional Genetics of the Comedy of Errors* (Urbana, 1965), pp. 226-84.

cult to believe he was ignorant of, or could have forgotten, such elementary facts as Cupid's disguise or Aeneas' report.

Still, these are "mistakes" in some sense, exactly as "Nell" and "Elinor" are mistakes: What are we to make of them? Here as elsewhere in Shakespeare, I believe that the interpreter has little choice except to assume that Shakespeare was fully aware of what he was doing and intended the "mistakes" to carry specific and discoverable meanings. These meanings, moreover, were sufficiently important to him to want to call attention to them by the apparent faults in which they were imbedded. What follows is an hypothesis of what Shakespeare could have meant. If the hypothesis seems unduly complex, I am ready to withdraw it in favor of a simpler one, if that one accounts for Shakespeare's having knowingly and deliberately committed such a cluster of "errors" as he does in the "Nell" speech. True, explanations to the effect that Shakespeare was plainly ignorant have the advantage of unassailable simplicity. The trouble with such interpretations is that they short-circuit interpretation. More than that—though they can never be proved false, they are in the highest degree questionable. If by 1592 Shakespeare knew anything, he knew that his university-trained rivals would eagerly pounce on just this kind of error; he also knew the first book of the *Aeneid.* It seems reasonable to grant him, likewise, the knowledge of the names of his major characters and the ability to tell "Elinor" from "Margaret." The burden of proof is on those who assume Shakespeare's unawareness of what he was doing, not on those who assume his deliberateness. An hypothesis based on the latter assumption *cannot* be disproved by the claim that it is disproportionately complex; but it *can* be disproved by a simpler one resting *on the same assumption.* If my attempt prompts the proposal of such an hypothesis, I shall feel that I have done the state (of Shakespeare interpretation) some service.

VI

I shall assume, then, that the "Nell" speech is part of Shakespeare's reply to Eleanor's "speeche" in Peele's *Edward I.* The first thing that must have struck him about the latter is, I should think, what later struck Peele's editors and forced them to amend the text at this point: namely, that here a show-piece speech had been inserted into the text *at great cost to the play's dramatic integrity.* Ostentatious pride, the will to assert one's superiority and outshine one's rivals, was more important than dramatic function. In other words, Eleanor and her "speeche" were the very embodiments of the principle of "ceremony" that had proved ruinous to England and now was proving equally ruinous to drama and the theatre.[15]

As such Eleanor is virtually identical with both the Eleanor (wife of Duke Humphrey) and the Margaret of Shakespeare's play. The quarrel of the roses has already gathered meaning and momentum; but it is still kept in check by the "good Duke." He, therefore, must be got rid of, and it is his wife's pride that furnishes the excuse for his removal. The quarrel between Margaret and Eleanor—entirely analogous to the Temple-Garden one in that it *is* a cause rather than having one—pushes England into full and open civil war; the last safeguard, the last "Lord Protector," is gone. Between Eleanor's

> Follow I must; I cannot go before
> While Gloucester bears this base and humble mind
> (I, ii, 61-62)

and Margaret's

[15] For a fuller account of this sense of "ceremony," see III.

[Is] this the royalty of Albion's king? . . .
Am I a queen in title and in style
And must be made a subject to a duke?
(I, iii, 48-52)

England founders.

Margaret's "Nell" speech is a set-piece very much like Eleanor's "speeche" in *Edward I.* But the decisive difference is this: unlike the "speeche," it *functions* as what it is. It is intended by Margaret to conceal a murderous plot under the cloak of grand rhetoric—and it almost succeeds. In other words, it has an object beyond itself, it does not mirror itself, Narcissus-like, in its own "glory" but moves under the direction of a larger dramatic purpose.

Since Shakespeare was intimately familiar with Book I of the *Aeneid,* he must have known not only of Venus' substitution of Cupid for Ascanius but also of her reason:

> At Cytherea *novas artis, nova* pectore versat *consilia,* ut faciem mutatus et ora Cupido pro dulci Ascanio veniat, donisque furentem incendat reginam atque ossibus inplicet ignem. quippe domum timet *ambiguam* Tyriosque *bilinguis.* (657-61, italics mine)

I propose that as the goddess, fearful of treacherous double meanings, substitutes a divine being for a human one to accomplish her purpose, so Shakespeare, similarly fearful, *reverses* the substitution and reinstates the true Ascanius. Moreover, in doing so he employs *novas artes, nova consilia*—a new art and a new plan. Where the goddess employs deception, Shakespeare resorts to what we may call "re-deception": by being "false" to the Virgilian story he restores the truth.

In other words, his new art will not avail itself of meretricious trickery, such as the blood-heating and bone-consuming "gifts" (*dona*) of Cupid—"dainty Cupid's candles," as Peele calls them. No close analysis is required to expose these "candles" as the seductive frumpery they are. Just as the whole "speeche" is simply meant to dazzle, so the "Cupid" lines are simply meant to seduce. Narcissus drowns in the delight of his own mirrored beauty, kissing his own mirrored lips, which—by a metaphorical extension not wholly illegitimate, since the self-embrace is consummated under water—bear the standard epithet "coral." But where do Cupid and his candles come in? If there is any liquor available, it can, within the terms of the metaphor, be only the clear (or rather, by now, muddied) water of the mirroring pool. The same profound dishonesty that has dictated the entire "speeche" has dictated these lines.

It would be a simple matter to pursue this dishonesty. We can see Peele beaming over the skill with which he turns out fine lines such as: "And I will stand on tiptoe for a kiss"—another Cupid's candle. These are the easy triumphs of vanity, the splendors of a peacock art. Peele's preening is so blatant that we almost suspect him of knowing what he is about. But no! this is display, not self-parody; pride, not humor. It is the poetic equivalent of the peacock nationalism, the peacock flaunting of degree and place which is the real cause of war in this ceremonial world—national, civil, or theatrical.

If not the aim, at least the effect of Cupid's gifts is arson. In the *Aeneid,* Virgil establishes a strange but real metaphorical identity between the burning of Dido—which stands for the destruction of Carthage by Rome—and the burning of Troy. Dido's fatal passion is described almost entirely in images of fire; and the phrase *donisque furentem/incendit reginam* is surely meant to remind us of the *dona ferentes* from what was probably the best known and most quoted line in the *Aeneid*: *quidquid id est, timeo Danaos et dona ferentes.* Indeed, what is Aeneas' story, up to and including the burning of Dido (Carthage) except an unfolding of the incendiary results of divine gifts. The first gift—triumphantly brought into Troy by Paris—was Helen; it was followed by the Trojan horse, which in turn was followed by the gifts of Cupid for Dido. The gods send presents, and cities crumble into ashes.

It would appear that Venus' new arts and plans are far from new; they have been tried long and often enough to make their results entirely predictable. At most they are novel tricks in a very old game. But in one respect they *are* new: in the *Aeneid*, unlike the story of Troy, they are employed toward the ultimate end of *founding* a city rather than destroying one. (And not of *a* city merely but *the* City—the almost universal order of Rome.) The burning of Carthage is not the tragic consummation of a divine quarrel, but the first, sorrowful act in a large and beneficent design—in a kind of "divine comedy." Even so, however, the plan and the devices were the Gods'; the new City, powerful and splendid in Virgil's day, was sacked in turn—by Goths, by Vandals, and, as recently as 1525, by the mercenaries of Charles V. The *pax Romana*, whether that of the Caesars or that more fragile one of the Popes, had been shattered; it looked as though the divine gifts still and forever carried within them the consuming flame that would ultimately destroy the "bewitched" recipient.

I suggest that by reinstating Ascanius Shakespeare serves notice that he means to write a *human* comedy, however bitter and tragic the opening act may appear. He has learned to fear the gods even when they bear gifts (as he has learned to fear demi-gods, or kings, like Peele's Edward giving a crown to Shake-spere). And at the same time he serves notice that he means to write a human *comedy*—i.e., a vast drama rather than an epic poem. Which brings us to the last "error": the making Ascanius rather than Aeneas the narrator of the "acts commenced in burning Troy."

In the *Aeneid,* action and narration are separate though parallel; even as Cupid administers the inflammatory gift to Dido, Aeneas tells of the inflammatory gift to Troy. God acts or directs action, while man in retrospect discovers the design and reports. When Cupid assumes the shape of Ascanius, therefore, he simply makes explicit what is implicit in the classical (and Renaissance) conception of epic poetry. The epic is essentially a report of God's purposeful action—a justification of the ways of God with, and to, man; man's seemingly confused gropings are shown to be intelligible and orderly within the divine "machinery" by which in fact they have been directed. Hence the setting at the end of Book I of the *Aeneid* is the precise embodiment of the epic situation: the human narrator (Aeneas) reporting the trials and glories of the past, while the divine planner (Venus through Cupid) directs the present.

By making Ascanius (rather than Aeneas) the narrator, Shakespeare transforms narration into *act,* epic into drama. In genuine drama, action is not something distinct from the telling of it; it is the telling itself. Nor are the "actors" mere mouthpieces and puppets, disguises that the divine planner puts on at will to achieve his purpose; they are actors in the true sense, pursuing their own ends and acting upon their own impulses. The dramatist's task is infinitely more difficult than that of the epic poet: he must create order without infringing on the liberty of his characters to be "themselves," just as he must achieve truth without infringing on their human prerogative to err or even tell lies. He cannot stand aside and report; he has no voice of his own. If he is to speak at all, it must be somehow through the mouths of those "apes" and "puppets" (as Greene had called them) whose speeches *are* in fact the dramatic action. And unless he realizes that these puppets have minds, passions, and purposes of their own, he will be a poor dramatist—not only in the sense that he will write inferior plays but, more importantly, in the sense that the design, the order he seeks to create, will shatter against the resistance and enmity of those whom he attempts so unwisely to rule.

It is my guess that at some point during the crisis years 1592-1594—when the theatres were mostly closed, the companies desperately struggling to stay afloat, when Marlowe was killed in a tavern brawl, Kyd imprisoned on suspicion of atheism, when Greene died in rage and destitution, calling upon his fellow playwrights to boycott the players and so reduce them to their former, miserable "estate" of vagrant jugglers—Shakespeare made a considered and profoundly serious choice to remain what he had been: a man of the theatre, an actor-dramatist. The external evidence for this guess—as for all surmises concerning Shakespeare's life beyond the barest vital and legal records—is of course scanty. Still, there are the dedications of *Venus and Adonis* and *The Rape of Lucrece* to Southampton (April 1593 and May 1594 respectively) ; there are possibly the sonnets, of mysterious import; there is the tradition (more authentic than most concerning his life) that Shakespeare was given a substantial sum of money by his patron for a "purchase he had a mind to"; there is Chettle's apology; and, lastly, there is the fact that for the court performances of Christmas 1594 Shakespeare was named for the first time as one of the payees of the Chamberlain's men and hence had presumably become a sharer. I believe the interpretation of Shakespeare's works might profit greatly from the hypothesis that during this time of troubles he both had the opportunity and was greatly tempted to leave the stage behind him and rise to the status of "poet": sustained by noble patrons, himself a gentleman, secure from the often demeaning necessities and limitations of the commercial theatre. We ought, I think, to entertain the idea that the money he was given was *in lieu* of such patronage and was invested by him as venture capital in the reconstitution of the Chamberlain's (formerly Lord Strange's) Men—in other words, that he threw in his lot, as a matter of deliberate choice, with his fellow players, the theatre, and his part. Even in his day Shakespeare was ridiculed for his determination to obtain a coat-of-arms and acquire the property necessary to maintain the status of a gentleman. But was not the point of this ambition that he managed to fulfill it *by remaining a player*—that a "degree" he might easily have attained had he been willing to renounce his past was proved attainable by a resolute acceptance of that past? What little we know of his life during these (surely crucial) years strongly suggests that he could easily have secured himself against ever again being called an "upstart crow," "rude groom," and "peasant." For a man then not quite thirty, raised in the provinces and without a university education, depending on the stage for his living and seeing that living seriously threatened, the prospect must have seemed brilliant. But the next we hear of him is in the company of Kempe and Burbadge, a "servant to the Lord Chamberlain," a motley to the view selling cheap what was most dear. I doubt that we will fully understand Shakespeare the *dramatist* unless and until we learn to take seriously the immense risk—financial, social, and poetic—he took when he *chose* to remain a player.

I must push my hypothesis one step further. If we suppose that Shakespeare had the opportunity of patronage and advancement I have surmised, what would have been his most likely effort to gain honor both for himself and for his patron? It is probable almost to the point of certainty that he would have set about writing a national epic. His attempt to write a national drama had come to grief; he himself had come under virulent personal attack, while the players were in great difficulties. The "matter" for the epic was practically given and pretty much at his command, since it was that of his earlier history plays: an epic version of Edward Hall's *Union.* (Samuel Daniel was shortly to publish the first four books of just such an epic and may even then have been at work on it, to the greater glory of himself and of his patron, the Earl of Pembroke.) Shakespeare knew that he could write verse narrative: the "facetious grace" of *Venus and Adonis* had amply proved his mastery of the Ovidian mode, while *The Rape of Lucrece* moved toward the weightier measure and matter of history. Epic poetry was the summit of Parnassus; writing an English *Aeneid* would have satisfied his own highest ambition, his patron's highest expectations, his nation's proud desire to prove herself the equal of Rome. There was no reason why he should not rival Spenser, protected by Essex as Spenser was by Raleigh; and, considering Essex' favor with the Queen, there was good reason to hope that, rather than finding himself exiled in Ireland, he would live honored in England, even at court.

It is a commonplace that when Shakespeare began in his career, players occupied a very low place in the social hierarchy. But I think we need to grasp the commonplace very firmly and concretely when we try—and how can we help trying?—to reconstruct Shakespeare's literary-moral biography. If we grant that at one point in his life he had the choice of joining the Spensers and Daniels, it would seem to follow that his refusal to do so was a profoundly revolutionary act. He was saying, in effect, that the accepted hierarchical ordering—social as well as literary—was false; that the true summit of poetry was the drama (or better, the play); and that the place of the true poet was with the players. His own achievement has borne him out so completely and magnificently that we are in danger of forgetting the revolutionary daring that was its precondition. I believe we must learn to read Shakespeare's Sonnet 94—as interpreted by William Empson—as *his* "Letter to Lord Chesterfield."

VII

I have admittedly speculated—but not idly. To repeat, the speculation has been directed toward the solving of a precisely defined textual problem: why did Shakespeare, though he clearly "knew better," make the multiple errors of the "Nell" speech in 2 *Henry VI*? The answer I have suggested is, in brief, this: The experience of the "war of the playwrights," the closing of the theatres in 1592, the opportunity of quitting the stage and assuming the rank of true poet—all these prompted Shakespeare to render a most searching account to himself of what it meant to be a playwright, more particularly one who hoped to do for England what Virgil had done for Rome. He discovered four things: (1) He could not avail himself of any supernatural machinery to bring his story to a genuinely constructive conclusion; the new and greater order must be achieved by *human* agency and effort. (2) He could not function as the epic narrator, telling of past deeds and of the divine purpose by which they were directed; he had to write in such a way that the telling *was* the action. He had no voice of his own, no means of revealing the design by which acts and actors were governed; the design could and must manifest itself only through the manner in which the actors spoke and, by speaking, acted upon one another. (3) The truth as well as the beauty of the whole and of any part inhered in their *function*, not in their congruence to any outside "authority," their splendor or "propriety." What was an "error" by external criteria might be a revelatory truth judged and interpreted by its function within the economy of the play; what was a most handsome line or wise *sententia* by itself might, within that economy, be a blemish or a stupidity. (4) This being the nature of genuine drama, the social order which rests and insists on "degree"—which compels the incessant assertion of one's "place"—is jealous of any challenge to it as inherently undramatic, in fact anti-dramatic. By scorning function and glorifying conspicuous consumption, it consumes the body dramatic as surely as the body politic; by its relentless ostentation and "state," it destroys state and stage alike.

These discoveries account precisely for the "errors" of the "Nell" speech; more accurately, I have analyzed what is essentially one discovery into four aspects corresponding to these "errors." The first is embodied in the reinstatement of Ascanius for Cupid, the second in his being made the narrator of Aeneas' acts and, by being that, the cause of Dido's burning love. The third accounts for *all* the substitutions in the speech: those of Ascanius for Cupid and Aeneas, as well as that of "Elinor" for Margaret. The last-mentioned (actually the first, the most repeated and the most obvious) serves as the figure and signal warning us that identity is determined by function rather than "state," so that "Margaret" and "Elinor," though seemingly signifying opposites like Red Rose and White, are in fact interchangeable. At the same time the "truth" of what Margaret/Eleanor says—and we have no reason to doubt the truth of her account of the crossing—becomes a dramatic lie, since its dramatic function is to conceal the truth. By the same token, Queen Eleanor's "speeche" in Peele is at least an untruth, since its function is to dazzle and seduce the audience (and Shake-spere) into acknowledging the playwright's superior rank, no matter what wounds are thereby inflicted on the body of the play itself. The fourth discovery, finally, accounts for Shakespeare's need to develop a new art and a new plan (*novas artes, nova consilia*) in his labor to write England's *Aeneid*—which is to say, to find, reveal, and help determine England's true role and function in the founding of a new Rome, a new universal order. The divinely founded Rome of the Middle Ages is no more; it has been shattered by the Reformation and by the pugnacious self-assertion of the new national states. Though England at long last is united, Europe is ravaged by wars. The rivalry of opposed gods—He of the Protestants and He of the Catholics, not to mention the demi-gods called "kings"—feeds the flames; so do the *consilia* of nationalist history (read: propaganda) and the *artes* of nationalist literature. A new plan is needed, and a new art: one whose mode is function rather than "state" and whose aim is a "Union" greater than that of Tudor history.

VIII

We are now in the position, I believe, to understand the full meaning of Henry's "King of Scots" analogy, both as a reply to Peele and, more importantly, as a key to *Henry VI*. Henry is by no means frivolous in discounting the "dumb significants" of partisanship—roses and crowns—as mere trifles. But he *is* profoundly wrong.

One way of describing his position is to call it "realist" (in the sense of medieval philosophy) or Platonist. He refuses to attach weight to the fact that, in choosing to wear a rose or crown, he cannot but wear a *particular* rose or crown. Though language and logic would seem to demand the prior existence and greater reality of the universal Rose or Crown, the inescapable fact is that he who chooses one must choose a red or white, English or Scottish, one. The wholeness and purity of conceptual forms is not sustainable in the world of choice and action; in action we become partial and partisan. In terms of language: the universality and permanence of conceptual forms is a linguistic illusion; as soon as we pass outside the charmed circle of words (*speaking* significants) into the realm of things (*dumb* significants), we discover that there is nothing answering to our expectation to possess *the* Rose or *the* Crown. What we have treated with contempt as "accidental" becomes in the highest degree "substantial"; in the world of action the redness or whiteness of a rose, the Englishness or Scottishness of a crown, is likely to be much more determinative than its conceptual "essence."

Henry seems to sense this; perhaps it is not quite accurate to call him a "realist." But this response is to retreat still farther into universality, to call even roses and crowns "as such" "things of no regard." For him reality is so inseparable from ultimate unity and harmony that even in the act of putting on dumb significants he can proclaim them insignificant. His essence lies in his "love," his devout and pious will to "still continue peace and love" and admonish others to do likewise.

But of course, reality makes him a liar:

> And therefore, as we hither came in peace,

So let us still continue peace and love.
Cousin of York . . .
And, good my Lord of Somerset, unite . . .
Go cheerfully together and digest
Your angry choler on your enemies.
(IV, i, 160-68)

What enemies? Why, the French: "Charles, Alencon and that traitorous rout." Suddenly the crown Henry wears turns out to be something far other than a trifle; his "peace and love" turn out to be of very limited application. Only a moment before, Somerset and York meant to digest their *choler* on their enemies, "enemy" then being defined by the *color* of the roses they wore; now they are instructed that "enemy" is to be defined by the kind of crown the king wears. Just as letters—another kind of "dumb significant"—are needed to determine whether "ko:lor" means "color" or "choler," so roses, crowns, or some comparable symbols are needed to tell me who are my enemies and who are my friends. If Henry can call the French a "traitorous rout," Burgundy can call the English a "pernicious faction." To whom these words apply is a matter of which dumb significant is chosen to be determinative.

The fact is that the world of *Henry VI*—of all nationalist history—is, in Virgil's words, a *domus ambigua* and *all* its inhabitants are *Tyrii bilingui*. God offers no solution; on the contrary, He is the most ambiguous and double-tongued of all. To influence events, he disguises himself in human form and speaks in the language of men—with the result that Dido and Carthage burn to ashes. Rome has seen to it that there will be no Carthaginian *Aeneid*; but, if there were, it might be of some interest just how the Dido-Aeneas story would be told. What the Roman Virgil blandly calls "new arts and plans" would, thus translated, very probably appear as "new lies and treacherous schemes"; and Cupid disguised as Ascanius might look more like an agent of Hell than of Heaven. Is Joan of Arc a witch or a saint? Tell me what dumb significant you have chosen and I will answer—except that my answer will be wholly superfluous, a mere tautology, since it is already determined by your choice. Are you my brother, to be embraced in "peace and love," or my enemy to be slaughtered? The answer is the same—and it makes a lie of Henry's noble and Christian admonitions. Not only is the world no *better* off for his high-minded discounting of the symbols of partisanship; it is much worse off. The dumb significants avenge themselves bloodily on those who disown them even while they wear them.

Henry makes his last dramatic appearance sitting on a molehill at Towton and dreaming of a life without crowns and roses. But Richard of York—whom no one will accuse of slighting the importance of dumb significants—ends on a molehill at Wakefield, a paper crown on his head, savagely abused and killed by Margaret. It seems that the wily and ruthless seizing of such symbols is as fatal as the disowning of them. Taken as substances, they kill as surely as when they are treated as mere accidents. What are they, then, or how must they be taken? I do not think Shakespeare finds the answer in his earlier history plays; but he comes close enough to have a reply for Peele.

Peele thought he could reestablish order within the world of the theatre by making it conform to the Elizabethan world picture: Let every man keep the degree assigned him by higher authority. Let the players (Scots) acknowledge the natural superiority of the poets (English), and all will be well. If there is a dispute among them, let the poets adjudicate it and thus keep peace.

The interesting thing about Henry's analogy is that, though it is disastrously wrong *within Shakespeare's play,* it is right as a reply to Peele. He who has to act within the world of the play cannot ignore dumb significants; but there is a world beyond—let us call it the republic of letters—which can and must achieve an impartiality transcending the inescapable partiality of symbols. If Henry were a playwright rather than the actor/king he is, he would be right. Which means that insofar as his analogy addresses itself to Peele's Shake-spere allusion rather than to the pugnacious partisans before him, he *is* right. In the world of playwrights, all this dealing in crowns and investitures and feudal degree is an empty masquerade; the sole determinant is function. Who's in, who's out, who wears this party emblem or that—all these are trifles, things of no regard. Arbitrational authority does not depend on degree but on the will and readiness to submit self-assertion and self-interest to a higher and common purpose.

V

KING JOHN: THE ORDERING OF THIS PRESENT TIME

> The Lady Constance speaks not from her faith,
> But from her need.
> (*King John* III, i, 210)

For a man or an age, the faith in order—that is, in justice and truth at the heart of things—is inversely proportional to the need. The need will seize upon an image of order, a "world picture"; but a dropped hint, and "Chaos is come again." The more perfect and encompassing the image, the more fragile also. It breeds barbarians within and without its borders, lawless fears, needs, and perceptions clamoring to be recognized. And when it falls, it may be dark ages before another is created to take its place.

The idea of *creating* order I shall, somewhat crudely, call modern. For medieval man, order *had been* created, once and for all, by God. Man's task was not to create but to contemplate, obey and—as the need arose—to imitate. And Elizabethan man, if we can trust Tillyard and others, was in this respect still essentially medieval. Archetypal order was eternal, divine, revealed, quite beyond man's tampering. Man's orders were no more than this order writ small; though they could be, and often impiously were, tampered with, ultimately they must and would be restored to their proper form and "correspondency." Vengeance, meanwhile, might be bloody, but it was always the Lord's.

KING JOHN: THE ORDERING OF THIS PRESENT TIME

It is natural to read Shakespeare—particularly the early Shakespeare—as an Elizabethan, that is to say as a poet who accepted the "Elizabethan world picture." But natural or not, I believe it is a mistake so to read him. I hope to show that when he wrote *King John,* or quite possibly in writing it, Shakespeare was or became a "modern." Ordering for him became a conscious, human, creative act—not the less creative for being desperately needed. It was not an act of restoration, but an act of discovery and shaping—not of imitation but of design. And it sometimes could be no more than an "ordering of this present time," answering to the urgencies of the moment, with no claims to indefeasibility.

I hope to show something more: that Shakespeare's modernity was not merely a "sense of life," but was itself the outcome of a conscious discovery. The Elizabethan world picture is imposing; we cannot displace it—anymore than Shakespeare could—by anything as soft-focused as the suggestion of a different "Weltanschauung." He saw that the picture was false and embodied the discovery in his play's "argument": in its plot and style as well as in its dialectic. And he worked into the text a pointer, small but unmistakable, to direct our understandings. I shall begin with the pointer.

I

When the dying Melun confesses the French plot to kill the rebel English lords as soon as John is defeated, he is explicit about what prompts him:

> Commend me to one Hubert with your King.
> The love of him, and this respect besides,
> For that my grandsire was an Englishman,
> Awakes my conscience to confess all this.
>
> (v, iv, 40-43)

The mention of Hubert is odd. Nowhere else in the play —nor in Shakespeare's sources—is there so much as a hint that Melun and Hubert have known each other or even been aware of each other's existence. Hubert appears here on Shakespeare's summons alone; that is why the lines are of particular interest. That, and possibly one "respect besides": among them is the only line which Shakespeare lifted bodily from his main source, *The Troublesome Reign of King John.*[1] *TR's* Melun also gives two reasons for his confession; he is even more methodical about it than Shakespeare's:

> Two causes, lords, make me display this drift;—
> The greatest, for the freedom of my soul,
> That longs to leave this mansion free from guilt;
> The other, on a natural instinct,
> For that my grandsire was an Englishman.
> (II, v, 24-28)

Melun observes the proper priorities; his soul's well-being is the dying Christian's foremost concern:

> And fearful thoughts, forerunners of my end,
> Bids me give physic to a sickly soul. (10-11)

"Natural instinct" is admitted only as a secondary mo-

1 Hereinafter cited as *TR*. I quote according to the edition by Furnivall and Munro, London, 1913.—The textual relationship of *KJ* to *TR* has been debated. Alexander (*Shakespeare's Life and Art*, 1939) and more recently Honigmann (introduction to *KJ*, Arden Edition, 1954) have argued that *KJ* must have been written before *TR*, hence before 1591. Like the great majority of critics I find their arguments quite unconvincing and accept what may reasonably be called the orthodox view: that *TR* was Shakespeare's main source, but that he consulted Holinshed again for some minor rectifications.

Another theory, proposed by Courthope in 1916, strikes me—for reasons that will be evident from my interpretation—as very attractive: that *TR* is Shakespeare's own work, probably somewhat contaminated by players' additions, and later completely recast by him as *KJ*. But the theory has not met with scholarly favor, nor is it in any way necessary to my case.

tive, an apposite reinforcement. Dependent on the accident of birth, it might easily have been lacking—and as easily omitted.

Surprisingly, this is the motive, and the very unmemorable line, Shakespeare chose to keep. What he omits is the primary, religious motive; for it he substitutes a totally unmotivated "love" of Hubert. The very wilfulness argues intent.

We are invited to look at Hubert's one great scene (IV, i), where, contrary to his pledge and the king's command, he lets himself be talked out of blinding Arthur. M. M. Reese finds Shakespeare's management of this scene baffling: "Hubert is strangely unsatisfactory. . . . The stage is . . . set for a classic discussion of the conflict between duty and conscience. . . . In the corresponding scene [in *TR*] Hubert acknowledges the traditional dilemma. The deed is bad, but 'a king commands, whose precepts neglected or omitted, threateneth for the default.' . . . Arthur prevails, but he does it here by reminding Hubert that he is imperilling his immortal soul; and Hubert desists because the 'great Commander counterchecks my charge.' Shakespeare deliberately refused this issue, and it is hard to see why."[2] Quite so: Shakespeare deliberately refused the issue. Perhaps it is hard to see why, but if we are concerned with Shakespeare's concept of order, it is imperative that we look for the answer. For the issue lies at the heart of any such concept—so that the answer will bear decisively on whatever we say about Shakespeare's world picture.

[2] *The Cease of Majesty* (London, 1961), p. 281, note. I have found Reese's book by far the most adequate and illuminating treatment not only of the history plays but of Shakespeare's general beliefs about political and universal order. Though he accepts and uses Tillyard's most important findings, Reese is much more perceptive in noticing divergencies between Shakespeare and his contemporaries, as well as changes in Shakespeare's own beliefs. I disagree basically with Tillyard and considerably with Reese, but it will be evident that I am deep in debt to both.

To show just how consistently Shakespeare altered this scene, I must quote *TR* at some length. In the earlier play Arthur pleads not so much *with* Hubert as *for* him:

> Ah, Hubert! makes he [John] thee his instrument
> To sound the trump that causeth hell triumph:
> Heaven weeps; the saints do shed celestial tears;
> They fear thy fall, and cite thee with remorse;
> They knock thy conscience, moving pity there,
> Willing to fence thee from the rage of hell:
> Hell, Hubert! trust me, all the plagues of hell
> Hangs on performance of this damned deed.
> This seal [on John's warrant], the warrant of thy body's bliss,
> Ensureth Satan chieftain of thy soul:
> Subscribe not, Hubert! give not God's part away!
> I speak not only for eyes' privilege—
> The chief exterior that I would enjoy—
> But for thy peril, far beyond my pain,
> Thy sweet soul's loss, more than my eyes' vain lack;
> A cause internal, and eternal too.
> Advise thee, Hubert! for the case is hard,
> To lose salvation for a King's reward.
>
> (I, xii, 63-80)

Straight out of Marlowe's *Faustus*. Hubert tries to argue that he owes the king obedience and is not morally accountable for evil done by royal command. But Arthur is the better Elizabethan theologian and political philosopher:

> Yet God commands—whose power reacheth further—
> That no command should stand in force to murther.[3] (83-84)

[3] I have emended "God's," as given in Furnivall and Munro's text, to "God"—as the sense of the passage demands.

When this appeal to the doctrine of passive resistance seems still not to persuade Hubert, Arthur invokes the ultimate sanctions:

> Let Hell to them—as earth they wish to me—
> Be dark and direful guerdon for their guilt;
> And let the black tormentors of deep Tartary
> Upbraid them with this damned enterprise,
> Inflicting change of tortures on their souls!
>
> (112-16)

At this, Hubert decides to opt for the higher power:

> My king commands; that warrant sets me free;
> But God forbids; and He commandeth Kings.
>
> (125-26)

As against the natural instincts of pity and fear of pain, the concern for a man's soul is incomparably "the greatest cause"; the merely human motives are barely mentioned. But more important to note is the fact that the terms of the argument are insistently *political*; the issue is one of authority and supervening authority, of lesser and greater sanctions. Perfectly in keeping with the Elizabethan concept of order, the moral, religious, and political question is one and the same, to be argued and decided within one universal, hierarchical frame, in which God, king, and subject merely occupy different rungs.

This, then, is the issue Shakespeare refused. His Arthur never once employs the argument of higher authority and more terrible sanctions.[4] The pathos of his pleading may strike us as somewhat forced and studied;

[4] He does mention "Heaven," but not as though it could issue commands or inflict punishment, not as part of an order. Quite the contrary: Heaven's influence is at most a "breath," easily counteracted by Hubert's "breath" (IV, i, 110), and hence powerless against what John has previously called "the free breath of a sacred king" (III, i, 148).

but there is no question that it is directed entirely at Hubert the *man*, designed to awaken in him that sense of compassion which, once admitted, will render him incapable of the cruel act. Instead of saints and fiends, Shakespeare's Arthur invokes the glowing iron, crediting it with greater mercy than Hubert shows. Instead of summoning up visions of eternal torture, he wishes only that a grain of dust might blow into Hubert's eye:

> Then feeling what small things are boisterous there,
> Your vile intent must needs seem horrible.
>
> (IV, i, 95-96)

The king's authority, or God's, is not once alluded to; the very words are studiously avoided—at times almost improbably. Even the sight of the king's hand and seal does not cause Arthur to exclaim against his uncle, nor Hubert to argue that duty compels him to execute what he, personally, finds abhorrent. Nothing is admitted into the scene that would remind us—or the characters themselves—of order and degree.

Instead, Arthur relies on sheer speech, the mere force of words unaided by any authority whatever. Shakespeare is not at his best here, but one thing is clear: he means language to do its own work. The tongue is mentioned almost as often as the eyes, and in significant counterpoint: but for the tongue, the eyes will be lost. At one point, Arthur promises not to "speak a word" more if Hubert will only send away the executioners and do the deed himself. But in this play full of broken promises, he too breaks his promise and continues his pleading:

> Hubert: Is this your promise? Go to, hold your
> tongue.
> Arthur: Hubert, the utterance of a brace of
> tongues

Must needs want pleading for a pair of
eyes.
Let me not hold my tongue, let me not,
Hubert. (97-100)

In a scene otherwise rather too rich in conceits and quibbles, the last line stands out as a *cri de coeur.* And in the end it is his tongue alone that saves Arthur—the "innocent prate" which Hubert rightly feared would "wake my conscience, which lies dead."

I believe Hubert's odd appearance in Melun's dying speech is now accounted for. Melun's love is not rooted in "fact" but in the knowledge he has been granted, by Shakespeare's poetic fiat, of Hubert as a figure in the play. "Prompted" in this sense by Hubert's dramatic example, Melun likewise refuses the issue of conscience against duty (or rather of higher against lower duty) as it was posed in *TR.* Shakespeare removes two major instances of right moral choice from the frame of order in which his predecessor had so carefully placed them. This is the more remarkable when we consider that England's existence hangs by these two choices. Except for Hubert's example, Melun would not have confessed; and except for Melun's confession, the barons would not have returned to John's side. Thus Shakespeare determines the great political issue of his day—submission versus rebellion—not by invoking the highest authority of all, but on the contrary by specifically and deliberately eliminating that authority where his source did invoke it. Hubert is exemplary because he has responded to speech that is literally unwarranted, utterly without warrant. For this he deserves Melun's and our love; but there is more at stake than our feeling about him.

II

Ulysses, in *Troilus and Cressida,* is a crafty manipulator, who puts his considerable eloquence at the service of some very dubious schemes. But among Shakespeare scholars his speech on "degree" has been curiously exempt from the distrust with which we would normally listen to anything said by such a man. Again and again his grand, "cosmic" lines are quoted as though they stated Shakespeare's own, certified convictions about the universe, the body politic, and man's proper place and role in them. Man's prime virtue, religious as well as social, is subordination and obedience. Rebellion is the worst of sins, the Satanic father of all others. Even a bad ruler must be suffered patiently as a divine visitation; the only limit to obedience is passive resistance, the refusal to execute manifestly sinful commands.

Obviously such a doctrine has its practical difficulties —especially where the ruler's title is doubtful. Does God command obedience to the *de facto* ruler or to the *de jure* one? Are there kings so utterly bad and criminal that rebellion becomes legitimate? For these questions Tudor doctrine provided practical answers very much in line with Tudor interest; and English history was told and retold to teach these answers by example.

So far so good; it would be unreasonable to demand perfect rational consistency of a politico-religious theory addressed to urgent practical problems. There are always borderline cases where difficulties arise. But one question is strangely skirted by the Homilies on Obedience and against Disobedience and Wilful Rebellion—and by its modern expositors. It is the dilemma of the subject finding himself confronted, at the same moment, by equal and opposite claims to his obedience. Here the entire doctrine must ultimately be tested, and here it miserably breaks down.

Tillyard has shown that Shakespeare's histories cover exactly that span of time and reigns which was crucial to the "Tudor myth." The only one that falls outside this "main sequence" is *King John.* Not that John's reign had not also been used to make a propaganda point. Bale had presented it as prefiguring the reign of Henry VIII, with John a martyr to Popish pride and treachery who perished in the effort to deliver England from Roman bondage. The author of *TR,* though much more candid about the ambiguities of John's rule and character, still presented him as Rome's stout antagonist and gave ample scope to anti-Catholic sentiment. But Shakespeare reduces precisely this element, hitherto pretty much the play's *raison d'être,* to an absolute minimum—so much so that he lays himself open to charges of poor craftsmanship. Why then did he choose the subject at all?

I suggest he chose it because it posed, as he found it shaped in *TR,* the decisive question raised by the doctrine of obedience and the entire world picture behind it. Two kings claim the obedience of the town of Angiers, not just by embassies but by armies at its gates. One full act is given over to the debating and settling of these claims. The dispute—not in the legal sphere only but more importantly in the physical staging of it—has the deadly balance, the test-case purity of Buridan's ass starving between two equidistant haystacks. The town of Angiers is the embodiment in dramatic fact of a crucial dilemma.

For it is at this point that the cosmic order should intervene and, by a spokesman of unquestionable authority, determine the issue. *Now* is the need for a sermon on Obedience: "Almighty God hath created and appointed all things in heaven, earth, and waters, in a most excellent and perfect order. In heaven, he hath appointed distinct and several orders and states of archangels and angels. In earth he hath assigned and appointed kings, princes, and other governors under them, in all good and necessary order."[5] Thus the Homily on Obedience, continuing in measured cadence and cosmic imagery. But who is authorized to preach it? It would appear—it must at any rate appear to the citizens of Angiers—that Almighty God hath assigned, all in good and necessary order, at least one king too many. The citizens are not rebellious or unwilling to listen; they positively beg to be instructed. But before Angiers all such instruction turns into empty noise, for lack of the one thing that alone could give it meaning: the truly authorized spokesman, the man bearing the warrant.

Where is the remedy? Medieval legal theory provided for such emergencies: God sometimes spoke through trial by combat, and battles and wars were interpreted to be large-scale trials of this kind. To minds not impregnably devout the solution verges dangerously upon the principle that might makes right, but it is nevertheless tried. The two kings do battle—and come up with a draw. Not even Fortune will determine the issue, let alone God.

Swords having failed, words are once more resorted to. The Bastard offers his "wild counsel": let France and England together attack these "scroyles of Angiers," level the town, and then fight it out between themselves. That would dispose nicely of the doctrinal problem, but in rather a self-defeating fashion, as John—though pleased by the idea—seems half to realize:

> I like it well. France, shall we knit our powers
> And lay this Angiers even with the ground;
> Then after fight who shall be king of it?
>
> (II, i, 398-400)

[5] *Certaine Sermons and Homilies*, as quoted by T. W. Baldwin, *On the Compositional Genetics of the Comedy of Errors* (Urbana, 1965), p. 140.

A less self-defeating counsel prevails; instead of Angiers, Arthur and Constance are sacrificed. Angiers finally opens its gates, not to its rightful king but to a bargain.

And now, finally, we get the homily:

> Mad world! mad kings! mad composition! (561)

The Bastard's great speech on Commodity—a perfect inversion of Ulysses' Degree speech, even to the honesty or dishonesty of the speakers and their intentions—is more than just a cynic's railing; its full force comes from its *placing*. In good Renaissance fashion the Bastard has looked at history for the lessons it has to teach; here is the lesson, with a Bastard, fittingly, to drive it home. And Shakespeare has seen to it that the event from which the lesson is drawn is not just one of many; its elaborate and careful balances show it to be a classical dilemma, the reduction of the problem of order and obedience to its pure form. So reduced, it turns out to be unresolvable, at least on the secular plane.

III

But Shakespeare is still not satisfied; he feels the need to push still further. Pandulph, the Papal legate, enters at this point, with an embassy from God's Vicar. Who if not he can adjudicate conflicting secular claims? Since the conflict has already been compromised and poor Constance's cause may seem too lost even to the man who has power to bind and loose, Pandulph might at least ratify the "mad composition" and bestow on it, after the fact, the sanctity it so embarrassingly lacks. But of course he has more serious business; he comes not to exercise authority but to defend it.

TR makes the legate the aggressor; his first words are:

> Stay, King of France! I charge thee, join not hands

With him that stands accurst of God and men.
(I, v, 63-64)

After so provocative an opening, John's peremptory counterclaim to be "Supreme Head over spiritual and temporal" is understandable. Little is left to be said: Philip of France quickly acknowledges Papal authority and considers himself absolved of his oath to John; there follow the standard threats and defiances, and in seventy lines the scene is concluded.

Shakespeare takes over two hundred lines. His legate begins with a handsome acknowledgment of royal dignity:

Hail, you anointed deputies of Heaven! (III, i, 136)

and then demands that John answer charges of usurpation of Papal authority. It is John who first enters, in the most insulting terms, the claim to unchallengeable supremacy:

What earthy name to interrogatories
Can task the free breath of a sacred king?
Thou canst not, Cardinal, devise a name
So slight, unworthy and ridiculous,
To charge me to an answer, as the Pope. (147-51)

What follows is a reenactment, on the highest possible plane, of the dispute over Angiers. Where Angiers stood, Philip of France now stands—between two irreconcilable claims to his allegiance. Shall he honor his oath to John and claim supremacy also for himself, or shall he acknowledge the Pope's authority? Again there is no higher voice; how could there be, with the Pope's legate standing beside him as one of the claimants? And this time there is no Arthur to be sacrificed for compromise and profit.

Pandulph's reasoning to persuade Philip that he can be truly loyal only by breaking his oath to John has often been condemned as mere casuistry. It is certainly involuted and paradoxical, but it is far more than verbal trickery. As Samuel Johnson recognized, it is "irresistible" once we grant that the voice of the Church, as uttered by the Pope, is the voice of Heaven. But in fact the argument has a still broader force.

The Elizabethan world picture is hierarchical not only in fact but by inner necessity; it collapses if there is no *one* ultimate authority. Of course, everyone is piously agreed that that authority is God; but since God does not speak *in propria persona,* the order must designate some*one* who is authorized to speak *for* Him. The crucial thing—except as a question of plain power—is not whether that someone is the Pope, the Emperor, or the King; the crucial thing is that there *be* one, and only one, such voice.[6]

The difficulty is that of kings there are more than one. Thus there was an unresolvable contradiction at the very center of the Tudor doctrine; and Shakespeare's structuring of *King John* seems to me clear evidence that he saw that contradiction, meant to lay it bare, and tried, somehow, to come to terms with the consequences. The mere fact that John enters his claim with another

[6] Of course there was the Bible, the directly inspired Word of God, acknowledged as such by all concerned. But unhappily the Bible was no more immune than the Church; in fact, its authority turned out to be inseparable from Church authority. For it was not *self-interpreting,* so that again God's voice could be reliably heard only through an "authorized" interpreter—the one man with the warrant. Even the Devil could cite Scripture—the sole repository of indubitably divine truth—for his purpose; and who was to gainsay him? I believe that Shakespeare was fully aware of the implications which the concept of a self-interpreting utterance had for his own work as a poet, and that he became aware of them when he saw how the traditional order collapsed the moment the Church's sole authority to interpret the Bible was denied.

king standing next to him exposes the doctrine as false. (Erastianism is the official name of the "heresy" in question; but Shakespeare was concerned, not with heresy and orthodoxy, only with the inner truth of the doctrine itself.) As soon as there is more than one king, each claiming to be answerable only to God and to speak for God, it takes no more than a single dispute between kings to destroy the whole beautiful cosmic structure on which the claim rests. To be sure, John limits his claim to "our dominions. . . . Where we do reign"; but it is his dominions that are in dispute. The claim has become tautological: his dominions are precisely those lands, and people, whom at any given moment he can compel to acknowledge his "supreme" authority. (In terms of the Bible: the authority of the Authorized Version extended to the borders of the English King's dominions, and not a foot beyond.) His "under God" has become mere noise; not only every other king but every other *man* can enter as valid a claim as he.

Pandulph is right. He is right when, at the outset, he hails the two kings, in the plural, as anointed deputies of heaven, for then he still assumes that they consider themselves answerable to heaven's one earthly voice. He is equally right later in announcing that

> All form is formless, order orderless,
> Save what is opposite to England's love (253-54)

provided we interpret England as standing for the doctrine of royal supremacy John has just proclaimed, and "form" and "order" as meaning what in fact they do mean in Tudor doctrine. Whatever we may think of that doctrine as a device to tide England and other post-Reformation monarchies over dangerous times, it was *essentially* flawed. It was at best a makeshift solution, a gorgeous old tapestry hung up by rebellious vassals to conceal the very breach by which they had entered and taken possession of the palace.[7]

Machiavelli knew this; and the well-nigh hysterical Elizabethan reaction to him suggests that he only said what his revilers secretly feared was true. The defense against him was disarmingly typical: he was assigned a place in the old tapestry. He became the Vice of the moralities, the "Machiavel"—villainous though jocular, unmistakably identified (usually by himself), dangerous enough to keep up a measure of suspense but sure in the end to be brought to ridicule and defeat. He was made part of the "picture" and so, it was hoped, rendered harmless.

Assuredly Shakespeare was no Machiavellian; but neither was he an ordinary Elizabethan. *King John* seems to me inexplicable on Tillyard's assumption that Shakespeare, like other Elizabethans, never really understood the full seriousness of Machiavelli's challenge. Presumably he too rejected the Pope's claim to ultimate authority; he certainly does so in *King John.* But he makes it clear that with this rejection the whole beautiful structure crumbles: the divinity of kings, the religious duty of obedience, even the sanctity of oaths. (Whether he owed this insight to the Florentine is of no importance here; I rather think that he came upon it by himself.) For as Pandulph knows and tells Philip:

> It is religion that doth make vows kept;
> But thou hast sworn against religion. . . .
> Therefore thy later vow against thy first
> Is in thyself rebellion to thyself. (279-89)

7 Within fifty years of Shakespeare's writing, when monarchs felt more secure of their possession than the Tudors could, all this was admitted in the frank principle: *Cuius regio, eius religio.* With that admission, kings surrendered all claim to sanctity; the titular

And Austria dutifully echoes the dread word: "Rebellion, flat rebellion!" The Pope, whatever we may think of him and his purposes, is at least not in rebellion against himself; unlike John, he does not put forth a claim that destroys its own foundation.

But consistency is one thing, matter of fact another. Constance, though Pandulph's passionate ally, has bitter firsthand experience that the world moves by laws other than the "picture" provides for. She doubts the efficacy of Rome's curse:

> For without my wrong
> There is no tongue hath power to curse him right.
> (182-83)

Pandulph rebukes her:

> There's law and warrant, lady, for *my* curse.
> [italics mine]

But she has the last and definite word:

> When law can do no right,
> Let it be lawful that law bar no wrong.
> Law cannot give my child his kingdom here,
> For he that holds his kingdom holds the law.
> (185-88)

Here, finally, the grim truth is said which all the events, claims and arguments have implicitly demonstrated: *He that holds his kingdom holds the law*. In Act I possession was about eight points of the law: Eleanor knows that John's title rests on "Your strong possession much more than your right" (i, 40). In Act II, by virtue of the question mark, it was still only nine; "Doth not the crown

phrase "by the grace of God" became a mockery. Still, myths have more lives than cats; another one hundred and fifty years later Europe was still stunned when the French dared behead a "sacred" king.

of England prove the King" (i, 273)? Now, since John's declaration of Supremacy, it is all ten.

There is no higher court of appeal left, only curses and prayer. We might think that cursing and praying do, after all, invoke a higher power, however remote. But Shakespeare is quick to block even that last escape from the dilemma. Constance chooses to curse, but by "need" not by "faith":

> Blanche: The Lady Constance speaks not from her faith,
> But from her need.
> Constance: O, if thou grant my need,
> Which only lives but by the death of faith,
> That need must needs infer this principle,
> That faith would live again by death of need. (III, i, 210-14)

Her son Arthur later chooses prayer; but, as we saw, it also is a prayer of need rather than faith—addressed to a man rather than God. God may still be there, but He can no longer be effectively invoked in the affairs of men, since He has neither voice nor sanctions.

France sides with Rome against England; we will hardly wrong the new allies if we classify their league also under "commodity." But there is no final speech from the Bastard this time; the matter now has become too serious for his high-spirited, almost innocent cynicism. Perhaps, also, he feels a trifle guilty, for it appears that John and Pandulph have followed the "wild counsel" which John and Philip had previously put aside. Angiers still stands, but between claim and counterclaim the cosmic order has been levelled to the ground. All that King and Pope have left to fight over is the debris.

IV

Even bardolaters have little good to say about the last two acts of *King John.* And I strongly suspect that Shakespeare himself knew that he was not bringing the thing off—not because he was bored with a theatrical chore and wanted to finish it quickly and anyhow, but because he saw no way to put Humpty Dumpty together again.

There is abundant evidence that he continued to work with the utmost care; Melun's mention of Hubert and the Hubert-Arthur scene stand in proof of that. But it seems that, with the Bastard turned serious, Shakespeare no longer had a language adequate to his real purpose. His problem was not just a philosophical one; inevitably it was at the same time a poetic—that is to say, a linguistic problem.

In the first three acts his task had been to expose an order and a language that had become false; and he knew he could leave most of that to the very men who acted in the name of that order and spoke its language. They were sure to do themselves in—with here and there a quick *coup de grace* by the Bastard. The Bastard—character and language—sparked Shakespeare's imagination as nothing else in the play did: his gay defiance of the proprieties, his unfailing ear for pretense and pomposity, the simple pleasure he takes in his own shrewd discoveries and in the exuberantly "low" language he finds for them—all these make him completely captivating. He is a great parodist, even self-parodist, having too much fun not to feel a certain affection for his victims. But Shakespeare is not blind to the Bastard's limitation. As second act rounds into third, the Bastard becomes increasingly repetitive, almost nagging. His invention runs dry—largely, I think, because his language allows of only one kind of effect. He does not so much speak a language of his own, it turns out, as a counter-language, an anti-ritual language. Like all cynics and parodists, he feeds parasitically upon the very thing he mocks; and when he has done his (very minor) part in killing it, he is at a loss for sustenance.

The difficulty is not one of character; under the impact of most disquieting events and novel responsibilities, the Bastard's character changes readily enough. But he cannot find a new language for himself. When he accepts the king's responsibilities—"Have thou the ordering of this present time"—he also takes over the king's language:

> Now hear our English King,
> For thus his royalty doth speak in me.
> He is prepared, and reason too he should.
> This apish and unmannerly approach,
> This harness'd masque and unadvised revel,
> This unhair'd sauciness and boyish troops,
> The King doth smile at, and is well prepar'd
> To whip this dwarfish war, these pigmy arms,
> From out the circle of his territories. (v, ii, 128-36)

And so on for twenty more lines. Even the French Lewis can garner, in response to such stuff, some otherwise undeserved dignity:

> There end thy brave, and turn thy face in peace;
> We grant thou canst outscold us. Fare thee well.
> (159-60)

Shakespeare may be a patriot, but he is not patriot enough to let the Bastard get away uncensured with *that.*

This is the "ritual" language, but something new has been added. And that something is identifiable—and clearly identified by Shakespeare himself. We may call the new style the "this 'once-again,' this 'paint-the-lily,' this double-coronation" style. Here is some more of it; the barons are expressing their dismay at the second coronation:

Pembroke: This 'once again,' but that your Highness pleas'd,
Was once superfluous. You were crown'd before. . . .
Salisbury: Therefore, to be possess'd with double pomp,
To guard a title that was rich before,
To gild refined gold, to paint the lily,
To throw a perfume on the violet . . .
Is wasteful and ridiculous excess.
(IV, ii, 3-16)

Shakespeare often finds ways to tell us *himself* what we are to think of a certain mode of speech (though he is not often as direct about it as he is here). The lines enact the very fault they censure, but beyond that we are told the *cause*. John feels the need to prop up his title, now bereft of its foundation in faith, by sheer iteration.

The effect, of course, is the exact opposite; again Shakespeare is quite explicit:

Pembroke: But that your royal pleasure must be done,
This act is as an ancient tale new told,
And in the last repeating troublesome,
Being urged at a time unseasonable.
Salisbury: In this the antique and well-noted face
Of plain old form is much disfigured;
And, like a shifted wind unto a sail,
It makes the course of thoughts to fetch about,

> Startles and frights consideration,
> Makes sound opinion sick, and truth
> suspected. (17-26)

Not only is the "once again" style wasteful and ridiculous; it raises doubts about the very legitimacy it wants to confirm. The Elizabethan world picture rested on the faith in a vast fabric of correspondencies: between universe and state and body, between God and king and sun and lion and eagle, etc., etc. These also furnished the basis and stock images of Tudor homilies, histories, and other propaganda, as abundantly documented by Tillyard. Here we see Shakespeare demonstrating the bankruptcy of the faith by the simple device of pushing it to its limits—not just to parody it but to show us exactly what linguistic and stylistic consequences it entails. (If a stylistic interpreter or New Critic finds himself hard pressed by an historian of ideas, I propose this passage as an impregnable pièce de résistance.)

There is, I think, something else implicit in "an ancient tale retold,/ And in the last repeating troublesome." Is it fanciful to surmise that just as Shakespeare makes this style comment upon itself, so he makes these lines comment upon the play as a whole? Is he not telling us here of the "troublesome" effect that the recasting and re-recasting of the old chronicle story of John's reign was bound to have on the audience? Or, rather, is he not telling this to the authorities, who, to strengthen the Tudors' position, "urged at a time unseasonable" the writing of such histories as propaganda vehicles?

However that may be, on himself the recasting must have had a very unsettling effect. What seemed, in the "plain old form," natural and innocuous enough must have gained a "startling" pointedness from the effort to make it serve the ends of Tudor propaganda. The condensations and confrontations which the dramatic form made necessary were bound to "fright consideration" still further. Above all: the imaginative effort demanded of the dramatist to translate merely narrated events into the direct utterance of live and lifelike characters could hardly help but make "truth suspected." Specious reasoning and fraudulent feeling are most tellingly revealed in the poet's work of recreation; for by that very effort he discovers how infinitely manipulable language is, how it can be bent to any purpose whatever. Passionate protest, proud patriotism, pious appeal—whatever it is—it is of *his* manufacture, the product of his calculating skill. And the more skillful he becomes, the more aware he must be that there is no feeling or conviction that is beyond the power of simulation. Commodity!

The reason speech is not to be trusted is a simple reason: speech receives what truth it has from *outside* itself. An oath is the essential form of speech, because it explicitly invokes that outside authority which will vouch for the truth of what is said. If that authority can be trusted—i.e., if the sanctions at its disposal are effective and certain to be applied—only then can speech be trusted. What *King John* presents us with is a world in which authority is totally untrustworthy. God is spoken for by voices which not only contradict each other but repeatedly belie themselves. Sanctions are applied not to enforce the truth and sanctity of words but to further unspeakable ends. (Literally unspeakable: witness John's unwillingness to *say* what he wants Hubert to do.) This world is so chaotic that as often as not oath-breaking must be considered more meritorious than oath-keeping; witness Hubert and Melun and, as an ambiguous but compelling rationale, Pandulph's irresistible argument. The play demonstrates the simultaneous disintegration of order and speech and truth.

That, I think, is why the Bastard cannot find a new, true language when he assumes the king's function. If he found one, it would mean that he had also found a new order to take the place of the shattered one, that he—the Bastard—had discovered a new legitimacy. It is not likely that he could. He is beset by too many and too radical ambiguities: that of his birth, or that of Arthur's death, to mention only two. He tries various languages on for size, as it were—Othello's, for instance:

> Your sword is bright, sir; put it up again.
>
> (IV, iii, 79)

But he cannot keep it up; immediately after this tone of calm, if somewhat posed, authority he relapses into his own former mode:

> Put up thy sword betime;
> Or I'll so maul you and your toasting-iron
> That you shall think the devil is come from hell.
>
> (98-100)

Or something more in the line of Horatio:

> Art thou gone so? I do but stay behind
> To do the office for thee of revenge,
> And then my soul shall wait on thee to heaven.
>
> (V, vii, 70-72)

(He does not quite say, "Good night, sweet Prince"; but considering that he is talking about John, he is even so treading the thin edge of the ludicrous.) There is little discoverable relation between these languages and their several occasions—except when he assumes the voice of "majesty." That, utterly exposed though it has been, is the only stable language available to him—exactly as the order, shattered though it is, is the only order within which he can act at all. At the very end, the real task:

To set a form upon that indigest
Which he hath left so shapeless and so rude
(v, vii, 26-27)

remains still to be done. Little wonder that we feel dissatisfied.

V

It remains to deal with an objection and—it will be the same thing—to draw the conclusion. The objection arises from analyses of *King John*—supported by many quotations—such as Campbell's, Tillyard's, Ribner's, and Reese's. These scholars are all pretty much agreed that the play, after some initial cynical doubt, concludes with a more or less ringing reaffirmation of the Tudor doctrine. (Reese is the most qualified; perhaps—he is not altogether unambiguous in his summary paragraphs—I differ from him in little more than emphasis. Ribner is the most absolute for orthodoxy.) To cite just one of the passages in apparent support of this view, here is Salisbury after Melun's confession:

We do believe thee; and beshrew my soul
But I do love the favour and the form
Of this most fair occasion, by the which
We will untread the steps of damned flight,
And like a bated and retired flood,
Leaving our rankness and irregular course,
Stoop low within those bounds we have o'erlook'd,
And calmly run on in obedience
Even to our ocean, to our great King John.
(v, iv, 49-57)

There are more such passages, with the standard images of order and degree; and there are a great many eloquent appeals to national unity and national purpose.

My reply is, predictably, that all the orthodox sentiments at the end are *faute de mieux*. I believe that for most of his creative life Shakespeare was driven by a passion for order; I would even call this the law of his development. But *his* need, too, was inversely proportional to his faith; his passion was so keen that it compelled him to test every order that offered itself against his incorruptible and rich sense of reality. An order that did not meet this test might still have to serve as an interim solution, an "ordering of [and for] this present time." But it was sure to betray itself—by its language. For in the real sense such an order has no language; or rather, the poet has no language for it.

I have tried to show that the play as a structure—in its plot, dialectic, and style—does not permit a more affirmative and orthodox interpretation than this: that the old order is suffered, in a greatly diminished form, as a makeshift structure. Such an interpretation accounts without difficulty for images like "to our ocean, to our great King John." A mere glance at John dying—not to mention living—exposes them as perilously close to sham:

> And none of you will bid the Winter come . . .
> Nor let my kingdom's rivers take their course
> Through my burn'd bosom. (v, vii, 36-39)

On the other hand I do not see how a more orthodox interpretation can account even for so small a fact as Melun's love of Hubert.

If there anything other than sheer need to take the place of dead faith? Melun's dying words hold the answer—or the promise. England, we recall, is saved from disaster and foreign conquest by two things: the ties of blood ("For that my grandsire was an Englishman"), and the example of Hubert's humanity. The first calls for that purely instinctual and limited affirmation of community which we call nationalism (*TR* calls it "natural instinct"); this obligation Shakespeare discharged, a little too conscientiously for some modern tastes, in this and other histories. Men no longer united by a common faith in a universal order must hold to what ties remain to them; and in the absence of higher claims to one's loyalty those of the blood are valid. But they are not enough; they are not even "the greatest cause." They are (for the poet) no more sufficient than the ties of language. They are the given, the raw material of true communion. Justice and truth, though communion cannot exist apart from them, does not by that fact alone dwell in them; before the national instinct can generate a just order and the national idiom a true language, something more is needed.

But this more, no longer resident in an "eternal city," lives for the time being only in shapeless intuitions. It has no language yet, just as Hubert has no language to tell us *why* he breaks his oath:

> Well, see to live; I will not touch thine eye
> For all the treasure that thine uncle owes.
> Yet am I sworn and I did purpose, boy,
> With this same very iron to burn them out.
> (IV, i, 122-24)

That is all; with the order gone, so are the stateable reasons. Melun speaks of "love"—surely the love which "alone is hugely politic," the only available answer to the Machiavellian "policy" into which this world must otherwise lapse. But it is a word and not a sentence, a feeling and not an order. A new "bond" must be found.[8]

Meanwhile there was the immediate need; the na-

[8] I believe that *The Merchant of Venice* represents a decisive turn in Shakespeare's search. Cf. my interpretation of the play, pp. 208-236.

tional cause demanded to be served. Without illusions Shakespeare met the need; his histories, from *King John* on, are a kind of holding operation, with the work of discovery going on beneath the surface. They are resolute and stirring—in a "damn the torpedoes" way and often in a "once again" style:

> But wherefore do you droop? Why look you sad?
> Be great in act, as you have been in thought.
> Let not the world see fear and sad distrust
> Govern the motion of a kingly eye.
> Be stirring as the time; be fire with fire;
> Threaten the threat'ner, and outface the brow
> Of bragging Horror; so shall inferior eyes,
> That borrow their behaviours from the great,
> Grow great by your example and put on
> The dauntless spirit of resolution. (v, i, 44-53)

This manner would do until *Henry V*: "Once more into the breach, dear friends, once more!" But that would be the end of it. Not because Shakespeare had discovered *the* order but because his continuing need was driving him beyond the confines of

> This royal throne of kings, this sceptred isle,
> This earth of majesty, this seat of Mars . . .
> This blessed plot, this earth, this realm, this
> England.

VI

"SWOLL'N WITH SOME OTHER GRIEF": SHAKESPEARE'S PRINCE HAL TRILOGY

> I speak of peace, while covert enmity
> Under the smile of safety wounds the world;
> And who but Rumour, who but only I,
> Make fearful musters and prepared defence,
> Whiles the big year, swoll'n with some other grief,
> Is thought with child by the stern tyrant war,
> And no such matter?
>
> (2 *Henry IV*, Induction)

IN *Der bestrafte Brudermord*—a seventeenth-century German version of the Hamlet story, which appears to be derived from the lost "Ur-Hamlet"—Hamlet rids himself of Rosencrantz and Guildenstern (as Shakespeare was to call them) by a neat and simple stratagem. As he marches between them, their pistols aimed at him from either side, he suddenly ducks; by sheer reflex, the two courtiers pull their triggers and shoot each other dead. The stratagem illustrates nicely how to win by the dialectical, *divide et impera* or *tertius ridens* method. The dialectician is not such a fool as himself to take arms against a sea of troubles; he divides his troubles into antitheses and makes them take arms against each other. If he can make no sense of "being," he pairs it off against "non-being," and presto! he emerges in possession of "becoming," historical process and metaphysical certitude. For a mere trick, dialectics has earned handsome (but unhappily only paper) profits.

Shakespeare does not allow his Hamlet to play it; perhaps that is one measure of his difficulties. The Prince likewise rids himself of Rosencrantz and Guildenstern, but not quite by the *tertius ridens* method. He has to do more than duck; he has to act and make himself co-responsible (with Claudius) for the courtiers' death. Now it is they who are in the middle, "between the fell, incensèd points/Of mighty opposites." Hamlet claims that they "sit not near [his] conscience"; but what about Ophelia, who perishes between the same fell points? And in any case he finds *himself* one of the mighty opposites; for him, "to be" and "not to be" do not cancel each other into a higher synthesis.

Dialectics is an ordering device; it orders by arranging disorder symmetrically. We do not resort to it as long as we know, or think we know, where and wherein order resides; we resort to it when we do not know, or pretend not to know, where our quest for order is taking us. The dialectician acts as though he had fully accepted the challenge of disorder and were seriously engaged in meeting it. What he forgets, or chooses to ignore, is that dialectical conflict is a question-begging device. Whatever victories are won in this way are won by prearrangement.

There are various possible images of order; traditionally, that of the Christian West has been the triad. Unlike the circle (the image of divine order), the triad allows for discord, as any image of human order must; the base points are seen as potentially or actually in conflict. But at the same time it provides the apex where conflict can be arbitrated and resolved. For any level where conflict can arise there is a next higher level of appeal—the whole forming a pyramid, with God or some other absolute as the supreme arbiter.

If this is our image of order, it is natural that we should think of disorder as a triad minus the apex—as conflict where there is no higher court of appeal. Dialectics undertakes to reconstruct the apex from the base points, once the former can no longer be assumed as known. But the fact is that the apex *is* known; it is given by the symmetry of the image. Dialectical conflict is an instance not so much of disorder as of order *manqué*. It is a duel, trial by combat. A duel differs from normal, "orderly" trials only in that the court speaks through the outcome rather than *in propria persona*. This may not be very consoling to the losing combatant, who may be so unreasonable and dialectically unenlightened as to feel that *he* was in the right and should have won. But it is most reassuring to the observing dialectician, who can persuade himself that once again disorder has brought forth order. If it had, the birth would be miraculous; in fact it is simply a *petitio principii*.

All this may seem an odd preamble to an interpretation of Shakespeare's Prince Hal plays. But I hope to show that in these plays Shakespeare took a much more searching look at the problem of disorder than he had in the earlier histories. He had long since discovered that the apex had disappeared or become inaccessible; he now finds that even the remnant is more than he can safely take for granted.

I

Symmetry is so satisfying an arrangement because it gives scope to our secret lust for combat and disorder even while reassuring us that we are ultimately safe. We may think as we wish of Hal's famous soliloquy in *1 Henry IV*—"I know you all, and will a while uphold" —we *are* reassured by it. Between rebellion and misrule, between hot pride and slippery wit, sword-edged honor and fat-bellied self-indulgence, we know there is an axis of symmetry and a *tertius ridens*. Order will emerge in the end, not necessarily because it has proved its superior title but because the two kinds of disorder will kill and cancel each other.

1 Henry IV seems to reach this point of satisfying resolution when Hal stands between what he assumes to be the corpses of Hotspur and Falstaff and speaks over each the appropriate obsequies. If the stage were simply a mirror of reality, its order and disorders, here the ordering would seem achieved. But of course it is not; no sooner has Hal walked off than disorder arises in massive palpability:

> 'Sblood, 'twas time to counterfeit. . . . Counterfeit? I lie, I am no counterfeit. To die is to be a counterfeit, for he is but the counterfeit of a man who hath not the life of a man; but to counterfeit dying when a man thereby liveth, is to be no counterfeit, but the true and perfect image of life indeed. . . . I am afraid of this gunpowder Percy though he be dead. How, if he should counterfeit too and rise? By my faith, I am afraid he would prove the better counterfeit. Therefore I'll make him sure; yea, and I'll swear I killed him. Why may not he rise as well as I? (v, iv, 113-28)

Not only *may* Hotspur rise but he *will*—as soon as the scene is ended and his "body" has been lugged off the stage. Like other leading actors in tragedies and histories, he makes a living by counterfeit dying, and to do so "is to be no counterfeit, but the true and perfect image of life indeed." Falstaff's rising destroys all kinds of reassuring symmetries, the first being that of stage and world. *Sub specie realitatis,* his claim to being Hotspur's killer is exactly as good, or bad, as Hal's, just as his pretense of having died on the field of honor is exactly as good, or bad, as Hotspur's. Simply by refusing to submit to the agreeable fiction that there is an axis of symmetry between on-stage and off-stage and that reality and its representation correspond to each other in perfect balance, Falstaff throws us and the play back into dizzying confusion.

The confusion is covered up—at a price. In order to reestablish the stage-world balance, Hal lures—not to say bribes—Falstaff back into fictionality:

> Come, bring your luggage nobly on your back,
> For my part, if a lie may do thee grace,
> I'll gild it with the happiest terms I have.
>
> (v, iv, 160-62)

He manages to sound magnanimous about it, but is he doing more than making a virtue of necessity? For the "truth," in this confusion of counterfeits, is with Falstaff; he is the only one at this point who is not a "double man":

> Falstaff: No, that's certain; I am not a double man. . . . There is Percy. If your father will do me any honor, so; if not, let him kill the next Percy himself. . . .
>
> Hal: Why, Percy I killed myself, and saw thee dead.
>
> Falstaff: Didst thou? Lord, Lord, how this world is given to lying! I grant you I was down and out of breath, and so was he. . . .
>
> (v, iv, 141-50)

Falstaff is ready to split the credit for Hotspur's killing: if Hal supports him in his "lie," he will sustain Hal in Hal's "lie." And this bargain does represent some sort of truth, or at least of justice. For no matter who has run his sword through Hotspur in the make-belief of the stage, dramatically and morally it is Falstaff's role to kill him and to be killed by him; in the dialectic of the play's structure, he is a hero, while Hal is the *tertius ridens.* Strangely, it is he, the creature of Shakespeare's imagination rather than of history, who in the end asserts himself as the reality principle incarnate, reminding us that disorder is not slain as neatly and inexpensively as the calculated symmetrics of dialectics would have us believe. Very likely his creator planned him as Hal means to use him: as a foil, with Hotspur as a counterfoil. But he would not stay so corseted; he outgrew his preassigned measure and function. In the end, while he does not seriously disquiet us—Shakespeare, when he has need, is a master at letting us have our cake and eat it—Falstaff *remains,* the bulky remainder of a division which was calculated at $2 \div 2 = 1$, but which would not come out even.

II

1 Henry IV is designed toward the release of combat. We watch the opponents quarrel; lay their plans, and gather their forces; march toward Shrewsbury, and fail in last-minute negotiations, until by Act v, scene iii, we are ready for that discharge of tension which of itself seems to create a sense of order.

2 Henry IV promises to repeat the design. Once again the rebels plot and march; once again the king takes countermeasures. But this time the encounter takes place in the first part of Act IV—and in Gaultree Forest of infamous memory. We are denied the release of battle; the confrontation ends in the treachery of John of Lancaster. The rebels, promised redress of their grievances, are tricked into dismissing their army; as soon as they have done so, they are seized and executed, while their dispersing soldiers are pursued and slain.

In the innocent days of moral and psychological criticism, John's bloody equivocation used to be roundly condemned; critics made no secret of their distaste for a play which seemed, for its satisfactory outcome, to depend on so mean a stratagem. Of late we have become more sophisticated; we talk about the larger political design, the education of Hal, and the utter wickedness of rebellion in Tudor doctrine. We are warned not to take Gaultree Forest too seriously: for an Elizabethan audience, rebels deserved no better. What Prince John dispenses is, after all, a kind of "justice," though somewhat "rigorous": "Temperamentally [Hal] strikes the balance between . . . John and . . . Falstaff. . . . The justice of John in his cold-blooded treatment of the rebels verges on rigour; Falstaff has no general standard of justice at all."[1]

I suggest that if an interpreter finds himself driven, by the tenor of his argument, into such euphemizing, there is something badly wrong with the argument. We always misread Shakespeare if our reading compels us to make light of cruelty and treachery—especially where these are not condemned and in some manner disowned in the play itself. More shocking even than Gaultree itself is the fact that it is accepted almost without comment. Prince John hardly troubles to justify himself; the transaction is between the rebels and "God":

> Strike up the drums, pursue the scattered stray.
> God, and not we, hath safely fought today.
>
> (IV, ii, 120-21)

The king, when he is informed by letter of "the manner how this action hath been borne," says nothing explicit about it. But his reaction is telling: it is upon receiving the news of victory that he falls into his final illness:

1 E. M. W. Tillyard, *Shakespeare's History Plays* (New York, 1962), p. 302.

And wherefore should these good news make me
sick?
Will Fortune never come with both hands full,
But write her fair words still in foulest letters?

(IV, iv, 102-04)

The only extended commentary is Falstaff's praise of sherris-sack, which invites comparison with the Bastard's "commodity" speech in *King John*. There a peaceful "composition," healing in itself though achieved at some cost in loyalty, was flayed in explicitly moral terms; now an act of slaughter, made possible by a signal abuse of trust, is described as a matter of metabolism. Gaultree Forest becomes more troublesome by being treated with cold matter-of-factness.

But our trouble is by no means simply moral; Shakespeare frustrates an almost physical need for a discharge of tension. Gaultree Forest is, to be sure, a "fact of history," but if Shakespeare felt that he could not, in honesty, leave it out of his account, he had the option of giving it little or no dramatic weight. He might have relegated it to a report—with the appropriate sad commentary on the questionable shifts kings sometimes find themselves driven to. Instead, he designs his play so that Gaultree looms as a second Shrewsbury, only to deceive our expectations both dramatically and morally. What is more, he gives us clear warning of what he is about:

I speak of peace, while covert enmity
Under the smile of safety wounds the world . . .
Make fearful musters and prepared defence,
Whiles the big year, swoll'n with some other grief,
Is thought with child by the stern tyrant war,
And no such matter.

(2 *Henry IV*, Induction)

These lines have usually been glossed—no doubt correctly—as alluding to contemporary political events, particularly to the false rumors of a Spanish invasion which alarmed England in 1596. But their much more immediate and revealing reference is to the play they introduce—to its false expectations and false promises of safety, indeed to its general sense of false pregnancy.

The question we must ask of *2 Henry IV* is, I think, quite different from those which have commonly been asked. Many critics have marked the play off as unworthy of Shakespeare, a chore he assumed unwillingly and discharged carelessly. More recently, under the leadership of Tillyard and J. Dover Wilson, it has been interpreted as the second step in Hal's *gradus ad regnum,* his preparation for the royal office. The newer criticism has the virtue of assuming a serious intention on Shakespeare's part; but I do not see, any more than Derek Traversi and Clifford Leech, how *2 Henry IV* can be interpreted as part of a continuous ascent. How does Hal say?

> From a God to a bull? A heavy descension! It was Jove's case. From a prince to a prentice? A low transformation! That shall be mine; for in everything the purpose must weigh with the folly.
>
> (II, ii, 192-96)

Here the immediate reference is to his disguise as a tapster; but we need only remember the Gadshill robbery and its sequel in *1 Henry IV* to see what broader meanings attach to this "heavy descension." There is, throughout Part II, a musty atmosphere as of stale air in closed rooms, of moral and physical debility. The tapster scene is to Gadshill very much as Gaultree is to Shrewsbury. The question to ask is: What is the purpose that weighs with such dramaturgical folly? What is that other, unexpressed, stifled grief with which *2 Henry IV* goes pregnant?

III

I quoted John's summing up of the "battle" of Gaultree Forest: "God, and not we, hath safely fought today." The piety is more offensive than the treachery, even though John seems to be saying no more than Harry will say after the Battle of Agincourt. Why? Because John perverts the very principle of trial by combat to which he appeals. Combat as a means of discovering truth and doing justice can have only one justification: that it be open, with the outcome in genuine doubt, so that God *can* render His verdict. At Agincourt there is some meaning to the claim that God has spoken; there is none at Gaultree. I believe that Shakespeare intends to underscore the difference when he has Harry say, after Agincourt:

> O God, Thy arm was here;
> And not to us, but to Thy arm alone
> Ascribe we all! When, *without stratagem,*
> *But in plain shock and even play of battle,*
> Was ever known so great and little loss
> On one part and on th' other. Take it, God,
> for it is none but Thine!
> (*Henry V*, IV, viii, 111-17—my italics)

I shall have to return to Harry's oddly strenuous insistence on the *non nobis, Te Deum* theme. (After Shrewsbury, God is not even mentioned.) At the moment my point is that John has not submitted his case and cause to God's judgment but has preempted that judgment and foisted his own treacherous equivocation off on us as God's voice. In terms of triadic order, he has construed the apex by identifying it with one of the base (very base!) points. And in doing so he has transformed the figure from a triangle into a line. We shall presently explore the implications of this "low transformation."

One thing is immediately clear: the order he represents—that of Lancastrian and post-Lancastrian England—has become *secular*. The sanctions it rests on are not divine or cosmic but at best pragmatic. The shift to secularity finds its most palpable expression in the unexpected fulfillment of the prophecy that Henry IV will die in "Jerusalem." Throughout the two parts of *Henry IV* the king speaks of his purpose to wash away the stain of Richard's sacred blood by leading a crusade to the Holy Land, but the very forces he has set free by his usurpation prevent his doing so. He cannot "get away"—get away, that is, from the consequences of the act to which he and all his successors owe the crown. Blindly he hopes that he can regain the lost religious sanction, only to discover on his deathbed that the prophecy on which his hope was based had a secular rather than a sacred meaning—that his final destination is not the Holy City of Christendom but a chamber in Westminster Palace.[2]

The age of holy wars is past. When, in the night before Agincourt, Harry disputes with Williams and Bates about the king's accountability for the afterlife of those who die in his wars, we need to be as much aware of

[2] The story of the prophecy, as of the intended crusade, Shakespeare found in Holinshed. What he did not find there was the stress on secularization. The effect of the story in Holinshed is that Henry IV died piously. The crusade is not a long-nourished, repeatedly frustrated plan, nor is it linked to Henry's guilt and doubtful title. Henry announces it for the first and only time shortly before his death and justifies it in thoroughly medieval fashion: "For it grieved him to consider the great malice of Christian princes, that were bent upon a mischievous purpose to destroy one another, to the peril of their own souls, rather than to make war against the enemies of the Christian faith, as in conscience (it seemed to him) they were bound." He is stricken, not upon receiving the news of Gaultree Forest, but while praying at the shrine of St. Edward; and the "Jerusalem" where he dies, though not the Holy City, seems at least to be in the Cathedral (it is "next at hand" and belongs to the abbot of Westminster) rather than in the palace.

what he *cannot* answer as of what he can and does answer:

King: Me thinks I could not die anywhere so contented as in the King's company, his cause being just and his quarrel honourable.
Will: That's more than we know.
Bates: Aye, or more than we should seek after; for we know enough if we know that we are the King's subjects. If his cause be wrong, our obedience to the King wipes the crime of it out of us.
Will: But if the cause be not good, the King himself hath a heavy reckoning to make. . . . I am afeard there are few die well that die in a battle. . . . Now, if these men do not die well, it will be a black matter for the King that led them to it. (IV, i, 132-52)

To which Harry has but one reply:

Every subject's duty is the King's, but every subject's soul is his own. (IV, i, 185-86)

This is cold, secular comfort. What he ought to be able to answer Williams is what Richmond told his men before Bosworth Field:

God and our good cause fight upon our side. . . .
Then, if you fight against God's enemy,
God will in justice ward you as His soldiers.
(*Richard III*, V, iii, 240-54)

Since the king claims to be God's representative, his cause ought to be God's cause, his wars holy wars, and those who die for him [Him] ought to be martyrs. To die for the king should *ipso facto* be a "good end," washing away prior sins and earning the reward of eternal salvation.

But of course Harry can answer nothing of the sort. His father's yearning to lead a crusade was already an anachronism and even as such tainted with policy:

> To lead out many to the Holy Land,
> Lest rest and lying still might make them look
> Too near unto my state.
>
> (2 *Henry IV*, IV, v, 211-13)

Bolingbroke's political testament undergoes exactly the same shift as the meaning of "Jerusalem." The holy war having been prevented by the very forces it was meant to check, the dying king urges his son to engage in "foreign quarrels" (in sharp contrast to his sentiments as recorded by Holinshed) :

> Therefore, my Harry,
> Be it thy course to busy giddy minds
> With foreign quarrels, that action, hence borne out,
> May waste the memory of former days.
>
> (IV, v, 213-16)

This is realism rather than cynicism: a clear-eyed recognition and acceptance of the fact that kingship, if it ever was divine, is no longer so. What is cynical is the pretense of John of Lancaster (and many statesmen since) that, though every subject's soul is his own when he is asked to fight *for* the king, it is *ipso facto* the Devil's if he chooses to fight against him.

IV

To return to the structural argument. Two things about 2 *Henry IV* are clear: it is designed to culminate in Hal's accession; and it disappoints our expectation (aroused by the play itself) of reaching that point through the "plain shock and even play of battle." To gauge our disappointment, we need only imagine the following: that Shakespeare had written *Henry IV* in one part, climaxing in the battle of Shrewsbury; that the king had died right after the battle, so that Hal's accession would have followed immediately upon his battlefield triumph; and that Hal had at that point exposed Falstaff's cowardice and lies, making them the occasion of rejecting him and signifying his own resolution to be a just and sober as well as valiant king. The distortion and telescoping of historical facts would have been no worse than what Shakespeare permits himself elsewhere; and I am by no means the first to suggest that such a way of managing the story would have been dramatically much more satisfying than the two-part arrangement Shakespeare chose.

What would have been lost? Very little of Falstaff; whatever Shakespeare does with him in Part II, except for the rather pathetic lechery, he has done already and better in Part I. To compare the capture of Sir John Coleville with the "killing" of Hotspur, for example, is to notice not just a repetition but a "heavy descension," analogous to that from Gadshill to the taproom and from Shrewsbury to Gaultree. We would miss Justice Shallow, but only as one more figure in Shakespeare's vast gallery of comic portraits. The only matters of dramatic weight that probably would have had to be sacrificed are the action involving the Chief Justice and the episode of the premature seizure of the crown.

No one, as far as I know, has tried to make much of the latter; so what is left is the Chief Justice, and it is hardly surprising that the play's defenders have made him the pivotal figure. The argument runs thus: of the two royal virtues, valor and justice, the Prince proves his title to the first in Part I and to the second in Part II. Moreover, the rejection of Falstaff must be adequately prepared; Shakespeare does so by showing how

Falstaff takes himself and his claims on Hal more and more seriously, until in the coronation scene he clearly overreaches himself and precipitates his own disgrace. The specifically political conflict, with its conclusion in Gaultree Forest, plays a very minor role in this account. (Some critics of this persuasion manage not to mention it at all.) The major antagonists, corresponding to Falstaff and Hotspur in Part I, are Falstaff and the Chief Justice; when Hal sides with Justice and rebukes Misrule, his *gradus ad regnum* is completed.

The interpretation has much to recommend it, especially neatness; but it will hardly bear scrutiny. I noted that it fails to account for the play's sense of debility and decline. But if that seems too subjective and intangible a factor, there is still the political action. Why would Shakespeare burden his play with this dramatic and moral abortion, if it did not even serve his end? Why, on the other hand, would he reduce to a mere mention the most famous and dramatic episode in the Hal legend: the striking of the Chief Justice? The episode had become virtually canonical; and it is difficult to imagine a scene better suited to Shakespeare's purpose, *if* that purpose were to show Hal learning to respect the law's majesty. Instead, what do we see of the Prince? Nothing in Act I; the Poins and tapster scenes in Act II; nothing in Act III and for most of Act IV; the seizing of the crown at the end of Act IV; and, finally, the elevation of the Chief Justice and the rejection of Falstaff in Act V. The rebels are given greater scope than that.

In fact, up to the point of his seizing the crown, it appears that Hal is quite deliberately being kept *out of* the play. Of the only two scenes he is given prior to that point, the second (II, iv) is almost wholly dominated by Falstaff and his gentlewomen; the Prince's puny jest is just sufficient—and is *meant*—to remind us of the lost glories of the corresponding scene in Part I (II, iv). And the first, with Poins, has no action; except for a good deal of aimless banter and the quick planning of the tapster scene, we hear only of Hal's weary resignation to the role of wild prince which common opinion compels him to keep up. Not only are his appearances grudging; they are intended for little else than to let us *know* that they are grudging.

If Hal's participation in the "low" action is designedly minimal, in the "action of state" it is, except for the very end, reduced to nothing. Again Shakespeare takes pains to make us conscious of the lack. At the conclusion of the tapster scene Peto enters breathlessly with news of the king's being at Westminster and receiving alarming reports from the North. Hal responds:

By heaven, Poins, I feel me much to blame
So idly to profane the precious time,
When tempest of commotion, like the south
Borne with black vapour, doth begin to melt
And drop upon our bare unarmed heads.
Give me my sword and cloak. Falstaff, good night.
(II, iv, 390-95)

Spoken like a Prince—and in orotund blank verse. But what happens? The next scene shows the king in Westminster, deeply troubled by the rebellion and resolving to meet it; Hal is not present. Nor is he with the king's forces in Yorkshire. In IV, iv, again in Westminster, the king inquires after him and is told that he is hunting at Windsor—or, it may be, dining in London, "with Poins and other his continual followers." In any case he is not at court; he arrives only after the king has been stricken and seems to be dead.

Again the inevitable comparison with *1 Henry IV* makes this absence even more pointed. In the great post-

Gadshill scene, Hal treated a summons from the king with wonderfully inventive levity; there was nothing in the style of "I feel me much to blame" and "Give me my sword and cloak. Falstaff, good night!" All the same, he did appear before his father, did pledge himself to fight Hotspur, and was given "sovereign charge" of the king's forces. And, of course, he went on to become the hero of Shrewsbury—rather more so, be it noted, than Shakespeare's sources gave warrant for. From *The Famous Victories* Shakespeare refused to take what seems to have been another noted scene in the legend: Hal's coming before the king in a cloak full of eyelet-holes and needles (to signify his being on needles until he has seized the crown) and with dagger drawn. Hal's "Give me my sword and cloak" is the only remnant of this scene—just enough to warn the audience that here again their expectation will be disappointed.

Thus *2 Henry IV* is littered with rejections of dramatic opportunities, or rather of dramatic obligations, incurred partly by the structure of the play itself, partly by what we will (and are carefully reminded to) expect from *1 Henry IV*, and partly by what we expect from the established legend. Shakespeare rejects not whole incidents but rather the scenes to which they would naturally give rise: the actual dramatic confrontation and "showdown." We *hear* of Hal's striking the Chief Justice but we do not see it; we *hope* for a major encounter between Hal and Falstaff but are disappointed; we *expect* a confrontation between Hal and the king but are denied it; we *are sure* that there will be a battle between the king's forces and the rebels but are cheated of it. The play seems a series of "fearful musters and prepared defense—and no such matter." The children of the "stern tyrant war"—confrontation, encounter, conflict, battle—are one by one killed in the womb; and since drama is conflict, it seems as though Shakespeare set about deliberately strangling his play.

Clearly the theory that in Part II Hal proves himself just (as in Part I he proved himself valorous), while it has a certain *a priori* plausibility, is sadly lacking in dramatic substance. But just as clearly the play is *about* Hal and culminates in his accession. What, then, is Hal's role; what does he *do*, except remind us that he is doing nothing? The answer is simple: prior to his accession, Hal has one role only—that of heir, of *successor*.

He nowhere shows the slightest concern with justice until after he is king. The serious part of his conversation with Poins turns on the succession: Poins cannot believe that Hal is sincerely grieved by his father's illness, which promises to speed him to the throne; and Hal wearily acknowledges that common opinion can hardly think otherwise. The scene with Falstaff has nothing to do with justice. In his soliloquy by the king's bed, Hal is full of resolution; but what he thinks about is the crown and how he means to keep it:

> Lo, where it sits,
> Which God shall guard; and put the world's whole strength
> Into one giant arm, it shall not force
> This lineal honour from me. This from thee
> Will I to mine leave, as 'tis left to me. (IV, V, 43-47)

In the following dialogue with his father, the latter does raise the problem of justice:

> Pluck down my officers, break my decrees;
> For now a time is come to mock at form.
> (IV, V, 118-19)

But Hal hardly responds to it; he is entirely taken up with convincing the king that when he took the crown he was not prompted by an unfilial wish to succeed before his time. With Hal on the scene, the dramatic focus is always on the succession.

I am not arguing that justice is irrelevant to *2 Henry IV*; on the contrary, it is manifestly the controlling theme of the subplot between Falstaff and the Chief Justice, with Justice Shallow in a subsidiary role. This subplot is concluded and determined by the young king at play's end; and in that sense and to that degree it does involve him. But I *am* arguing that this involvement is designedly minimal and late. To describe Hal as playing the same role with respect to justice that he played in Part 1 with respect to valor is to distort and ignore the play's dramatic logic for the sake of a far too neat and symmetrical scheme—for the sake of a symmetry, I might add, to which the play bids a troubled, anxious farewell.

Our seeing Hal as stripped of all roles except that of successor helps us account for several oddities. It accounts for the omission of the scene in which Hal strikes the Chief Justice; it accounts for his non-appearance at court and his non-participation in the affairs of the realm. It also brings into focus another oddity, which has attracted some critical attention. In his soliloquy, Hal apostrophizes the crown; when he justifies himself to the dying king, he claims to quote this apostrophe:

> I spake unto this crown as having sense,
> And thus upbraided it: . . . (IV, V, 158-59)

But, strangely, what he quotes himself as having said differs from what we have just heard him say. If the difference were great and intended to deceive the king about Hal's true feelings, we would simply conclude that Hal is being hypocritical. But that is clearly neither the case nor the intention; there is no reason why he should not quote himself as exactly as he claims to be doing. Why the misquote?

I believe this is one of the many instances where Shakespeare does something odd because he wants to startle us into paying close attention. If we do so, we find that the difference between the two apostrophes is one of metaphor rather than of feeling or motive. In his soliloquy, Hal calls the crown a "*lineal* honor" (rather strangely, since the one standard attribute of a crown, other than its being gold, is that it is a circle, a round or "rigol"). He is determined to keep the *line* of succession unbroken. But in his subsequent self-quoting, he uses a different metaphor:

> Thus, my most royal liege,
> *Accusing* it, I put it on my head,
> To *try* with it, as with an *enemy*
> That had before my face murdered my father,
> The *quarrel* of a true inheritor.
>
> (IV, V, 165-69—my italics)

Now it is combat—more precisely trial by combat—that is insisted on. The crown comes to Hal not as a lineal honor but, paradoxically, as both the object of combat ("true inheritor") and the antagonist ("enemy"). The Prince, in his capacity as successor, sees himself as the challenger in a just "quarrel" which he is eager to "try."

What are we meant to make of this mass of oddities? It would seem that we need to think carefully about the problem of *succession*. What is it? What does it rest on? What does it entail? It is time to think before we can go back to quoting.

V

Not that the question of succession has been ignored

by Shakespeare scholarship. It has been shown that the governing theme of the history plays, derived by Shakespeare from Hall's *Union of the Noble and Illustre Famelies of Lancastre and Yorke,* is that of the disturbed succession. But I shall argue that for Shakespeare the disturbance was vastly more radical and encompassing than we have realized; that it involved not merely England but the entire moral universe; and, most importantly, that its consequences were *irreversible.* To put it somewhat provocatively: in the deposition of Richard II Shakespeare discovered the decomposition of a world picture; we are wrong in assuming that his world picture was still that of Hall and Tudor doctrine.

Succession in the usual sense—the transfer of sovereign power—is actually only a special case of succession. The transfer of sovereign power is an event very much like other events involving the transfer of energy; if we assume that the universe in its physical-moral totality is governed by uniform laws, it makes no difference, in principle, whether the force being transferred is kinetic energy passing from one billiard ball to another or sovereign power passing from one magistrate to another. The reason it does seem to make a difference is that we have come to think of the physico-moral universe as two distinct universes and of the laws governing them as two distinct kinds of law. For us a law of succession (in the narrow sense) is man-made, changing with time, place, and social circumstances; whereas for most of us even today, and for all of us until quite recently, a law of physical succession is, or was, universal and eternal in its operation. In terms of legal philosophy: we regard social laws as *positive* (man-made) and scientific laws as *natural* (inherent in the structure of the universe or given by its creator).

On the whole, when it came to succession, the sixteenth century did not make this distinction. The law governing the transfer of sovereign power—primogeniture—had all the prestige and sanctions of divine prescription; it was a "natural" law like other natural laws, instituted by God for the ordering of events. The physical and moral universe was still one and indivisible, a basically juridical order in which "law" had the sense of rule or decree. The immense success of the natural sciences since then—especially when coupled with the ill success of our efforts to find just, stable, and universal social arrangements—destroyed that faith and that unity. Still it was by no means as naïve as we thought. We are now beginning to realize that scientific laws are no more "natural," universal, and immutable than social laws. The universe is coming to be *one* again, the only difference being that its laws—i.e., the order we find in it—are positive rather than natural or divine.

We know now that scientific laws imply "models"; the models are man-made and stand or fall by their ability to order events. The model of the world underlying the concept of mechanical causality is no "truer" than the model underlying primogeniture, is in fact very much of the same kind. If, and as long as, it is successful in ordering the transfer of force, it will serve; if it proves inadequate for that purpose, we start looking for a better model. In other words, the real change that has taken place over the last three hundred years is that the world, which used to be seen (and more importantly, felt) as divinely ordered, now appears to us as ordered by our needs and for our ends. Still, the belief in natural law dies hard, because it answers to our profoundest need: to find, in the purposeless flux of time and energy, that ultimate permanence without which, it seems, we cannot make sense of our experience. We have made a religion of science not because we revered science but because we needed a religion; now that this religion is also failing us, we must see how we will orient ourselves in a universe that is wholly secular. Will we learn to manage a world that is entirely ours to manage?

Laws of succession, then, order the transfer of sovereign power, that power being conceived not as the property of the particular "body" or magistrate who at a given moment holds and exercises it, but as inhering in and emanating from some being or entity which is considered eternal or almost so. God, the nation, the sovereign people, even the "blood royal" all share this quality of permanence. Nevertheless it is not a matter of indifference where a given society believes that power to reside, and hence how it orders its transfer from one bearer to another. For the mode of transfer implies a model of the universe, a picture of how events must succeed each other to be orderly, intelligible, *legitimate.* A man who has a concept of legitimacy different from mine lives not just in a different society but in a different world.

At first glance it seems obvious that Shakespeare's histories recognize only one mode of succession as truly legitimate: primogeniture. Other modes—particularly succession by combat, as described in Frazer's *Golden Bough*—seem clearly illegitimate; indeed they are not alternate modes so much as lapses into chaos. (Succession by popular election can readily be interpreted as a variant of succession by combat.) All the same it would be very easy for an anthropological critic to read the history plays as recording a series of successions by combat, in which kings who are lacking in potency are supplanted (and usually killed) by others who prove their right to the title by their ability to seize it. Indeed, if this critic were rigorously descriptive and inferred the law of succession in the histories strictly from the actual events, he could not possibly arrive at the law of primogeniture. Richard II to Henry IV, Henry VI to Edward IV, Edward V to Richard III, Richard III to Henry VII—by the combat mode this succession is close to "unbroken," certainly much less broken than under the mode of primogeniture. Depending on the model we choose, the same sequence will appear as either reasonably orderly or disastrously chaotic.

Of course, if we chose the combat model we would completely pervert the meaning of Hall and other Tudor historians and do at least some violence to Shakespeare's. Still I cannot help asking: how much violence? Tudor political theorists and propagandists were always ready to quote St. Paul to the effect that all power is from God, whence it followed that the subject owed obedience, as a matter of religious duty, to the *de facto* ruler. It does not take much thought to discover that this argument implies a combat model of succession; a little more thought may even lead to the suspicion that there is a remarkably close, perhaps necessary, connection between this model and a divinely ruled universe. However that may be, the Tudors were not foolhardy enough to rest their title on the Pauline principle alone; a great deal of effort and ingenuity was expended in proving that the title was (primogenitively) legitimate. Tudor propaganda left little to chance; it worked both sides of the royal road. The title was legitimate beyond question; and even if it was not, it still was. Heads the king won, tails the doubting subject lost—his head most likely if he was rash enough to ask for the toss.

I do not mean that the deception was conscious; the apologists of the Tudor establishment were, I expect, all honorable men, and in any case there is hardly a limit to the inconsistencies men manage sincerely to believe where their needs and vital interests are at stake. Without question the Elizabethans believed that legitimacy and orderly succession went by primogeniture. But the idea that combat was an acceptable way of discovering God's will and verdict was still very much alive—vestigially even in the ritual of succession. (The English coronation ceremony provides for a "King's Champion," who offers to prove his sovereign's title by combat against any and all challengers.) The sense was still strong that there are important occasions where the truth of a claim and the justice of a cause can be determined only by an "appeal to arms," the presiding judge in this court of last appeal being God. Under these circumstances it was natural that even thoughtful men should, as occasions demanded, feel quite untroubled about applying one or the other of these concepts of legitimacy, or even both simultaneously, without realizing that they entailed mutually inconsistent world pictures. But I believe that Shakespeare—who was a more than ordinarily thoughtful man—did see the inconsistency.

VI

Shakespeare's presentation of Richard II departs significantly from tradition. Tradition had bracketed Richard with Edward II as a bad king, extravagant, ruled by selfish and wicked favorites, arbitrary and neglectful of his duties. Since nonetheless he was the legitimate king, it was sinful for Bolingbroke to depose (let alone murder) him; but at the same time it was clear that, humanly speaking, Richard had brought his misfortunes upon himself. In Shakespeare's play we *hear* something of this (especially from John of Gaunt), but we *see* very little of it; Shakespeare's managing of the story is altogether different from Marlowe's in *Edward II*. What we do witness at inordinate length is the history and preparation of a duel which at the last moment Richard prevents from being fought; this takes up almost all of Act I. We then witness Richard's preparations for the war in Ireland and, as part of that, his dispossession of Bolingbroke upon John of Gaunt's death (first part of Act II). By Act II, iii Bolingbroke has returned to England and the rebellion is underway. All Richard has done to deserve it (other than his duty in making war upon the Irish) is to stop a duel and to prevent an exiled heir from assuming his title and possessions.

These do not seem such terrible crimes, but it is worth noting that they in effect abrogate the two modes of establishing legitimacy: combat and primogeniture. York makes it clear that by dispossessing Bolingbroke Richard dispossesses himself:

> Take Hereford's rights away, and take from Time
> His charters and his customary rights;
> Let not tomorrow then ensue today;
> Be not thyself; for how art thou a king
> But by fair sequence and succession? (II, i, 195-99)

With primogeniture thus abrogated, Richard finds himself reduced to proving his title by combat. But how can he, since he has already outlawed even single combat as a form of civil war?

> For that our kingdom's earth should not be soiled
> With that dear blood which it hath fosteréd;
> And for our eyes do hate the dire aspect
> Of civil wounds plowed up with neighbors'
> sword . . . (I, iii, 125-28)

therefore he has stopped the duel and exiled the would-be combatants. He cannot reconcile his concept of kingship with the necessity of defending his title, as though his title were separable from his person and God's decision as to the true claimant were still, or again, open. If the title is true, *God* will defend it:

> For every man that Bolingbroke hath pressed
> To lift shrewd steel against our golden crown,
> God for his Richard hath in heavenly pay
> A glorious angel. (III, ii, 58-61)

If God will not defend it, it isn't true:

> I have no name, no title;
> No, not that name was given me at the font,
> But 'tis usurped. (IV, i, 255-57)

So he refuses combat and in doing so rejects any possibility of succession. As Richard understands kingship —the complete identity of title and name (or person)— there *can* be no successor; true kingship ends with him.

Richard, then, "solves" the problem of succession by rejecting both possible modes of it—and paying the price. We can put it this way: he rejects both senses of the word "cause": the juridical sense of "cause at law," with God as the supreme judge of "quarrels," *and* the primogenitive sense of "cause-effect," with God as the first and final cause, beginning and end of an infinite chain. He rejects the first because he finds it too bloody and chaotic, an institutionalizing of civil war, as it were; he rejects the second because it puts unacceptable constraints on his sovereign authority. His fate indicates that his is not the right way to solve the dilemma.

I have introduced the term "cause" because it was of interest to Renaissance historians. The authors of the *Mirror for Magistrates,* for example, considered Hall's chief excellence to be the noting of "causes":

> But seeing causes are the chiefest things

That should be noted by the story writers,
That men may learn what ends all causes brings,
They be unworthy of the name of chroniclers
That leave them clean out of their registers.

Unworthy, among others, was "unfruitful" Fabyan, because he only

followed the face
Of time and deeds but let the causes slip.

I think Fabyan might have had reason to protest; he, like other chroniclers before him, probably knew quite well what the cause of historical events was: it was God. The issue was not one of noting or neglecting to note causes; it was one of defining "cause." Everyone was agreed that God governed events; the question was how *directly* He governed them. Implicit in the medieval chronicler's simple narrative is the picture of history as a court of law in permanent session, in which God determines case after case, now finding for plaintiff, now for defendant. Each event was literally the "outcome" of a battle or trial, related to all others not as effect to cause but as verdict to verdict; the historian's task was to "register" the verdicts. The Renaissance historians deplored this as a chaotic way of ordering events—civil war rather than orderly rule by primogeniture. To find the "lessons" of history, they required a lineal succession of events, in which God's will was made known through some mediate cause or chain of causes. The historian's job was so to tell his story that these causes would become manifest. Like Polonius and like most subsequent historians, he was expected to be a man "of wisdom and of reach," who could "by indirections find directions out."

The trouble is that once indirections are admitted,

there is no limit to how they may be applied to find the directions one wants: witness Polonius. Witness also the historians, more particularly the Tudor historians, who duly discovered that the operation of causes led inevitably to the fulfillment of God's true purpose: the accession of Henry VII and the Tudors. By a lineal succession of events—most of them, to the uninitiated, diabolically or barbarously illegitimate—legitimacy was achieved. (In a sense, everything must have been legitimate all along the chain, since nothing can be in the effect that is not a cause.) It was a sad puzzle. History from Richard II to Henry VII was little more than a bloody chain of men lying, murdering, and perjuring themselves to achieve legitimacy. As Henry IV, one of the lesser offenders, tells Hal:

> God knows, my son,
> By what bypaths and indirect crooked ways
> I met this crown.
>
> (2 *Henry IV*, IV, v, 184-86)

On the record it was not easy to see how the succession became morally much more intelligible when it was told lineally rather than as a series of divine verdicts. By either model the ultimate wisdom seemed to be that nothing succeeds like succession. Even under primogeniture succession seemed to be by combat—except that the combat had become much less direct. Instead of being settled by the "plain shock and even play of battle," it was determined, more often than not, by equivocal and secretly murderous "stratagems."

VII

I am aware that my ideas on the meaning of "succession" must seem wholly un-Shakespearean in spirit. Few things are as firmly established as that the history plays adopt and follow the great scheme of Tudor history. Far from being caused by the law of primogeniture, England's troubles from Richard II to Henry VII were both the result of and the punishment for the *breach* of that law. (We note in passing how in this account the two models—causal and juridical—are mixed.) Of all the lessons to be learned from history, that is the one most insistently pointed by Hall, as well as by many of Shakespeare's characters. Even Henry V recites it when he implores God's help in the night before Agincourt.

The argument, I grant, looks strong; all the same I find it less and less tenable. What does the orthodox scheme entail? Most importantly it entails the belief that in the long run, if not in the short, the movement of history is *restorative.* The cosmic order has been disturbed by man; after a while, and often at great cost to man, it reasserts itself. The scheme of Hall's *Union* satisfies this assumption perfectly; it traces English history from the fatal breach to the happy restoration. But Shakespeare's histories do *not* satisfy it; his second tetralogy ends in the middle of the story, with the usurper Henry V at the high tide of glory and good fortune.

Even Tillyard—to whom Shakespearean criticism will remain indebted for having restored the picture *against which,* as a background, Shakespeare must be understood—betrays a certain uneasiness over this divergence. He surmises that the second tetralogy may be Shakespeare's revised version of some very early, lost plays of his. If this were so, Shakespeare would have followed Hall's scheme in its structural as well as chronological integrity: from breach to restoration. But there is no evidence whatever for the surmise.

I doubt that we will ever know what prompted Shakespeare to begin his dramatization of Hall at the half-way mark rather than at the beginning. What we do know is that he dramatized the first half *after* he had done the second—in fact long after, if we reckon the intervening time by his development as a dramatist rather than by calendar years. It is also clear that the arrangement of the first tetralogy is restorative, exactly like Hall's. That Shakespeare begins in the middle does not greatly matter; he lets us know, by expository scenes and speeches, when and how England's troubles began. Having done so, he takes us to the final restoration.

The structure of the second tetralogy, on the other hand, is *not* restorative. It moves toward the accession and "victorious acts" of a king whose title is almost nonlineal, one short link removed from the breach. This king is not sent by God as a redeemer; we observe him grooming himself for his role with the cool calculation of Richard III (though of course by wholly different means). I think we need to be cautious about calling Henry V Shakespeare's "ideal king"; but to a remarkable degree he is *self-made*. His title is legitimized largely by his self-nurtured qualities and by his achievements; when God "crowns" him with victory, that legitimation is *ex post facto*.

To put the case differently: instead of surmising the existence of four lost plays, let us suppose the loss of four extant plays—the first tetralogy. Our conclusion about Shakespeare's view of English history and political order would then have to be inferred from the second tetralogy and *King John*. (For the purpose of this argument, we can ignore *Henry VIII*.) I do not see how, in that case, we could conclude that he meant to embody and enforce the lessons he found in Hall and others. To be sure, we would still have a good many passages teaching these lessons; but though such passages undoubtedly express the views of their speakers and of most of Shakespeare's contemporaries, they can hardly be taken as expressing his own. *His* meaning lies in the dramatic structure; and the structure of the second tetralogy, the logic of its events, undercuts Tudor doctrine. How could a reasonably perceptive spectator, having watched the not undeserved misfortunes of Richard II and the predictable and predicted troubles of Henry IV, leave the theatre at the end of *Henry V* with the conviction that the breach of primogeniture is a crime for which God, through the operation of "causes," will punish the perpetrators until legitimacy is restored?

It is a question of surrendering to the dramatic present, of not forcing that present into a chronology that is not its own. If we surrender to the dramatic present of the first tetralogy, we do not have to read Hall to know that we have been moving toward a restoration. In the end, a frightful disturbance has run its course, a curse has been lifted. "The bloody dog is dead," and "this long-usurped royalty" has returned to "the true succeeders of each royal house." Though Richmond and Elizabeth are "true" succeeders because they are lineal, the movement of the action is the very opposite of lineal. A line moves into an undetermined, undeterminable future; but at the end of *Richard III* we are meant to feel, and do feel, that things have finally come "round": they are back to where they always should have been. So it is entirely appropriate that the restorer—Richmond—has no history; he is *only* the restorer, coming into the play by divine dispensation, from a realm beyond time. It is Richard III who has a history; for fifteen acts we have watched him scheming and reaping the fruits of his scheming. The events of the drama occur more and more by Richard's will, are ordered by his purpose; when Richmond descends, the action stops. It is as though action and time—i.e., history—were adjuncts of evil, from which by God's grace we are finally delivered. That we are delivered by, and to, lineality is a contradiction the play does its successful best to ignore.

We misread the second tetralogy if we think of it as "really" the first. The chronology that counts is not that of English history but that of Shakespeare's plays—which is to say, of his development as a dramatist. There is no evidence for considering the second tetralogy a revision of some lost plays; but there are some very good reasons for considering it as a revision of the first tetralogy—as a revision dictated by the discovery that restoration is a false ideal. Time, like a line, moves in one direction only; and drama, especially historical drama, is action in time.

The first tetralogy is dominated by men—preeminently Richard—who seek to *make* themselves (or others) kings and whose efforts are and cause evil. The second tetralogy is dominated by a man who expects to *become* king and who in the end deserves well of his country. In the first tetralogy the crown is striven for as though it were a final goal—as though time would stop once the goal were reached. In the second tetralogy it is the symbol of an office, simultaneously desired and feared, a goal and at the same time a beginning. The methods of attaining the crown are correspondingly different. To Richard lineality means a counting of the heads he must chop off before the crown comes to rest on his own; that, therefore, is how he prepares for the kingship. (Tate's famous "Off with his head! so much for Buckingham!" catches this quality perfectly.) Time for him moves by "strokes" rather than continuously. Prince Hal, as the immediate heir, can afford to let time work for him; even so Shakespeare carefully eliminates from his version of the story almost all elements—his sources contained many—which would make Hal appear impatient for the crown. (Others suspect him of such impatience, but they are mistaken.) Time moves (especially for Falstaff), but not as though Hal expected it to stop with his accession; his arrival is a setting out.

Of course, any properly constructed play, or series of plays, must leave us with a feeling of finality, of things having come "round." The natural stopping points are death and marriage. The first tetralogy, following Hall, combines the two; it ends with Richard's death and the "union" of Richmond and Elizabeth, Lancaster and York. The second tetralogy ends with a marriage only, the union of Henry and Catherine, England and France. The difference is greater than it seems. The restoring marriage of Richmond and Elizabeth is made in heaven; at least it is not made on earth. No courtship leads up to it, nor even negotiations; prior to Richmond's formal announcement of it, it is mentioned once briefly by two secondary characters. This is even more striking when we consider other courtship scenes and marriages in the tetralogy. Shakespeare composed such scenes with obvious relish and exploited to the full the opportunities his story offered for writing them. There is the marriage between Henry VI and Margaret, arranged by Suffolk's ambition and adulterous passion and costing England dearly in blood and treasure. There is the marriage between Edward IV and Lady Grey, dictated by lust and plunging England back into civil war. There is the marriage between Richard and Anne, perpetrated (no better word comes to mind) in what must be the most outrageous and sinister courtship scene in literature. There is, finally, the long (235 lines) and elaborate scene in which Richard tries to win the dowager queen's consent to marry Elizabeth. Considering how crucial the marriage between Elizabeth and Richmond was in the whole scheme—how it was, in fact, its true terminal point—we might surely expect that Shakespeare would give the last of these scenes to Richmond rather than Richard. Better still, he might have split the scene between them, in perfect correspondence to the "split" scene in which the two antagonists dream their counterposed dreams before the battle. What could be more appropriate than to show Richard and Richmond striving for the same goal—Elizabeth's hand—the true heir succeeding where the tyrant miserably fails? But no; the "true succeeders" are "by God's ordinance conjoin[ed] together"—and *only* by God's ordinance. It is as though Shakespeare refused to take credit for this union—as though he wanted to exempt it also from the evil of human design and passion. He disclaims the role of creator. Man's efforts to create order are sinful pride and lust and come to nothing or worse; his task is not to make history but piously to retrace God's providential and restorative design.

The second tetralogy has no courtship and marriages except the concluding one. And this marriage does not descend from heaven; it is the effect of human action, both political and personal. It restores nothing, but points to the future; it is not a conclusion but a hope (the more so because we know that the hope will not be fulfilled). As all human unions must, that between Harry and Catherine crosses barriers—most concretely the barrier of language; for while God is One and all is one in Him, man is many and separate. The marriage does, nevertheless, heal a wound, or at least envisage the hope of healing it: the breach between England and France. The scene and scope of the action have changed and broadened, as has the concept of "civil war": the final union, if only it held what it promises, would end the civil wars of Christendom. That it does not hold does not mean that man's creative efforts are wicked and must come to naught; it means at most that he has not yet found the right way, the true language. The sword has still done more than the word to found this union, has in fact done just about all. But however incomplete the design, however faulty the instruments, they are *man's*. Much more than a precursor of Richmond, Henry V is a descendant of Richard III redeemed from the curse which, under a restorative view of history, damned all genuinely human action and denied the dimension and meaning of time.

VIII

I find myself engaged in the ironic enterprise of "restoring" the second tetralogy to its true place in the succession of Shakespeare's plays by showing that it is *not* restorative. And I do not think that this irony is simply a play on words; it reflects, I believe, a question Shakespeare faced and tried very seriously to answer: what was the true succession in *his* plays? How were *they* legitimized? When, some four years after writing the first tetralogy, he undertook to write the second, what chronology was he to follow: the seemingly God-given one of Hall's history, or the very different, creative one of his own development? Was he reverently to "restore" a missing piece in the great design, writing as though his own intervening conquests and discoveries were irrelevant? Or was he to accept the fearful responsibility of writing as though he, a mere man, *made* history? Whose "order" was he to obey: that of his life, or that of God's (presumed) design?

He was caught in a paradox either way. For if he gave priority to the lineality of his own development, how could he deny it to the events he meant to chronicle? On the other hand, if he claimed the right, by virtue of his creative power, to determine the succession as he saw fit, what order, what succession was there unless he could simultaneously (and contradictorily) claim that his power was in fact not his but God's, for God to dispose of as He saw fit? And God *had* disposed: the reigns of Richard II, Henry IV, and Henry V did not follow those of Henry VI, Richard III, and Henry VII but preceded them.

In other words, he found himself exactly in the predicament of Richard II: neither model of legitimacy, of succession, was acceptable. He must have felt tempted to follow Richard's example: to rid himself of the burden of genuine sovereignty and genuine succession, to enclose himself in the prison of ineffectual, self-generating imaginings and enjoy the unlimited sovereignty of the "pure" creator:

> I have been studying how I may compare
> This prison where I live unto the world;
> And for because the world is populous,
> And here is not a creature but myself,
> I cannot do it; yet I'll hammer it out.
> My brain I'll prove the female to my soul,
> My soul the father; and these two beget
> A generation of still-breeding thoughts,
> And these same thoughts people this little world.
> (v, v, 1-9)

The thoughts *are* "still-breeding"—simultaneously ever fertile and sterile, the parthenogenetic offspring of the self-sufficient imagination, a "little world" or drama that leaves no successor. We know that Shakespeare refused to follow Richard into this prison of rejection; but what principle of generation was he to accept? Was the only choice to be "with child by the stern tyrant war"—to adopt the combat model of dramatic succession—or, like John of Lancaster, to speak of, and on the surface to protect, the "peace" of strict lineality, "while covert enmity/Under the smile of safety wounds the world?" Was he to be the purposeful, unrelenting plotter, a Richard III of the drama, or its Tamburlane, rushing from battle to bloody battle? Or was he to mix the two models, use one or the other as it suited his purpose, ignoring or disguising their inconsistency?

For the last "solution" there was ample precedent and justification; we have seen that it was that of Tudor doctrine, the *via media* of having it both ways. The inconsistency was concealed under a thick coating of pious rhetoric and rich imagery. It was concealed also in another way: by nationalist fervor. The trick was simple and has been used with great success ever since. One model was applied to internal affairs, the other to affairs between nations. Internally, the horror and waste of civil war demanded the proscription of the combat model and the combat ethic; decisions as to legitimacy could not be safely left to God. The king took God's place and claimed to speak for Him; since he fell somewhat short of the required immortality, primogeniture was given sacred status as the sole true mode of succession. But externally, the combat model was in full force, its ethic sedulously inculcated; in "foreign quarrels" God was appealed to. What were crimes inside the border became acts of higher justice beyond; wicked pride and ambition turned into valor and honor by travelling abroad. Passing from one country to another was like passing from one moral universe to another, was in fact practically the same thing: deeds and values came to bear totally different names. As Catherine's English lesson in *Henry V* illustrates, words that are perfectly innocent in one language sound like obscenities in another.

The combat model, though it seemed (except to the most devout) an institutionalizing of disorder, had some compensating virtues. Under the lineal system, since God worked by indirection, the king, being God in little, could claim the same privilege. Rebels had no status as legitimate challengers; the code of honor did not apply to them. "Due process," considered causally, is something altogether different from due process considered juridically; as in ballistics, it is determined by whether the target is hit. John of Lancaster observes this kind of due process in Gaultree Forest; both the French and the English observe the other kind at Agincourt (with one bad lapse on either side). The model decides which is which. If Gaultree Forest strikes us as hasty and Agincourt (e.g., the endless comings and goings of the French herald) as somewhat absurd, the reason is that we cannot accept either model in its pure form. We cannot settle for the notion that anything as serious as war should be played purely as a ritual or game, in which man observes the rules and God renders the verdict. But neither can we settle for the notion (though we are learning fast) that war can be treated simply as the most efficient use of causal law, the sole aim being the most economic and complete extermination of the enemy. If human conflict is to remain human at all, it must be both formal and functional, conducted by both juridical and causal due process. It is far from easy—it may in fact prove impossible—to discover a model of moral order which satisfies both these needs without contradiction. But it is fatally easy to pretend that there *is* no contradiction, so that one can be both vicious and absurd and feel fully legitimate in being either. Each several model has some healing properties; it is the mix that is wholly poisonous. In the words of Hal's second apostrophe of the crown:

> Therefore, thou best of gold art worst of gold.
> Other, less fine in carat, is more precious,
> Preserving life in medicine potable;
> But thou, most fine, most honoured, most renowned.
> Hast eat thy bearer up. (*2 Henry IV*, IV, v, 161-65)

The burden of my argument—the point of this interpretation of the Hal trilogy—is this: Shakespeare, having discovered that the "most fine, most honoured, most renowned" golden unity of the Elizabethan world picture was in truth a lethal mixture of two mutually inconsistent and severally inadequate models of succession, but that to reject both meant imprisonment and sterility, first tried a dialectical solution (*1 Henry IV*) and next a dis-solution (*2 Henry IV* and *Henry V*). The solution, he found, rested on a *petitio principii*; the several dissolutions entailed severe sacrifices—most importantly, the sacrifice of true legitimacy. Each in its own way was "swoll'n with some other grief"; but it was a grief that had to be borne and born, if bearing, generation, succession was to continue.

I realize that I have credited Shakespeare with what appears to be a very modern and still largely scientific concept: that of the *model*. I must now credit him with another, closely related one: *complementarity*. I am in fact saying that, some three centuries before Niels Bohr, Shakespeare discovered the need of complementarity—i.e., of operating with two mutually inconsistent and severally inadequate models because, and as long as, a single, consistent, and adequate model has not been found. Complementarity differs from and is superior to mixing because it remains aware of its "illegitimacy" and *pays the price* of choosing one model or the other. It does not pretend to be a solution, hence does not close the road of discovery but on the contrary compels us to take the risk of following it. Its passionate demand for order forces us to leave the safe prison of a static, once-for-all world picture, to suffer the grief of imperfection and disorder and the joy of genuine action and creativity. Complementarity, in short, asserts the value of *human action in time*—which is to say, of history, of drama.

I credit Shakespeare with discovering these concepts not because I want to "modernize" him but because I see no other way of accounting for the observable facts of the second tetralogy. How else are we to explain the sequence Shrewsbury-Gaultree Forest-Agincourt? How else are we to explain the strange frustration of our combativeness, which appears to be the "law" of *2 Henry IV*, and on the other hand the almost total indulgence of this same combativeness which governs most of *Henry V*? How—to descend to the level of textual cruxes—are we to explain the oddity of Hal's two apostrophes of the crown? How—to mention one more item from what could easily be extended into a very long list—are we to explain the fact that the crown comes to Hal both by seizure and by lineal descent—that he takes, before the appointed time, what becomes his at the appointed time? Why this filial, lineal piety so oddly yoked with creative impatience? Wherever we look, we find complementarity.

Hal's seizure of the crown is the figure of Shakespeare's "seizure" of history. Of course, he found the episode in his sources, but that is precisely the point. He likewise found other episodes in his sources—most signally that of Hal's striking the Chief Justice. Many of these he reduced to dramatic insignificance, but this one he makes his own. Not wilfully, not for theatrical effect, but because in it he discovers the very metaphor of his effort and enterprise: to write "creative history," to find meaning and order both in the succession of historical events and in the succession of his dramatic explorations. Truly and reverently looked at, recorded history answers *to* his quest and question; but it does not *answer* it. Instead of providing him with the definitive model of succession and success, to be retraced by him in simple piety —or instead of meeting him with blank silence and leaving him free to impose on it whatever pattern happens to suit him—it supplies him with a metaphor. And the metaphor is one of *complementarity*, of either-or. It is neither a mixture nor a synthesis, but a metaphor: that strange entity which demands to be analytically dissolved because it *means* and creatively "made good" because it *is*. It is pregnant, hence promises birth; but the birth is never certain, while labor and pain *are* certain. Is even the father certain? Can we be sure of legitimacy? Will the offspring be the child of passion or of duty, of self-assertive lust or submissive routine? There are no guarantees, only the risk and the will—the need—to order.

IX

To state my argument in terms of the "price paid," the following schema emerges. Richard II, refusing to pay any price whatever, in the end pays most heavily; he finds himself compelled to retreat into the sterile though poignant pathos of non-success and non-succession. Prince Hal of *1 Henry IV* tries to avoid paying the price by dialectical design: he exploits the combat model by pitting disorder against rebellion, but hopes to escape the consequences of this model by superior management. He is literally the "know-you-all," the omniscient and almost omnipotent dramatist, seemingly involved but actually secure. And he almost brings it off; *1 Henry IV* is not by accident the "best play" of the trilogy. If the problem of succession were solvable by dramaturgic skill, here it would be solved; if dialectical "wit" were the ultimate wisdom, Hal's obsequies over Hotspur and Falstaff might be the last word. But, as we saw, Hal's solution is half a lie; to sustain it, he must also sustain Falstaff's half-lie. Disorder is not vanquished; Falstaff survives by playing dead, and the rebellion survives, at least in part, by Northumberland's playing sick. If disorder has lost a good deal of its vitality, so has order (witness *2 Henry IV*), for the simple reason that order, under the dialectical scheme, depends on disorder as symmetry depends on contrast. Without two such splendid foils as Hotspur and Falstaff to flash in mock-heroic combat, Hal finds himself sadly reduced.

In *2 Henry IV* he (and Shakespeare—the two are the same) accepts the necessity of paying the price; and the price is self-denial, withdrawal. Now there is no theatrical cashing in on the combat model: on exciting clashes and encounters, on tense confrontations; the "due process" of lineality prevails. A fetid domesticity, a weary rather than vigorous air of expectancy, blankets the whole. What vigor there is comes from Falstaff and even so is generated by contrast:

> If you do not all show like gilt twopences to me, and I in the clear sky of fame o'ershine you as much as the full moon doth the cinders of the element, which show like pins' heads to her, believe not the word of the noble. (IV, iii, 54-60)

As usual, he is in the right; for if the capture of Coleville was not exactly an act of heroism, it shines brightly in comparison to the victory won by John of Lancaster.

But there is no longer room in England for the combat kind of disorder—which is not exactly to say that order has prevailed. Disorder has taken the meaner and more indirect forms of corruption and equivocation: partial justice, bribery, false promises, and bad debts—disorders rather than disorder. The body politic no longer suffers from a raging fever but from ill humors—that's the humor of it. The "high terms" of a proud and combative nobility have deteriorated into the ludicrous fustian of Pistol, the gentle poetry of ladies into the grubby prose of Doll Tearsheet:

> She bids you on the wanton rushes lay you down
> And rest your gentle head upon her lap,
> And she will sing a song that pleaseth you
> And on your eyelids crown the god of sleep.
>
> (*1 Henry IV*, III, i, 214-17)

but:

> Ah, you sweet little rogue, you! Alas, poor ape, how thou sweat'st! Come, let me wipe thy face, come on, you whoreson chops. Ah, rogue! i' faith, I love thee.
>
> (2 *Henry IV*, II, iv, 233-36)

A world seems to have come to and end.

True, there is the Lord Chief Justice. But there are likewise the little justices, the Shallows, in whom the current of the law, however pure at the fountainhead, will ultimately stagnate. The new England seems to have little room for high drama; it breeds the comedy of humors and of satire. John of Gaunt's "sceptred isle" has become Nashe's *Isle of Dogs*. At the top, the lineal succession is by way of being secured, justice is being maintained, order upheld; why do we miss the bright spark of metal on metal? Why do we feel oppressed by the insistent organicity of this order, the sequence of growth and decay?

Shallow: Death, as the Psalmist saith, is certain to all; all shall die.
How a good yoke of bullocks at Stamford fair?
Silence: Be my troth, I was not there.
Shallow: Death is certain. Is old Double of your town living yet?
Silence: Dead, sir.
Shallow: Jesu, Jesu, dead! A' drew a good bow; and dead! John a' Gaunt loved him well, and betted much money on his head. Dead! . . . How a score of ewes now?
Silence: Thereafter as they be. A score of good ewes may be worth ten pounds.
Shallow: And is old Double dead? (III, ii, 41-58)

Yes, old "double" is dead. Succession is no longer won by competition and at hazard; it breeds. Let time and nature have their course, and it will come to you: death is certain. Order is no longer something wrought, the reward of struggle and design, but something self-perpetuating, the endless sequence of cause and effect. The blood royal, too precious to be shed on the battlefield, flows sluggishly through sober veins. It is sadly in need of artificial stimulation:

> The second property of your excellent sherris is, the warming of the blood; which, before cold and settled, left the liver white and pale, which is the badge of pusillanimity and cowardice; but the sherris warms it and makes it course from the inwards to the parts extreme. It illumineth the face, which as a beacon gives warning to all the rest of this little kingdom, man, to arm. And then the vital commoners and inland petty spirits muster me all to

> their captain, the heart, who, great and puffed up with this retinue, doth any deed of courage; and this valor comes of sherris. (IV, iii, 110-22)

Even valor is a matter of what "comes of" what.

This is the quality of by far the largest part of *2 Henry IV*. We are constantly aware of Hal, to be sure, but only as the "next in line." He no longer directs the action or designs the confrontations; he lets himself be carried where, by lineality and with the aid of his brother's indirection, he is destined to be carried: to the throne.

Once there, however, he is no longer passive and withdrawn; he takes charge. *Henry V* obviously returns to the combat model, but it does not return to *1 Henry IV*. Harry is no longer the *tertius ridens*; he is himself a combatant. With a sense of elation and relief, he surrenders the function of arbiter to the "Lord Chief Justice"—to the human judge in England, to the divine Judge in the battlefields of France. To put it bluntly, he *escapes* into France—which is to say, into a world where the combat model still seems applicable and sufficient. He rids himself of the impossible burden of sovereignty, of having to be both chief arbiter and chief designer. For a brief moment of gloriously simple action, he gives himself over to the plain shock and even play of battle.

Shakespeare would not be Shakespeare if the matter were quite that simple. There are still many reminders that this is an escape, not a solution; I shall have to deal with some of them. But I think the zest of the play as a whole—its clear and uncomplicated line of action, its simple camaraderie and gaiety—is explicable only as the self-reward of a man who feels he has earned a vacation. Harry permits himself the luxury of being a participant, of taking part and leaving the cares and ironies of design to a higher power.

But again he pays the price. The choruses of Henry *V*, with their repeated apologies for the limitations of drama, have properly attracted attention. Some critics argue that the choruses are later additions, inserted without much regard for consistency. Others see in them Shakespeare's effort to ward off the attacks of classicists such as Ben Jonson, who scoffed at the popular theatre's violations of the unities and of verisimilitude. Still others stress the "epic" quality of *Henry V* and regard the choruses as Shakespeare's acknowledgment of this quality. None of these explanations strikes me as adequate. What Shakespeare does is to refuse a certain responsibility and to claim a certain right. The responsibility is that of making a world; he insists that the world of the play is in large part *ours*, given fulness and continuity by our imaginations. The correlative right he thereby obtains is that of direct address: since he has resigned the playwright's quasi-divine sovereignty, he can speak to us as man to fellow man. Unlike God, he now has a language other than the mute and infinitely difficult one of design, and the language is *English*. Only if we understand "epic" in this sense does it help us in the interpretation of the play. The lyric poet speaks the language of the self, the first person singular. The epic poet speaks the language of the tribe, the first person plural. The true dramatist has neither person nor voice; he must speak the "language" of God. Once he has discovered the true nature of his craft, therefore, he cannot be a "nationalist." The choruses tell us that *Henry V* is a brief final escape into the ease and fellowship of nationalism.

As I said, things are not quite that simple; quite a few ironies remain, and many of these have caused disputes among the critics. There is the "justification" of the war against France—obviously exposed as mere rationalization by Shakespeare himself. Not only does the dying Henry IV urge Harry to engage in "foreign quarrels" for reasons that have nothing to do with those later given; not only does John, immediately after the coronation, reveal the young king's purpose to invade France; the churchmen who elaborately "prove" Harry's right to the French crown have told us previously what they hope to gain by doing so. The proof itself is transparently ironic. It is pompously, pedantically lineal, is in fact—and quite aside from its specific validity or invalidity—a *reductio ad absurdum* of the lineal argument. If title must be proved by retracing genealogies for millennia—to King Pharamond, say, "Who died within the year of our redemption/Four hundred twenty six"—what title is true? The inevitable next step is the rebellious peasant's unanswerable question:

> When Adam delved and Eva span,
> where was *then* the nobleman?

If the legitimacy of an event depends upon our showing that the chain of causes has continued unbroken from the beginning of time, how can it ever be proved? But if, by a "gentleman's agreement," we settle for less and make precedence and title depend on the relative length of chain each claimant can present, then the French king's claim is incomparably stronger than Harry's own. For at least it goes back to Hugh Capet, while Harry's puny little two links cannot even be called a chain. To speak to *him* of "crooked titles/Usurped from you and your progenitors" is to raise dangerously recent and unquiet ghosts—or would be, if national sentiment could not be trusted to drown memory, common sense, and elementary logic.

Shakespeare undercuts the lineal argument in every possible way. He exposes it beforehand as *ad hoc*, he shows it to be both doubtful and absurd within its own terms—*and* he does not even use it at the point of bearing. The French ambassadors hear not a word of it; the actual declaration of war is issued purely as the defiance of a challenge—i.e., under the combat model. After all the ponderous legalities and linealities, it appears that the war will be fought over a barrel of tennis balls! The language is entirely that of the duel, of a "quarrel" between champions:

> But this lies all within the will of God,
> To Whom I do appeal; and in Whose name
> Tell you the Dauphin I am coming on
> To venge me as I may, and to put forth
> My rightful hand in a well-hallowed cause.[3]
> (I, ii, 289-93)

If Shakespeare makes anything clear, it is that Harry is spoiling for a fight; what he wants from others is not reasons but excuses, and these are duly and plentifully supplied.

Many people find *Henry V* offensive, though they argue whether it is offensively foolish or offensively knavish. Was Shakespeare nationalist fool enough to believe such stuff, or was he theatrical knave enough to exploit

[3] To be sure, this is Harry's answer to the Dauphin's challenge; the formal declaration of war, based on the "memorable line" of Harry's genealogy, is made later (II, iv). But here again Shakespeare, though on the whole he follows Holinshed closely, has made a significant change. In Holinshed, the Dauphin's taunt is removed from the arguments for war; it comes *before* the calling of the Parliament at which the prelates offer their genealogical chart and war is resolved on. Nor does the Dauphin's message include any political matters (as it does in *Henry V*); it is personal. Shakespeare, by placing it as he does, gives it much greater political weight; Harry's defiance becomes the actual declaration of war and the later, "lineal" declaration is reduced to a superfluous formality. I am convinced that every untutored reader or spectator will remember the tennis-ball scene as the decisive one; I doubt that he will remember the later scene at all.

it? Both questions miss the point, I think. The point is that Shakespeare takes a rest from the labor of discovering the unifying model and knowingly chooses a partial and partisan clarity. The mark of knaves and fools is that they mix their models of legitimation; the mark of an honest and wise man is that when he accepts an inadequate one, he accepts it fully and with all that it entails.

By this standard, Shakespeare is scrupulously honest, and *Henry V* is attractively simple. If it were his only play, we might justly think the simplicity unearned, mere naïveté. Take the piety:

> Come, go we in procession to the village;
> And be it death proclaimed through our host
> To boast of this or take that praise from God
> Which is His only. (IV, viii, 118-21)

Fluellen asks a prosaically causal question:

> Is is not lawful, an't please your majesty, to tell how many is killed? (22-23)

Yes, it is "lawful,"

> but with this acknowledgment,
> That God fought for us. . . .
> Do we all holy rites.
> Let there be sung *Non nobis* and *Te Deum.*
> (24-28)

But this is *after* the battle. Before, the invocations of God are no more frequent or emphatic than the challenge-defiance ritual calls for. And at the point when the issue of the war's justice comes into sharpest focus—in Harry's nocturnal dispute with his men—Harry is unable to cite God as his guarantor. This, we saw, is no holy war but a trial, a testing of God's judgment. The victory is God's—not in the sense that His cause has won but that His verdict has been made known. No claim is made that the English are privy to God's intent, the chosen instrument of divine policy, the executors of a manifest destiny. Nothing is manifest until God has spoken, and He speaks only in the event. Harry fights for a claim, not a Cause. Hence the play's nationalism is, by modern standards, singularly nonvirulent. Where God's purpose is assumed to be known, man can hardly escape the conclusion that the end justifies the means; function overrules form. Under the lineal model, only the end can have moral identity; of the means nothing can be said except that they are more or less appropriate. (The dishonesty of historical dialectics—whether Hegelian, Marxist, or Spencerian—lies in the implicit claim that issues are being put to the test of battle while at the same time it is known which outcome of any given battle would be "right" and which would be "wrong.") Has there ever been a nation, party, or class which drew from a defeat the conclusion that the fittest had survived and God or History had definitively spoken? The conclusion drawn from a defeat is almost always that the wrong means have been employed, while the conclusion drawn from victory is invariably that the true cause has prevailed.

Henry V avoids this mixing of models. Shakespeare was an English dramatist writing for a fiercely self-assertive young nation. It would have been impossible for him to write of Agincourt as anything other than a victory for the right side; nor, I am sure, did he *want* to write otherwise. The whole play is animated by the joy of combat and victory. But what it blessedly lacks is the insufferable (and usually cruel and unscrupulous) self-righteousness of those who know themselves to be fighting God's battles. Shakespeare does his dramatic best to keep God out of it until *after* He has "spoken"; but then he gives Him sole credit for the decision.

This, then, is the price he pays; he surrenders his claim to "authorship": "Take it, God,/For it is none but Thine!" The piety is sincere, no doubt; but it, too, has its ironies. Shakespeare has made it quite clear that one has to be an Englishman to find the world of *Henry V* —for which he piously refuses to take credit—attractive. Pistol, for one, does not follow the wars in order to escape into a simpler world of combat and due process:

> Let us to France; like horseleeches, my boys,
> To suck, to suck, the very blood to suck!
> (II, iii, 57-58)

And when, before Harfleur, Harry threatens to unleash his soldiery, he leaves little to the imagination about what war is, or can be, like:

> filthy and contagious clouds
> Of heady murder, spoil and villainy,

committed by "the blind and bloody soldier with foul hand" (III, iii, 31-34). Or as Williams describes it: "all those legs and arms and heads, chopped off in a battle," which "shall join together at the latter day and cry all 'We died at such a place'; some swearing, some crying for a surgeon, some upon their wives left poor behind them, some upon the debts they owe, some upon their children rawly left" (IV, i, 141). *Henry V* is not an anti-war play of course (though even that interpretation has been attempted); but it might easily become one if Shakespeare did not resolutely limit our moral vision.[4]

[4] I say "resolutely" because Shakespeare wants us to *know* what he is doing. His treatment of Harry's cruel command to kill all the prisoners is a case in point. He makes the command appear much less justified than Holinshed does. As in the tennis-ball episode, it is

His piety is almost defiant; he says to God: "*You* made me English; *You* made English my language and did not provide me with a divine Esperanto or with an audience that would understand it if I had it. I know that from *Your* vantage point this must seem a bloody civil war. Perhaps you have a master design, a model of order under which these events are intelligible, necessary steps toward a greater harmony. All *I* have to make sense of them is the combat model, with You at the apex and myself one of the combatants. Under such a model, this is how the war looks. Now *You* take it; it's Yours."

Thus it would not be false to say that in *Henry V*, Shakespeare, though choosing the opposite model from that of 2 *Henry IV*, pays the same price: withdrawal. Where before he withdrew into passivity, he now withdraws into simple, partisan action. Because drama is action and conflict, *Henry V* seems at first blush altogether unlike a withdrawal, altogether "dramatic." And it is true that there is a natural affinity between drama and the combat model. But that is precisely the problem: is

---

a question of *sequence*. Holinshed first tells of the French attack on the English camp and the killing of the servants; Harry, hearing the "outcry," fears that the French are rallying for a "new field" and orders the prisoners killed. Thus the French outrage precedes and—by the instinctive causality of *post hoc, ergo propter hoc*—in a measure justifies the English outrage. Shakespeare could easily have read Holinshed in this sense and made Harry's order an act of retaliation. He carefully avoids doing so. Harry hears an "alarum," concludes that the French "have reinforced their scattered men," and issues the order. Only in the following scene do we hear of the French "knavery"; so that when Gower says: "Wherefore the king, most worthily, hath caused every soldier to cut his prisoner's throat. Oh, 'tis a gallant king!" the conclusion, *we* know, is both false and grimly ironic. I believe more is at issue here than Harry's moral stature—namely, legitimation. Gower's reasoning rests on the typically nationalist mixture of causal and juridical legitimation: Harry's order is justified as the effect of the French outrage and also as an act of "gallantry." If you hit me, I gallantly hit back twice as hard—and anyhow, you hit me first. (The up-to-date word is escalation.) Shakespeare takes pains to expose this reasoning for what it is; as to the facts of the matter, he keeps them in exact balance.

drama—are Shakespeare's plays—to be no more than the litter of the "stern tyrant war"? Does his craft compel him to fight battle after battle, court case after court case, under the arbitration of the Lord Chief Justice of the universe? Is he condemned to being "unfruitful" like Fabyan and let the causes slip? Is he to make a living from counterfeit dying and killing—and at the same time resign his creative sovereignty to God (or History, or Fortune)? If so, what is *his* legitimation; wherein does the continuity and intelligible order of *his* work consist?

Even in *Henry V* these troubling questions will out. Harry's soliloquy on Ceremony, to be properly understood, must be read against the background of its counterpart in the first tetralogy: the "split-dream" scene in the night before the battle of Bosworth Field. What is most significant about it is that Harry does *not* dream, is not either damned or promised success and succession by divinely sent messengers and messages. He has to face his trial—ambiguous as for human beings these always are—in full consciousness, and alone. He may pray, but he is not answered; the distinguishing attribute of God is not His omniscience, omnipotence or boundless love—these are simply human attributes raised to an infinite power—but His unwillingness, or inability, to *speak*. What language would He use? We may fool ourselves into believing that He does speak; on Bosworth Field, where everyone talks English, it is natural to think that God and His messengers do also. But at Agincourt the illusion is hard to sustain; we can hear the French chattering across the field.

Also, Harry in the night is one, alone; at this point in the play, "double is dead." At other times, though king, he is subject to the King of kings and can pass the heaviest part of his burden on upwards. But now he realizes that (to quote another Harry) his throne is where the buck stops:

> Upon the King! Let us our lives, our souls,
> Our debts, our careful wives,
> Our children, and our sins lay on the King!
> (IV, i, 247-49)

On Bosworth Field the problem was avoided by a neat split, with God above in charge and sending the appropriate messages to the pious and the wicked. Double was still alive—and in a much subtler form he has been revived for most of *Henry V*. But at this point the revival is exposed as an artifice; the messages Harry receives do not come from above to be passed down, they come from below, from Williams and Bates—and there is no way of passing them on. The discovery has a remarkable effect on Harry: as soon as he is compelled to think of himself as *the* King rather than as one king under the King of kings, he seems to forget where he is and what he is about to do. He is no longer on the battlefield preparing for the French attack; he is in his throne room, contemplating the burdensome pomp of kingship and the simple content of the peasant's life. He is not the warrior but the watchful and sleepless designer; his thoughts are not of combat but of peace:

> The slave, a member of the country's peace,
> Enjoys it, but in gross brain little wots
> What watch the King keeps to maintain the peace,
> Whose hours the peasant best advantages.
> (IV, i, 298-301)

Only after being interrupted by Erpingham does he turn his mind back to the present and to the "God of battles," to Whom he offers a troubled, unsure prayer.

Harry dies young and in the full flush of glory, a warrior King. God, or history, has spared him the full burden of his solitary office. I do not think we are meant to begrudge him his glory; he has earned it. Not because he has achieved a true ordering; if he had, he would have achieved a true succession, and we know what happens under his son. But in three plays he has discovered what lesser means of ordering are possible, what it costs to use any one of them, and, above all, what it costs to confuse them. His success (ion) will be short-lived; considering how it was obtained, it could hardly be otherwise. Not even England is better off for his reign, let alone Christendom. But we are gainers nevertheless: by the purity and valor of his rejections and acceptances we know far more clearly what to fear and what to hope for.

X

So far I have talked about *Henry V* as though it ended with Act IV, with Agincourt rather than the marriage of Harry and Catherine of France. I have done so because I believe that the last act is an epilogue to the history plays as a whole—an epilogue that points into the future.

The Chorus to Act V—famous for its allusion to Essex—asks us to imagine Harry's triumphant return to England and London. But why should we *imagine* it? England at peace and rejoicing, united in spirit and purpose, powerful and respected abroad; nobles and citizens alike welcoming the king as the true embodiment of *res publica*; the king himself, gracious and assured, giving due praise to God and concluding with a ringing affirmation of England, "if to herself she be but true"—surely this could have been managed on the stage! Since he is now closing his cycle of English history plays, surely Shakespeare might have *shown* us all this instead of leaving it to "the quick forge and working house" of our imaginations.

Once again, however, he does the unexpected; he hurries us on with harsh commands:

> Now in London place him.
> And omit
> All the occurrences, whatever chanced,
> Till Harry's *back-return again to France.*
> *There must* we bring him; and myself have played
> The interim, by *rememb'ring you 'tis past.*
> Then brook abridgment, and your eyes advance
> After your thoughts, *straight back again to France.*
> (italics mine).

"Back-return again to France" and "straight back again to France" within five lines—is he running out of words and ideas? No, he "must"; this is the iteration of a man who acts under compulsion: the compulsion to "remember" us that the expected glorious and satisfying conclusion is *past,* that the union of Lancaster and York has long since been enacted; that "this earth, this realm, this England" is too small a stage for a designer of worlds and world orders who is about to move to the *Globe*; that larger and more difficult unions need to be achieved. And these unions will not be "by God's ordinance conjoined together"; though we cannot but believe that they are God's will, they are man's task. We must "back return again"—"straight back"—not to a divine restoration but to the outward journey. For a moment of respite, we have been permitted the nostalgic simplicities of a world picture in which we can be unreflective actors and leave the judgment to God (the more so since we already know what it is), in which gallant combat is the mode and victory the divine affirmation. But now the *line* must be resumed; time in its irreversible forward motion claims us as its own.

Must we be "Time's fools" then, carried forward by the current of events, fettered in the chain of causality? Is this the only alternative to being the spectators and victims of a series of savage spectacles put on by a divine dramatist for no better reason than that one cannot have drama without conflict? Or is it possible to discover a model of order and succession—dramatic or political or universal, it is the same thing—in which the needed continuity is no longer vested in a silent and inscrutable God but is generated by, and from within, the equally needed confrontations and conflicts of human beings in the dramatic encounter of passion and purpose?

These, I have argued, are the questions with which the Hal trilogy is pregnant; and it is to them that the last act is meant to supply the answer. The answer is by no means earned yet; it does not arise with compelling inevitability from within the design of *Henry V* or even of the trilogy as a whole. As yet it is *imposed,* dictated by force and as unstable as force. It is a model, seized by a creative rape, as it were; it must still be "verified" —made true and "made good." The answer, the model, is marriage.

I have suggested that Harry's courting of Catherine must be understood as a "revision" of Richard's courting of Elizabeth—or, better, as the fusion of Richard's unsuccessful courting and Richmond's unearned getting. It is a strange scene. While Harry plays the persistent and pleading wooer, we know that on the inner stage the treaty is being concluded of which the marriage is the "capital demand, comprised/Within the forerank of our articles." Is the courting mere pretense, a cynically transparent curtain drawn before the harsh varieties of *Realpolitik*? I do not think so. It is, rather, the transposition or translation of the combat model into terms where success means succession, where victory generates a *line*.

"Soldier" is the dominant word of the scene, as its structure is that of a siege. We think of Harfleur; more immediately we think of Burgundy's lament that in times of war children

> grow like savages,—as soldiers will
> That nothing do but meditate on blood,—
> To swearing and stern looks, diffused attire,
> And everything that seems unnatural. (v, ii, 59-62)

Burgundy wants France restored to her "former favour," her "former qualities." But this is not the line Harry takes to the same goal:

> I speak to thee plain soldier. . . . If thou would have such a one, take me; and take me, take a soldier; take a soldier, take a king. . . . If ever thou beest mine, Kate, . . . I get thee with scambling, and thou must therefore needs prove a good soldier-breeder. Shall not thou and I, between Sain Denis and Saint George, compound a boy, half-French, half-English, that shall go to Constantinople and take the Turk by the beard?[5] . . . Now beshrew my father's ambition! He was thinking of civil wars when he got me; therefore was I created with a stubborn outside, with an aspect of iron. (v, ii, 156-244)

Even language is something to be conquered:

> It is as easy for me, Kate, to conquer the kingdom as to speak so much more French. (v, ii, 194-96)

[5] Even this "Turk" will, at the end of a long "voyage," find himself included in the marriage model—*The Tempest*:

> Oh, rejoice
> Beyond a common joy, and set it down
> With gold on lasting pillars: in one voyage
> Did Claribel her husband find at Tunis. . . . (v, i, 206-209)

Peace and union are the intent, but not by way of a return to former favor and qualities. Here again the thrust is outward and forward, toward the begetting of soldier sons and the bearding of the Turk. Peace, for Harry, is not a restoration but a continuing *instauratio magna*, a never-ending conquest.

Yet it is not mere conquest, the ultimate "pacification" of Europe and the world by the imposition of one man's or country's will. Shakespeare/Harry does not see himself as bravely shouldering the white man's burden. He knows he has no language but English, but he does not think that God speaks it. His "winning" Catherine is a foregone conclusion, but his courting ends in failure:

> Our tongue is rough, coz, and my condition is not smooth; so that, having neither the voice nor the heart of flattery about me, I cannot so conjure up the spirit of love in her, that he will appear in his true likeness. (v, ii, 313-317)

In the end the two are joined by "articles" of peace that are hardly distinguishable from articles of war.

But the failure, in one respect analogous to Richard's, is in another very different. The final part of Richard's courting consists in his vain effort to find something he can swear by:

> Now, by my George, my Garter and my crown. . . .
> (*Richard III*, IV, iv, 366)

The queen rejects one proposed oath after another as already invalidated by Richard's prior crimes. (Only the appeal to the horrors of civil war and the promise of a happier future for England seem to make her waver.) The point is that, to make his pleading successful, Richard must be able to invoke some guarantor of the truth of his words who stands outside and above them: the model for marriage, like that for combat, is triangular, with God at the apex (which is why, for God's own Richmond, courting is quite superfluous). Hence Richard's failure is absolute; for lack of the guarantor, the apex, his words can have no "binding" force.

Harry's failure is not absolute; he has been unable so far to break the "language barrier," so that at this point the sword speaks more authoritatively and compellingly than the word. But given time, the language can be conquered, even if it costs greater pain and labor than the conquest of kingdoms. Unlike Richard and Elizabeth (but like Richard and Anne), Harry and Catherine confront each other directly, as the base points of a hypotenuse; no triangular structure, no apex is required. Marriage is that balanced confrontation which generates a "line," a true succession.

Is it the final solution then, the ultimate model, the definitive answer to the question of dramatic and universal order? Yes and no. If I am permitted a concluding and perhaps rather fanciful simile, the model Shakespeare envisages at the end of his history plays is expressible by the square root of two, $\sqrt{2}$, the "irrational number." The number was born of the effort to find the single-expression, numerical solution to the Pythagorean theorem, which defines the relation between the sides of an (isosceles) triangle. We *know* that the sum of the squares of the sides is equal to the square of the base; but what is the length of the base? It turns out that it is not an integer but an "irrational," a number that is forever unfinished, exists in time as well as in space. It can never be "closed" but only more and more closely approximated. It "proceeds" by ever-continuing divisions, and these divisions can never come out even. The Pythagoreans, I believe, kept their discovery of irrationals secret; they were terrified by the notion that the universe is not integral, reducible to and expressible in integers. This is the Platonic terror; the Elizabethan world picture was still shaped by it. The picture was an effort to accommodate the need for causal order, continuity in time, to the need for static order, immutability in space. But terror is a poor guide to discovery; at most it prompts a frantic and confused kind of expediency, a running from the threats implicit in one model to the imagined security of the other—and back again. Shakespeare was not, I think, immune to this terror; but the need to find a model of order which would give meaning and function to his creative energy was more imperious than the need for impregnable security, unquestionable legitimacy. Thus he discovered what for brevity's sake I call the irrational number, not as a fearful secret but as a liberating truth. It was a truth that was never finished, a truth that not even God could reveal. It was a laborious truth, to be worked out by man in infinite divisions, "growing together" with smaller and smaller remainders. It was a marriage, like that between the Phoenix and the Turtle:

> So they loved, as love in twain
> Had the essence but in one;
> Two distincts, division none.
> Number there in love was slain.
>
> Reason, in itself confounded,
> Saw division grow together,
> To themselves yet either neither,
> Simple were so well compounded.

VII

THE MERCHANT OF VENICE: THE GENTLE BOND

I

THE danger of literary source-hunting is that it abets our natural tendency to discount things we believe we have accounted for. The source, once found, relieves us of the effort to see what a thing *is;* we are satisfied with having discovered how it got there. Shakespeare's plots—especially his comedy plots—have generally been at a discount; we have been content to say that the poet took his stories pretty much as he found them and then, as the phrase goes, "breathed life" into them, enriched them with his subtle characterizations and splendid poetry. That the dramatist must make his plot into the prime metaphor of his meaning—this classical demand Shakespeare was magnanimously excused from, the more readily because by the same token we were excused from the labor of discovering the meaning of complex and "improbable" plots.

But with the plot thus out of the way, other problems often arose. *The Merchant of Venice* is a case in point. Audiences persist in feeling distressed by Shylock's final treatment, and no amount of historical explanation helps them over their unease. It is little use telling them that their attitude toward the Jew is anachronistic, distorted by modern, un-Elizabethan opinions about racial equality and religious tolerance. They know better; they know that, in the play itself, they have been made to take Shylock's part so strongly that his end seems cruel.

Nor does it do them much good to be told that Shakespeare, being Shakespeare, "could not help" humanizing the stereotype villain he found in his sources; Richard III and Iago are also given depth and stature, but we do not feel sorry for them. If we regard *The Merchant* as a play of character rather haphazardly flung over a prefabricated plot, we cannot join, as unreservedly as we are meant to, in the joyful harmonies of the last act; Shylock spooks in the background, an unappeased ghost.

The source of our unease is simple enough: Shylock gets more than his share of good lines. This is nowhere more evident than in the courtroom scene, where he and Antonio, villain and hero, are pitted against each other in a rhetorical climax. Shylock is powerful in his vindictiveness:

> You'll ask me why I rather choose to have
> A weight of carrion flesh than to receive
> Three thousand ducats. I'll never answer that;
> But say it is my humour. Is it answer'd?
> What if my house be troubled with a rat
> And I be pleas'd to give ten thousand ducats
> To have it ban'd? What, are you answer'd yet?
> Some men there are love not a gaping pig;
> Some, that are mad if they behold a cat;
> And others, when the bagpipe sings i' th' nose,
> Cannot contain their urine: for affection,
> Master of passion, sways it to the mood
> Of what it likes or loathes. Now, for your answer:
> As there is no firm reason to be render'd
> Why he cannot abide a gaping pig;
> Why he, a harmless necessary cat;
> Why he, a woollen bagpipe; but of force
> Must yield to such inevitable shame

> As to offend, himself being offended;
> So can I give no reason, nor I will not,
> More than a lodg'd hate and a certain loathing
> I bear Antonio, that I follow thus
> A losing suit against him. Are you answer'd?
> (IV, i, 40-62)

Antonio is grandiloquent:

> I pray you, think, you question with the Jew.
> You may as well go stand upon the beach
> And bid the main flood bate his usual height;
> You may as well use question with the wolf
> Why he hath made the ewe bleat for the lamb;
> You may as well forbid the mountain pines
> To wag their high tops and to make no noise
> When they are fretten with the gusts of heaven;
> You may as well do anything most hard,
> As seek to soften that—than which what's harder?—
> His Jewish heart. (IV, i, 70-80)

Both men use the triple simile in parallel structure, but the similarity serves only to bring out the difference. The toughness of Shylock's argument is embodied in the toughness of his lines, his passion in their speed and directness; this is a man who *speaks.* We might simply say that Shakespeare here is writing close to his dramatic best; but if by this time he was able to give his devils their due, why does he leave his hero shamed? Antonio's lines are flaccidly oratorical; his similes move with a symmetry so slow and pedantic that our expectations continually outrun them. He strains so hard for the grand that when he has to bring his mountainous tropes around to the point of bearing, they bring forth only a pathetic anticlimax: "You may as well do anything most hard." True, the burden of his speech is resignation; but it is feeble rather than noble, a collapse from overstatement into helplessness.

The historical critic may protest at this point that such a judgment reflects a modern bias against rhetoric, a twentieth-century preference for the understated and purely dramatic. But the qualities which make us rank Shylock's lines over Antonio's have long been accepted among the criteria by which we seek to establish the sequence of Shakespeare's plays, on the assumption that where we find them we have evidence of greater maturity and mastery. Nor is this only an assumption. In *The Merchant* itself there is a crucial occasion where these qualities are preferred and where, had the choice been different, the consequence would have been disaster for Antonio. The occasion is Bassanio's choice of the right casket; he rejects the golden one, because it is "mere ornament," and prefers lead:

> thou meagre lead,
> Which rather threat'nest than dost promise aught,
> Thy plainness moves me more than eloquence.[1]
> (III, ii, 104-06)

At a decisive moment, Bassanio's critical judgment is the same as ours; so that, when we find ourselves more moved by Shylock's plainness than by Antonio's elo-

1 My interpretation here rests on an emendation; F and Qq read "paleness," not "plainness." But the emendation has the support of most editors since Warburton—and of sound sense. Bassanio means to contrast the three metals; and though both silver—"thou pale and common drudge"—and lead are pale, it is contrary to his purpose, and to the logical structure of his speech, to fix on the one quality in which lead is *like* silver. The line as F has it would have to be read with a strong emphasis on "Thy"; but even then there is no reason why the paleness of lead should move Bassanio, when that of silver left him unmoved. Moreover, and most decisively, the word is clearly antithetical to "eloquence"; and while "plainness" yields a natural antithesis, "paleness" does not.

quence, we have the best possible reason for feeling sure that Shakespeare intended us to be.

For Bassanio's judgment is "critical" in more senses than one: the play's happy outcome hangs on his taste. Had he judged wrongly, Portia could not have appeared in court to render her second and saving judgment. In the casket scene, the action turns on the *styles* of metals, conceived as modes of speech; the causalities of the play assume a significance which is, initially at least, only obscured by our being told that Shakespeare's plot is to be found in *Il Pecorone* and the *Gesta Romanorum.* Why does Portia come to Venice? Because Bassanio chooses plainness over eloquence. And how is Bassanio put into the position to make that choice? By Antonio's having bound himself to Shylock. That is how the causal chain of the story runs; it does not run from Fiorentino to Shakespeare.

And as in any good play, so here the causality reveals the meaning of the whole. It shows that the plot is *circular*: bound in such a way that the instrument of destruction, the bond, turns out to be the source of deliverance. Portia, won through the bond, wins Antonio's release from it; what is more, she wins it, not by breaking the bond, but by submitting to its rigor more rigorously than even the Jew had thought to do. So seen, one of Shakespeare's apparently most fanciful plots proved to be one of the most exactingly structured; it is what it should be: the play's controlling metaphor. As the subsidiary metaphors of the bond and the ring indicate, *The Merchant* is a play about circularity and circulation; it asks how the vicious circle of the bond's law can be transformed into the ring of love. And it answers: through a literal and unreserved submission to the bond as absolutely binding. It is as though Shakespeare, finding himself bound to a story already drawn up for him in his source, had taken it as the test of his creative freedom and had discovered that this freedom lay, not in a feeble, Antonio-like resignation, which consoles itself with the consciousness of its inner superiority to the vulgar exigencies of reality, but in a Portia-like acceptance and penetration of these exigencies to the point where they must yield their liberating truth. The play's ultimate circularity may well be that it tells the story of its own composition, of its being created, wholly given and intractably positive though it seems, by the poet's discovery of what it is.

II

The world of *The Merchant* consists of two separate and mostly discontiguous realms: Venice and Belmont, the realm of law and the realm of love, the public sphere and the private. Venice is a community firmly established and concerned above all else with preserving its stability; it is a closed world, inherently conservative, because it knows that it stands and falls with the sacredness of contracts. Belmont, on the other hand, is open and potential; in it a union—that of lovers—is to be founded rather than defended. The happy ending arises from the interaction of the two realms: the bond makes possible the transfer of the action to Belmont, which then *re*-acts upon Venice. The public order is saved from the deadly logic of its own constitution by having been transposed, temporarily, to the private sphere.

But it is not a matter merely of transposition. Each realm has, as it were, its own language, so that the process is better described as a retranslation. Antonio's bonding is a necessary condition for Bassanio's winning Portia, but it is not a sufficient cause; the riddle of the caskets must be correctly *interpreted.* And in exactly the same way the winning of Portia is a necessary condition but not a sufficient cause for the redemption of the bond; it likewise cannot be bought but must be correctly interpreted. The language of love and liberality does not simply supersede that of "use" (=usury) and law; it must first be translated from it and then back into it. Love must learn to speak the public language, grasp its peculiar grammar; Shylock, to be defeated, must be spoken to in his own terms. That he compels this retranslation is his triumph, Pyrrhic though it turns out to be.

The Jew draws his eloquence and dignity from raising to the level of principle something which by its very nature seems to deny principle: *use.* Antonio's most serious mistake—or rather failure of imagination—is that he cannot conceive of this possibility. He takes a fearful risk for Bassanio, but he cannot claim full credit for it, because he does not know what he is risking. Not only is he confident that his ships will come home a month before the day; he is taken in by Shylock's harmless interpretation of the "merry jest," the pound-of-flesh clause:

> To buy his favour, I extend this friendship.
> (II, i, 169)

He is sure that the Jew wants to *buy* something, to make some kind of profit, and pleasantly surprised that the profit is to be of so "gentle" (=gentile) a kind; he cannot conceive that a greedy usurer would risk three thousand ducats for a profitless piece of carrion flesh. His too fastidious generosity prevents him from reckoning with the generosity of hatred:

> . . . his flesh. What's that good for?
> To bait fish withal. (III, i, 54-55)

So he blindly challenges the usurer—the very man he is about to use—to do his worst:

I am as like to call thee so again,
To spit on thee again, to spurn thee too.
If thou wilt lend this money, lend it not
As to thy friends; for when did friendship take
A breed for barren metal of his friend?
But lend it rather to thine enemy,
Who, if he break, thou mayest with better face
Exact the penalty. (I, iii, 131-38)

(Little wonder that his later words about Shylock's hardness come off so feebly.) The worst he expects is the exacting of "barren metal"; that it will turn out to be a pound of his own flesh does not enter his haughtily gentle mind.

But the play, thanks largely to Shylock's imagination, insistently makes the point that metal is not barren; it does breed, is pregnant with consequences, and capable of transformation into life and even love. Metal it is which brings Bassanio as a suitor to Belmont, metal which holds Portia's picture and with it herself. When Shylock runs through Venice crying: "My ducats and my daughter," we are as shallow as Venetian dandies and street urchins if we simply echo him with ridicule. Jessica and Lorenzo turn fugitive thieves for the sake of these ducats; it is only at the very end, and by the grace of Portia, that they are given an honest competence:

Fair ladies, you drop manna in the way
Of starved people. (V, i, 294-95)

In this merchant's world money is a great good, is life itself. When Antonio, again through Portia, learns that three of his argosies are "richly" come to harbor, he is not scornful of mere pelf but says:

Sweet lady, you have given me life and living.
(V, i, 286)

(Which makes him Shylock's faithful echo: "You take my life/When you do take the means whereby I live.") Bassanio, with Shylock's ducats, ventures to Belmont to win "a lady richly left" and so to rid himself of his debts; it is a good deal worse than irrelevant to blame him (as some gentlemen critics, of independent income no doubt, have done) for being a fortune hunter. One, perhaps *the* lesson Antonio is made to learn is a lesson in metal-breeding.

Shylock is imaginative not only about money and flesh but about speech. We are, I am convinced, meant to understand that he draws his bloody inspiration directly from Antonio. In the lines just before the stating of the clause, we are shown how intimately and subtly the Jew responds to words, how they trigger his imagination, which thus proves more charged and sure than Antonio's. (That is why he has the better lines.) When Antonio proudly says: "I do never *use* it," Shylock begins his story of Jacob's *ewes*; shortly thereafter, when his calculations—"Let me see, the *rate* . . ."—are brusquely interrupted by Antonio's impatient: "Well, Shylock, shall we be beholding to you?," he picks up the thread again but with a new twist:

> Signior Antonio, many a time and oft
> In the Rialto you have *rated* me. (II, i, 107-08)

This is how he is brought to the idea of making his metal breed flesh. Unlike Antonio, he does not speak in set pieces leading to sententious commonplaces, "as who should say, 'I am Sir Oracle,/And when I ope my lips, let no dog bark!' " *His* speech is for *use,* as it is of ewes; that is the secret of its effectiveness. Out of context his lines are not as quotable as many of Antonio's; but then we have reason to be suspicious of Shakespeare's quotable lines; Polonius is probably the most quoted of his characters. Shylock and Antonio provide the first major instance of Shakespeare's exploration of the conflict between noble-minded orators and less scrupulous but more effective speakers: between Brutus and Antony, Othello and Iago. The words of genuine speakers are so fully part of the dramatic situation, so organically flesh of the play's verbal body, that they resist excision. They grow, as truly dramatic speech must, from their circumstances and in turn change them; since the literal meaning of "drama" is "action," they are what they ought to be: language in action. It is because Shylock speaks this language that he is able to transform barren metal into living substance; the very mode of his speaking here becomes the mode of his doing.

III

In Belmont the Jew's money promises to breed in a more literal sense: it helps to unite lovers. The equation money = offspring is pointed up by Gratiano, in a line which echoes Shylock's "My ducats and my daughter":

> We'll play with them the first boy for a thousand
> ducats. (III, ii, 216)

More precisely, the money makes the union possible; the consummation turns out to be rather more complicated.

I have stressed the differences between Belmont and Venice; but in one respect they are alike: both are governed by rigorously positive laws, which threaten to frustrate the very purposes they are meant to serve, but which must nevertheless be obeyed. In fact, the rule which governs Belmont—the covenant of the caskets—seems even more wilfully positive than that of Venice. More rigidly even than the law of the bond, it puts obedience above meaning, the letter above the spirit.

The harshly positive character of Venetian law is evident enough. When Bassanio pleads a kind of natural law, man's intuitive sense of justice, he is sternly corrected by Portia:

Bassanio: If this will not suffice, it must appear
That malice bears down truth. And I
beseech you,
Wrest once the law to your authority;
To do a great right, do a little wrong,
And curb this cruel devil of his will.
Portia: It must not be; there is no power in Venice
Can alter a decree established.
'Twill be recorded for a precedent,
And many an error by the same example
Will rush into the state. It cannot be.
(IV, i, 213-22)

But Portia here can still appeal to reason, can show that the law which is at the mercy of man's "sense of justice" fails of its purpose, even though, taken as positively binding, it may also frustrate that purpose. Nerissa, defending the wisdom of the casket test against Portia's rebellious complaints, has no argument to fall back on except authority and faith:

Portia: I may neither choose who I would nor refuse who I dislike; so is the will of a living daughter curb'd by the will of a dead father. Is it not hard, Nerissa, that I cannot choose one nor refuse none?
Nerissa: Your father was ever virtuous, and holy men at their death have good inspirations.
(I, ii, 24-31)

The wisdom of the father's will can be proved only in the event.

The law of Belmont, then, demands submission quite as much as that of Venice; it too disallows mere feeling. But it differs in one decisive point: it permits, in fact (as the result shows) requires interpretation by *substance* rather than by letter. Aragon and Morocco fail because they try to interpret the lines inscribed on the caskets rather than the substance; they calculate which of the inscriptions correctly states the relation between their own worth, Portia's worth and the risk of choosing wrongly. For them the caskets are mere clues; what they are really concerned with is themselves and the object of their suit. It is this intrusion of their selves and their purposes that misleads them; they are enmeshed in their reckonings. The noteworthy thing about Bassanio is that he disregards the inscriptions; he lets the metals themselves speak to him (quite literally: he apostrophizes them as speakers). Once before the caskets, he seems almost to forget Portia, himself, and his purpose. He does not look for signs, pointers along the way to his goal; he stops—and listens to the things themselves. And so he wins.

This being the quality of his choice, I am both intrigued by and suspicious of the ingenious theory that Portia surreptitiously gives Bassanio a clue through the "-ed" endings (rhyming with "lead") in the song: "Tell me where is fancy bred." If we think of the rhyme as having this effect on Bassanio, the theory is consistent with the tenor of his response to the caskets; the phonetic substance of the words would be what he unconsciously responds to. But if we think of the rhyme as a clue in the ordinary sense, intentionally placed and consciously interpreted, it would be out of tune with the quality of his choice, which lies in the rejection of even such clues as are legitimately provided. As often in Shakespeare, music liberates from the slavery of intention; it suspends, in a momentary harmony, the endless chase of means and meanings. Portia is eminently useful, and she is sought after, at least in part, because she can be of use; but that is not how she is won. At the moment of choice, purpose is in abeyance, and the things themselves are given voice.

Yet this release into pure fancy is in its nature momentary; in human existence—and so in drama—purpose and use cannot long be set aside. "Fancy" is bred neither in the head nor in the heart, neither by will nor by thought; it is the child of pure vision. But being that, it lives only in the moment; its cradle is its grave. When the predestined pair is happily united and everything seems to have dissolved into pure concord, we are promptly reminded that there is an accounting still due back in prosaic Venice. Belmont is bound to Venice as surely as Antonio is to Shylock. If the bond were not acknowledged, the bliss of the lovers would remain private, encapsuled in the barren half-fulfilment of fancy and sheer, useless poetry, while in the public world of prose and use time and the law would run their deadly course. The parthenogenesis of fancy has no lasting issue; the union of Portia and Bassanio must remain unconsummated until after the retranslation to Venice:

> First go with me to church and call me wife,
> And then away to Venice to your friend;
> For never shall you lie by Portia's side
> With an unquiet soul. (III, ii, 306-09)

IV

At this point I had better deal with a question which may have troubled the reader for some time. I suggested that for Shakespeare the play he had been commissioned to do, or rather to rework (with a three-month deadline?) from a story already fixed, became the metaphor of the bondage he found himself in, and that the way to freedom he discovered was Portia's way of a radical and literal acceptance. Obviously this theory, if it is to be more than idle speculation, implies that Shakespeare did follow his source religiously; the question is: is this in fact true?

It would mean, for one thing, that Shakespeare did not, as used to be thought, graft the casket story from the *Gesta* onto the Fiorentino tale, but that this graft had already been made by the author of his immediate source. The evidence for such a source seems to me as conclusive as we can expect under the circumstances. In *The School of Abuse* Gosson mentions a play, no longer extant, which bore the title *The Jew* and showed "the greediness of worldly choosers and the bloody minds of usurers." The description fits the two main actions of Shakespeare's play so closely that we can hardly avoid regarding *The Jew* as his source; and so it has been regarded by most recent editors.

But the fact is that, as far as we can tell, Shakespeare did depart from his source in at least two important instances. The first of these is the inscription on the leaden casket. Gosson's phrase—"the greediness of *worldly* choosers"—shows that *The Jew* must still have had the *Gesta* inscription: "Whoso chooseth me shall find that God hath disposed to him." Shakespeare, while taking over the other two inscriptions as he found them, changed the leaden one to read: "Whoso chooseth me must give and hazard all he hath." If the very point of the play for him was that he felt bound to it and by it as it was, how did he come to take a liberty here?

His second assertion of independence is more substantial, although, as I shall try to show, less substantive; it is the Jessica-Lorenzo plot. It contains some echoes of Marlowe's *Jew of Malta,* but as a whole it appears to have been freely added by Shakespeare; no analogue to it has been found in any of his possible sources. Again: if he felt bound, whence this sudden flight of invention?

Before I take up these questions singly, I must note that they have one element in common: there seems to be no necessity for the departures. Bassanio, in choosing the leaden casket, gets no guidance from the inscription; insofar as his reference to threats and promises is an implicit allusion to the inscription, it is of a kind rather to frighten him off than to attract him. With the Jessica plot the puzzle is even greater; for not only does it not serve any useful purpose, it seems a perversely extraneous element in a story which was, to put it mildly, complicated enough without it. Yet I am persuaded that my general interpretation is confirmed—I would almost say verified—by these two elements.

To begin with the simpler one: In the Jessica plot Shakespeare breaks free of the bondage to his source and elopes into the untrammeled freedom of invention. Pure, spontaneous feeling governs the conduct of these lovers; they brush aside, without much compunction, the impediments to their union and celebrate careless honeymoons in Genoa, Belmont, or wherever their fancy and Shylock's ducats take them. The one theme that accompanies them quite faithfully, however, is the difference of their religions; we are never allowed to forget that Jessica was a Jewess and Lorenzo is a Christian.

One of the important stipulations in the judgment on Shylock is that he become a Christian; and the compulsion leaves a bitter taste in our mouths. Again, *pace* the historians, who assure us that Shakespeare's audience understood the shot-gun, or rather halter, conversion as an undeserved mercy, since it was Shylock's sole chance of salvation. I do not know whether so totally mechanical a view of an adult's conversion and baptism was then seriously held. However that may be, Shakespeare takes particular pains to impress on us the violence and merciless secularity of this act of "grace." Gratiano has the last word on it and places it in the proper metaphorical context:

> In christening shalt thou have two godfathers:
> Had I been judge, thou shouldst have had ten more,
> To bring thee to the gallows, not the font.
>
> (IV, i, 398-400)

We might think that the union of Jessica and Lorenzo would have offered a more harmonious means of conversion; the subplot, if it is designed for anything, seems designed to that very end. There could—I am tempted to say "should"—have been a final scene following the judgment, a scene with the satisfying, conciliatory finality and completeness we expect in comedies. As thus: Jessica and Lorenzo enter (perhaps from Genoa, bearing good tidings about Antonio's argosies) ; Shylock, already crushed, is urged by all to forgive his daughter and accept Lorenzo as his son-in-law; he still resists, claiming his religion; but finally Jessica's prayers prevail: he embraces Christianity and his newfound children. Antonio magnanimously renounces his claim to half of Shylock's property in favor of the lovers; Portia and Nerissa reveal themselves and are claimed by Bassanio and Gratiano; Antonio is asked to be honored guest at the triple wedding and godfather to Shylock. Curtain. I shall be so bold as to say that some such conclusion would have been a "natural": all the main characters on stage and in harmony, no need to return to Belmont and the business of the rings, no unresolved residue. As it is, Shylock exits unreconciled, while Jessica and Lorenzo moon in Belmont to no intelligible purpose, as they were brought there for no intelligible reason. I find it hard to imagine that Shakespeare, when he thought up the Jessica action, was not thinking of a conclusion somewhat along these lines, and that he was not fully aware of the complications and difficulties he needlessly created for himself by rejecting it. Why, then, did he?

The answer I am bound to by my interpretation—that it was not "so nominated in the bond," the source—only makes matters worse. Neither was the Jessica story in his source; if he felt free to invent that, why could he not take another liberty and tie it into the main action, as he might so easily and satisfyingly have done? As it stands, the play would have more unity and coherence if the subplot were simply left out; if Shakespeare felt the need to add to it, why did he not at least add something that would help round matters out? Worse: why did he perversely refuse to make the addition serve the one end it seems so manifestly intended for?

Of course, a purpose for it *has* been discovered. As Quiller-Couch puts it: "But here Shakespeare comes in. His audience, conventionally minded, may accept the proffer of the bond as a jesting bargain made with bloodthirsty intent, to be bloodthirstily enacted; but a gentle Shakespeare cannot. There must be more incentive to hate, to lust for a literally bloody vengeance, than any past insult, however conventional, put upon him on the Rialto by Antonio, mildest of men, can dramatically supply."[2] This, chastened into a prose somewhat more in keeping with the admirable precepts of the essay "On Jargon," would pretty well represent the critical consensus on the function of the Jessica plot. But it is not only implausible; it is demonstrably false. "Gentle Shakespeare"—the creator of Richard III and company—cannot create a vengeful Shylock? "An-

[2] Cambridge edition, 1926, p. xix.

tonio, mildest of men"—who spits on Shylock, calls him a cur, and promises to do so again even as he is asking him for a loan—did not give Shylock ample cause for bloody hatred? But we need not even speculate about sufficiency or insufficiency of motive; the text is perfectly explicit and unambiguously refutes the theory that Shylock needed the elopement of his daughter to confirm him in the resolution to enforce the bond. In Belmont Jessica reports:

> When I was with him [i.e., *before her elopement*],
> I have heard him swear . . .
> That he would rather have Antonio's flesh
> Than twenty times the value of the sum
> That he did owe him.[3] (III, ii, 287-91)

It is as though Shakespeare, suspecting that the subplot might be misinterpreted, had taken particular pains to prevent the misreading. But to no avail; the motive-mongers got the better of him. Here, as so often, the "psychological" explanation fails miserably—not because it is psychological, but because it is *ad hoc*, got up to explain away one difficulty and in doing so engendering a litter of others.

As almost always when Shakespeare puzzles us, the question to ask is not: why? but: what? If once we see the thing as it *is*, the question of its purpose will commonly answer itself. As lovers, Jessica and Lorenzo stand in the sharpest imaginable contrast to Portia and Bassanio.

[3] The most recent attempt to account for the Jessica action in this way (by John H. Smith, JEGP, LX [Jan., 1961], p. 19) has at least the virtue of dealing with these lines as a trouble spot. But the inevitable response is to explain them away; Jessica's statement, we are told, is neither true nor untrue; it is, rather, a Shakespearean stratagem to prepare us for Shylock's transformation into a bloodthirsty villain. Since Shakespeare, had he meant to prepare us for this, could have found any number of other ways of doing so, it remains unintelligible why he should have chosen the one way which was bound to confuse us about his real intentions.

Their love is lawless, financed by theft and engineered through a gross breach of trust. It is subjected to no test: "Here, catch this casket; it is worth the pains," Jessica says to Lorenzo to underscore the difference. The ring which ought to seal their love is traded for a monkey. They are spendthrift rather than liberal, thoughtless squanderers of stolen substance; they are aimless, drifting by chance from Venice to Genoa to Belmont. They are attended by a low-grade clown, who fathers illegitimate children (Launcelot), while Bassanio and Portia are served by a true jester, who marries in due form (Gratiano). Wherever we look, the Jessica-Lorenzo affair appears as an inversion of true, bonded love.

More: the spontaneous love-match remains fruitless and useless; it redeems no one but is itself in urgent need of redemption. There is one qualification to be made here; Jessica does have a function, which is repeatedly insisted on: she is to be the torchbearer in the impromptu masque. But the light she casts is ambiguous and flickering as that of a torch; it illumines only her own shame:

> Lorenzo: Descend, for you must be my torchbearer.
> Jessica: What, must I hold a candle to my shames?
> They in themselves, good sooth, are too
> too light.
> Why, 'tis an office of discovery, love;
> And I should be obscur'd. (II, vi, 40-44)

Also, the dramatic enterprise she is meant to serve in is

> vile, unless it may be quaintly order'd,
> And better, in my [Solanio's] mind, not undertook.
> (II, iv, 6-7)

But in any case nothing comes of it:

Antonio: Fie, fie, Gratiano! where are all the rest?
'Tis nine o'clock; our friends all stay for you.
No masque tonight; the wind is come about,
Bassanio presently will go aboard.
(II, vi, 62-65)

The play of bonded and tested love, which was in danger of being delayed by these improvising masquers, is underway once more. A "strumpet wind" propels loves like Jessica's and Lorenzo's:

How like a younker or a prodigal
The scarfed bark puts from her native bay,
Hugg'd and embraced by the strumpet wind!
How like a prodigal doth she return,
With over-weather'd ribs and ragged sails,
Lean, rent, and beggar'd by the strumpet wind!
(II, vi, 14-19)

But now the wind has changed; blowing sternly and steadily, it drives the main action on its set and narrowly plotted course.

What, then, does this torchlit subplot accomplish; why, it is now safe to ask, is it there at all? It is there to discover its own shame and uselessness and so, by contrast, to make clearer and firmer the outlines of bonded love. It is the abortive "masque," first planned by Shakespeare (I surmise) as an escape from the harsh letter of his bond, a means of rendering his intractable material more manageable. But when he discovered the much more hazardous and satisfying solution of unreserved submission, he turned the subplot to a new purpose, made it into something that should be "obscur'd," the *oscuro* in the chiaroscuro of the whole.

If this judgment of Jessica and Lorenzo seems too narrowly puritanical—and at odds, moreover, with their gorgeous lines about night and music at the opening of the last act—two things are to be remembered. *The Merchant* is a play of *use*; this word, among others, is rescued alike from Shylock's malice and Antonio's contempt. The people who ultimately count—Antonio, Bassanio, Portia, and, in a negative way, Shylock—have all been useful, have freed and united not only each other but also the state. And they have done so—to repeat—by accepting the given, the letter of the law, as binding; something to be fulfilled, not evaded. The play's ethos, the standards by which we must judge, are defined by its causality: and the causality is wholly unambiguous. Here, as in the sphere of speech, it is action that counts, not sentiment, effect, not attitude; here too Shakespeare teaches us—and perhaps himself—the true meaning of "drama." Mere lyrical splendor is, in the world the play defines, a kind of sentimentality, a parasitical self-indulgence, possible only because, and insofar as, others bear the brunt of the law.

Which brings us to the concrete setting of the lyrical interlude. It opens with the oddly ambiguous hymn to night; what we are given is the genealogy of fly-by-night love: betrayal (Troilus and Cressida), disaster (Pyramus and Thisbe), desertion (Dido and Aeneas), sorcery (Medea), and theft (Jessica). Only with the arrival of good news from Venice does the tune change to the beautiful praise of music. And even then the music Lorenzo commands is not his but Portia's ("It is your music, madam, of the house"). She who pays the piper calls off the tune; to Lorenzo's borrowed authority ("Come, ho! and wake Diana with a hymn") there answers the real authority of the owner:

Peace, ho! the Moon sleeps with Endymion
And would not be awak'd. [*music ceases*]
(v, i, 109-10)

Portia is known "as the blind man knows the cuckoo,/ By the bad voice." Compared to the heavenly harmonies Lorenzo has summoned the voice *is* bad for it is the voice of daylight, of action. The scapegrace lovers have an unearned, nocturnal grace which transcends all that is earned and useful; if we are not moved by their concord of sweet sound, we are not to be trusted. But neither, clearly, were Jessica and Lorenzo to be trusted. Our surety lies in the sterner sound of redeemed prose which is won by the hazard of making the ethereal music of love answer to the letter of the law.

V

If the Jessica story is thus a kind of inverse demonstration of the play's point, the changed inscription goes directly to the core of Shakespeare's meaning.

In writing *The Merchant* Shakespeare learned, by my interpretation, that his work as a commissioned playwright need not be servile, money-grubbing prostitution of his talent, that he need not make himself a motley to the view, gore his own thoughts, and sell cheap what was most dear. There was dignity in his trade, truth and worth in the two hours' traffic of the stage. Antonio's sadness at the outset is, by his own description, that of a man who has to play a "part" arbitrarily assigned him; his restitution to happiness begins when he—though not fully aware of what he is doing—pledges his life to a binding contract and a literal "deadline." With this pledge things start to happen; "circulation" sets in. Trading with his talent is not in itself contemptible, an exploitation of something that should be employed only freely, for "gentle," liberal ends. It is, or can be, the beginning of action.

But this discovery entailed another—and a formidable risk. It meant that Shylock, the prophet of use and the bond, had to be built up—that his language had to be given the force and dignity which would sustain the claim Shakespeare was entering for profit-poetry. (Marlowe's Barabas was of no help to him; Barabas was a merchant-prince, with a language much more like Antonio's than like the lowly usurer's:

> What more may Heaven do for earthly man
> Than thus to pour out plenty in their laps,
> Ripping the bowels of the earth for them,
> Making the Sea their servant, and the winds
> To drive their substance with successful blasts?[4]
>
> (*Jew of Malta*, I, i, 145-49)

That is Antonio's grandiloquence, as Antonio's humbling is the humbling of Marlowe's "mighty line.") Characters who spoke in Shylock's idiom and cadence had been comic figures, meant to earn goodnatured smiles if they were good and to be despised if they were malicious. For the language they spoke was that in "common use," employed by common men for the mean and illiberal ends they are compelled to pursue. It was not gentle, noble—the idiom designed to give the poet's patrons and protectors a properly idealized image of themselves. The language of the stage—at least of characters deserving serious regard—was one of representation rather than action, or if action, then of "actions of state." Or it was a language of feelings—the "gentle" feelings allowed for within the conventions of courtly love. It moved in set pieces—lofty commentaries

[4] C. F. Tucker Brooke, *The Works of Christopher Marlowe* (London, 1962).

on an action that moved independently. If the action ended tragically, it was because the protagonists were star-crossed, or because the wheel of Fortune turned, or because they were guilty of *superbia* or some similar grand and splendid sins and crimes. If it ended happily, it did so because the proper feelings, dressed in the properly gentle language, had won out over loud-mouthed braggarts, mealy-mouthed parasites, foul-mouthed usurers, and other ill-spoken folk. In either case the dramatic question was begged; the convention predetermined the issue and the judgment of the audience. Gentle was as gentle did; gentle talked as gentle did; ergo: gentle was as gentle talked—the syllogism of aristocratic sentimentality.

Had Shakespeare written three hundred years later, he might have had to fight free of a different kind of sentimentality—that of the naturalists. As it was—and because he was Shakespeare—he confronted the word "gentle" in all its tricky ambiguity: as meaning something purely external (well-born; Christian) as well as kind, generous, loving. He did not think that churlishness proved a man honest and uncorrupted; nor was he satisfied with making the tritely pious point that, alas! not every gentleman is a gentle man. His problem was a different one: to vindicate gentleness under conditions—social and (it is the same thing) linguistic conditions—which did not beg the question but put it.

Shylock puts the question. In his mouth the common language assumes a force which puts all genteel speech to shame and reduces gentle speech to impotence. It mocks, and makes a mockery of, all sentimental claims to a "higher truth," clothed in elevated and elevating rhetoric, which cannot produce its credentials in the only court there is: the state's. Shylock's language is positivism triumphant, scornful of gentle pretensions, forcing the gentles to confess that, when all the ornament is stripped away, they too have been relying on the positive laws of the social order. If Shylock were silenced by force or fiat—even by divine intervention—his triumph would only be more complete; for he would then have compelled the gentiles, or their god, openly to profess his own faith: positivism. An overruled Shylock would be what (I think it safe to guess) his predecessor of *The Jew* could never have been: a tragic hero.

The question the Jew puts is not confined to the class meaning of "gentle"; it probes with equal rigor the religious meaning. We have good reason to suppose that the language of Shakespeare's source begged the question of gentility; we *know* that it begged the question of Christianity. That is the point of the changed inscription. Simply by making the clearly labeled Christian choice, by proving himself a devout rather than a worldly chooser, the gentile of the earlier play gained the truth by which the Jew was vanquished. The test did not involve a risk but asked for a correct response; so that *The Jew* as a whole was not a drama, an action (with the absolute risk all true action involves), but a teaching machine, which in the end rewarded and reinforced the right answer with redemption, bliss, and victory over the evil one. The Christian proved his superiority over the Jew merely by showing that he *was* a Christian and had learned his catechism—a religious tautology exactly analogous to the social one. To sum up: Shakespeare sees that the word "gentle" evades the social and religious issue by institutionalizing it. Through the power he gives to Shylock's dramatically ungentle speech and through the elimination of the religious solution, he submits to the hazard of a genuine test—not a schoolmaster's but a chemist's. His play is, so to speak, the *aqua regia* into which the word "gentle" is dropped to see if it is more than fool's gold.

It may be objected here that changing the inscription was, after all, no real risk. The plot was laid out for the poet and was sure to lead to a happy ending; not even the device by which that ending was achieved—Portia's judgment—had to be invented. But beyond the risk involved in changing the moral and dramatic balance between the usurious Jew and the noble Christian, Shakespeare had to confront, in simple fidelity to his source, the hazard that was its very meaning. He did not alter the story but restored it to itself by freeing it from a pious falsification. For its meaning was that it sprang from a series of ventures, of hazards; it was propelled by the risks Antonio, Bassanio, Portia, and, up to a point, Shylock were willing to take. Its ethic was that of venture capitalism raised to the moral level; so that to make it pivot, at the decisive juncture, on an option to invest in God's own, gilt-edged securities was to deprive it of its truth. Shakespeare's change here, though of a kind opposite to that of the Jessica plot, is directed toward the same end: while through the "free lovers" he accented the outlines of the composition by adding shadows, in the test scene he removed a layer of pious overpainting. The picture as he leaves it is not changed but more itself than when he took it in hand; he is a restorer, not an adapter.

VI

To return to the plot. Belmont, left to itself, would end in sterile self-absorption; Venice, left to itself, would end in silence. There is an odd logic working in Shylock's bond: with its seal and letter it gradually deadens even the Jew's powerful speech. Increasingly his lines become monotonous and monomaniacal; where we heard him, earlier, responding acutely and flexibly to Antonio's hard scantness, he now grows deaf:

> Antonio: I pray thee, hear me speak.
> Shylock: I'll have my bond; I will not hear thee speak.
> I'll have my bond; and therefore speak no more . . .
> I'll have no speaking; I will have my bond. (III, iii, 11-17)

The theme is continued in the trial scene;

> I'll never answer that . . .
> I am not bound to please thee with my answers . . .
> Till thou canst rail the seal from off my bond,
> Thou but offend'st thy lungs to speak so loud.
> (IV, i, 42-140)

And finally:

> There is no power in the tongue of man
> To alter me. I stay here on my bond. (241-42)

Thus, "bond," in Shylock's mouth, comes to mean the opposite of speech and hearing; and since the state must sustain him, we come to the point where the community, to preserve itself, must prohibit communion. He who stands on the bond is no longer answerable and need no longer listen; the instrument of exchange threatens to render the body politic tongue-tied. A gap opens between the private and utterly ineffectual speech of men as men and the deadening, unalterable letter of the law. Portia's oft-quoted lines about the quality of mercy are remarkable not so much for their eloquence as for their impotence; they are of no use, fall on deaf ears, *do* nothing and so remain, in the literal sense, undramatic.

But at this point there is a reversal. Very much as Shylock learned, from Antonio's hardness, how to transform metal into flesh, so Portia now learns from Shylock himself the art of winning life from the deadly letter. So far she has given no hint that she has come with the solution ready; her last plea, interrupting as it does her already begun judgment, has the desperate urgency of a final, hopeless effort. When she asks Shylock to provide a surgeon to staunch the blood, does she know yet that it is on this point she will presently hang him? Or is it not rather Shylock himself who leads her to the saving inspiration?

Shylock: Is it so nominated in the bond?
Portia: It is not so expres'd; but what of that?
'Twere good you do so much for charity.
Shylock: I cannot find it; 'tis not in the bond.
(259-62)

We cannot read Portia's mind and purposes, but this much is clear: here the crucial word is forced from her which then recurs in:

This bond doth give thee here no jot of blood;
The words *expressly* are "a pound of flesh."
(306-07—my italics)

The same process is at work as that which led to the framing of the bond; language, and with it Antonio and the state, have been revived and freed to act.

If we read Portia's judgment as a legal trick and Shylock's defeat as a foregone conclusion, the Jew's final humiliation must appear distressingly cruel. But there is good reason for reading the scene differently. Portia's ruling is one more hazard, and Shylock's moral collapse does not demolish the bond and all it stands for, but rather proves him unequal to the faith he has professed. Even after the judgment the issue is in doubt; it is still in Shylock's power to turn the play into a tragedy, to enforce the letter of the bond and to take the consequences. But at this point and before this choice he breaks, turns apostate to the faith he has so triumphantly forced upon his enemies. Having made the gentles bow before the letter of the law, he is now asked to become, literally, a blood witness. But he reneges and surrenders the bond's power, and like a renegade he is flogged into gentleness.

That it is the apostate rather than the bond that is brought into contempt is made clear in the last act: the ring episode. We the spectators can view it as a mere frolic; because we know of Portia's double identity and so understand her threatening equivocations as being, in truth, binding pledges of fidelity. But Bassanio does not know and understand; to him the ring seems to continue the vicious circle of the bond. The cost of redeeming the public bond has been the forfeiture of the private one, the pledge of love; he now stands before Portia as Antonio stood before Shylock. His explanations, his appeals to circumstances, and motives are in vain; she insists on the letter of the pledge and claims the forfeit. What redeems the bond of true love is not good intentions but the fact that Portia speaks with a double voice, functions both in Venice and in Belmont, is both man and woman ("the master-mistress of my passion," we may call her with Sonnet xx).

The ring is the bond transformed, the gentle bond. Since "bond" has dinned its leaden echo into our ears for the better part of four acts, "ring" is now made to ring out with almost comic but still ominous iteration:

Bassanio: If you did know to whom I gave the ring,
If you did know for whom I gave the ring,
And would conceive for what I gave the ring,
And how unwillingly I left the ring,
When nought would be accepted but the ring,
You would abate the strength of your displeasure.

Portia: If you had known the virtue of the ring,
Or half her worthiness that gave the ring,
Or your own honor to contain the ring,
You would not then have parted with the ring. (v, i, 193-202)

Like the bond, the ring is of a piece with flesh, so that we can hardly tell whether it has made flesh into metal or has itself become flesh:

A thing stuck on with oaths upon your finger,
And so riveted with faith unto your flesh. (168-69)

Flesh, therefore, may have to be cut for it:

Why, I were best to cut my left hand off
And swear I lost the ring defending it. (177-78)

And in the end Antonio must once again bind himself:

Antonio: I once did lend my body for his wealth,
Which, but for him that had your husband's ring,
Had quite miscarried. I dare be bound again,
My soul upon the forfeit, that your lord

Will never more break faith advisedly.
Portia: Then you shall be his surety. (249-54)

Only with this renewal of the bond is the secret discovered, the true meaning of the equivocations revealed. Shylock has been defeated and dismissed, but the words which he almost succeeded in making synonymous with himself are not. They enter into the gentle contract of love, are requisite to the consummation; union, truth, and faith are impossible without them.

So the action ends; or rather, the circle closes. The play comes round with Shakespeare's happy discovery that poetry is an equivocal language, public as well as private, common as well as gentle, useful as well as beautiful. The poet draws upon the social order's legal currency and so is bound and fully accountable. But by binding himself with Antonio instead of stealing with Lorenzo, he frees energies which will save the order from becoming deadlocked in a vicious circle of self-definition; by hazarding all he has on the chance of making personal unions possible, he frees himself from the twin futilities of uselessness and parasitical exploitation of the public currency. For himself and for Venice he gains Portia—the indefinable being who speaks most truly when she sounds most faithless, who frees us through an absolute literalness, who learns the grim prose of law in order to restore it to its true function. The gain will serve him for the time of the great romantic comedies; when, with *Julius Caesar* and *Hamlet,* he confronts the fact that the social order has neither the stability nor the good will he supposed, a new and much grimmer search will begin. The gentle bond will hold until Brutus speaks the tragic epilogue to *The Merchant of Venice*: "Portia is dead."

VIII

KING LEAR: THE QUALITY OF NOTHING

In his fine preface to *King Lear,* Granville-Barker settles the old critical problem of the implausibility of the two opening scenes with refreshing simplicity: "Shakespeare asks us to allow him the fact of [Gloster's] deception, even as we have allowed him Lear's partition of the kingdom. It is his starting point, the dramatist's 'let's pretend,' which is as essential to the beginning of a play as a 'let it be granted' to a proposition of Euclid." This is sound sense and should put an end to all tortured reasoning about the play's opening, at least where it springs from the question: "How could Shakespeare have done it?"[1] But it must not put an end to the very legitimate, in fact necessary, question: "*What* are we expected to pretend?" The more willing we are to grant the poet his premises, the more necessary it is to know exactly what we are granting; else the demonstration will make no sense.

The first two scenes have usually been read as a concentrated exposition of two characters, one rash and despotic, the other weak and gullible, who because of these flaws fall into error. But the scenes are more than that: they are *events*—events which determine the future action. Undoubtedly Lear is rash and Gloster gullible; but since through such different failings they commit exactly the same fault—the banishing of the true

1 Harley Granville-Barker, *Prefaces to Shakespeare* (Princeton, New Jersey, 1946), p. 313. [We have let stand Burckhardt's preference for the older "Gloster" over "Gloucester." R.C.E. and R.H.P.]

and loving child and the preferment of the false one—we are compelled to ask what it is that accounts for the difference in the subsequent fates of the two men—the blindness of one and the madness of the other, for example. If such reasoning sounds forbiddingly rigid in a literary interpretation, I submit that Shakespeare, in this tragedy and in no other, constructed parallel plots of considerable rigor, and that we must assume that he meant something by this structure. He cannot have meant the plots to be merely parallel, one reinforcing the other; for then the subplot would become a mere redundancy, and if ever an action needed no reinforcement of its impact, it is Lear's. There is every reason to think that the apparent similarity of the two plots is like that of controlled experiments, and that the meaning of both lies in the one element which accounts for the difference.

Shakespeare commonly satisfies the positivistic axiom that we can get answers only if we ask the right questions. He certainly does in *Lear*. At the very outset he points up both the sameness and the difference of the two plots by the thematic use of "nothing." This is the word which both Lear and Gloster stumble over; with it, or their response to it, their falls begin—first Lear's:

> What can you say to draw
> A third more opulent than your sisters? Speak.
> Nothing, my lord.
> Nothing!
> Nothing.
> Nothing will come of nothing. Speak again.
> (I, i, 87-92)

And then Gloster's:

> What paper were you reading?
> Nothing, my lord.

No? What needed, then, that terrible dispatch of it
into your pocket?
The quality of nothing hath not such need to hide
itself. Come, if it be nothing, I shall not
need spectacles. (I, ii, 30-36)

The point of this insistent echo cannot be simply the similarity of the two men. It must be subtler and more precise, and it must lie in the quality of "nothing."

I

Had Shakespeare only meant to present us, in the first scene, with a wrathful and imperious old man, he could have found a more plausible way to do so. But what he seized upon in the fairytale motif and makes the substance of his "Let it be granted" is a particular *speech* situation. The king lays down conditions of discourse under which his daughters' words will have an automatic validity; he acts on the premise that what they say will be true by virtue of their saying it. He will not test their professions of love against the matter of fact of their previous behavior, will not treat the words as signs that are true or false to the degree that they correspond to an extraverbal reality. Rather, he treats them as substances, as entities, which carry their own truth within them; they create for him his daughters' loves, as they are to create—a kind of physical precipitate of this verbal creation—their realms. "Which of you shall we say doth love us most?" Lear asks and therewith engages to settle this question as though it were a poetry contest. It is false to ascribe to him here a despot's greed for praise or fawning submission; he makes a fearful mistake, but the mistake is the regal one of taking people *at their word* in the most radical and literal sense. He refuses to submit to the demeaning necessity ordinary men are under: the necessity of suspiciously grubbing for facts by which to judge words. Suspicion, the "looking beneath" words for what, as often as not, they hide rather than reveal, would seem to him a diminution of his royal dignity. He *cannot* be lied to by his daughters, because, in transferring his sovereignty to them, he also endows them with its noblest attribute and prerogative; to speak creatively, substantially, with automatic truth.

The error is a noble one, but it compels both Lear and those who wish him well to a disastrous rigor. It is idle to speculate about Cordelia's pride, her share of responsibility for the consequences of her unbending "plainness." As her asides make clear, she has no choice; the covenant under which she must speak has its own logic. Where there can be no lie, there can be no truth; and since the essential function of speech is to transmit truth, for Cordelia no speech is possible. Her "nothing" is the simple statement of this fact, and her following attempt to return discourse to the sphere where it can be true (or false) is condemned from the start to futility.

For Lear is already committed. He has not yet sworn, as when he later answers Burgundy: "Nothing. I have sworn; I am firm." But he might as well have; with his "Nothing will come of nothing" he has stated the very formula of his belief. He has no choice either—none, that is, except to give up his conception of himself, his royalty and truth. If words are substantial and creative, then his answer to Cordelia is the only possible one. And by the same token he is compelled to banish Kent. What prompts him is not the vanity of the tyrant who cannot bear criticism, or of the king who cannot bear discourtesy; he does not deign even to notice Kent's desperate ill manners, and he enters into no argument about the substance of Kent's charges. Kent's guilt is that he has sought

To come betwixt our sentence and our power,
Which nor our nature nor our place can bear.
(I, i, 173-74)

Lear here tries to banish the inherent "between-ness" of all discourse; with Kent he means to rid himself of the degrading intrusion of "mere" fact into the gapless identity of "sentence" and "power," of sovereign speech and the power of that speech to create what it states.

Thus the king's wrath and rashness receive the precise definition of a verbal *act*. He has rashly committed himself to a particular conception of himself and his office, his nature and place, has in fact identified the two; and he wrathfully resists all attempts to question this conception as questioning his identity. This he sees in, let us say, *immediacy*, in the possibility of getting at truth directly, without any circuitous "between." I shall try to show how this "verbal" reading of the first scene makes explicable, not simply Lear's fall (that can be explained in other ways as well), but the specific kind and direction and even depth of his fall. For the remarkable thing about *King Lear* is that in it the tragic error is "made good" as a word is made good: not by contrition and amendment but by an unyielding perseverance in it, a determination to live by it and its bitter consequences until it has yielded its core of truth.

But first Gloster's analogous stumbling demands attention. Had he responded to Edmund's "Nothing, my lord" as Lear did to Cordelia's—had he taken Edmund at his word—the letter scheme would have come to nothing. But for Gloster speech is the opposite of substantial; he sees in it "mere words," insubstantial signs which, as likely as not, have been made to point in the wrong direction. He is familiar with "the dark and vicious place" of illicit union and has learned the subject's craft of "looking beneath" for the matter of fact. He will not be taken in by words but will trust only to what he can see with his own eyes; there is an ignoble greediness for "the real thing" in his thrice repeated "Let's see" (antiphone to Lear's threefold and royal "Speak!"). And because to him words are merely a medium, he falls victim to a *mediacy* far more abject than Goneril's and Regan's lies; in his eagerness for the matter of fact he gets hold of a forged letter, an indirection squared. (Edmund shrewdly calculates on his father's affinity for the indirect: he tells him that the letter was thrown in at the casement, not delivered in person —"there's the cunning of it." To a mind like Gloster's, this increases the probability of the tale.) Determined as he is to distrust the direct word, he is at the mercy of report, of hearsay, of signs. With this scene, the letter becomes the emblem of the illicit and dangerously mediate—so clearly so that the sight of Lear reading a letter would strike us as somehow incongruous; for a letter is speech reduced to signs, discourse become manifestly indirect. Gloster's belief in signs and portents, ridiculed by Edmund, is further evidence of this affinity; not that it is necessarily wrong, but that it is slavish, implies an abdication of the creative will and a wish to get at the truth by an "outguessing" which Lear would never stoop to.

Gloster, like Lear, will attain his measure of truth—not by abandoning his error, but by being delivered over to it more absolutely than he and we had imagined possible. The problem of immediacy and mediacy, of confrontation and report, of being and meaning, is a true paradox, and the truth of paradoxes does not lie in the golden mean between the extremes; it lies in a man's readiness to penetrate through illusion and despair to his particular extreme and at the pole to find himself.

II

Shakespeare would be no poet if he gave equal dignity to the two errors; the poet is bound to err on Lear's side: that of thinking speech creatively substantial and truth direct. Every poet, I should guess, is an ironist; knowing, more intimately than the rest of us, the deceptiveness of words, he is condemned to being circuitous, to trying to get the better of his untrustworthy medium by stratagems and indirections. But precisely for this reason the true poet is an ironist *in spite of himself*; what he longs for is creative immediacy. From Iago to Melville's Confidence Man and Mann's Felix Krull, poets have portrayed themselves as tricksters and sought the release of truth in this self-exposure. But that is the roundabout way, the way of irony.

The difference between Lear and Gloster is to be measured by what one is granted and the other denied: the dignity of direct confrontation. In the end Lear sees Cordelia face to face, and we see both; all Gloster's sufferings never earn him this fulfillment. He can never, literally, *see* Edgar; even in the recognition he is dependent on report, and what is more, this event is withheld from us, buried in Edgar's story. His final release must reach him, and us, mediately.

For this reason it is a mistake to think of Gloster as being, by the loss of his eyes, given "true sight." To be sure, he now becomes aware of things he had been blind to; but we will do well to mind our metaphors in speaking of that awareness. (The trouble with treating *King Lear* under the categories of appearance and reality is not that doing so is false, but that is translates the play's realities too directly into the realm of metaphysics and so loses sight of the metaphorical substance. Both protagonists are deceived by appearance and discover reality; but as their ways of being deceived are not the same, neither are their sufferings and discoveries.) Always a led man, he is now led in the literal sense; always in the dark, he is now enclosed with darkness and made to *feel* the mediacy of report. He is guided to the truth, not by learning to see with an "inner vision" or "the mind's eye," but by a palpable thickening of the wall between him and reality. "I see it feelingly," he tells Lear, or:

> I stumbled when I saw. Full oft 'tis seen,
> Our means secure us, and our mere defects
> Prove our commodities. (IV, i, 21-23)

("Commodities" is to be understood in this play as related to "accommodate" and "unaccommodated" and thus having the secondary meaning of "clothes.") Similarly, Edgar tells the dying Edmund: "The dark and vicious place where thee he got/Cost him his eyes," thereby likening that place to the darkness into which Gloster is thrust. There is truth in discovering how densely we are enclosed in darkness; that, fittingly, is Gloster's truth.

Seen this way, his painful progress comes to its proper goal at what he thinks the edge of Dover Cliffs. Here we see him, who had swept aside "nothing" as an insubstantial nothing, totally delivered over to the creative power of the word. Edgar's cliff—a poetic lie creating a purely verbal reality—for Gloster assumes the substantiality of fact, because he no longer has any matter of fact to judge it by. Edgar acts from motives and for ends altogether opposite to Edmund's; but for all that he *does* the same thing: he lies. Though the motives will direct our moral judgment, the fact must determine our interpretation. And the fact is that Gloster is saved from despair and suicide by the very deed that plunged him into them; the difference is that now, he being blind, the lie can be "grosser."

There is another difference: Gloster suffers Edgar's lie, while he invited Edmund's. His assertions of superior insight were as mistaken as his desperate attempt to pit his will against the gods'; *his* truth and wisdom lie in obedience, the virtue of the natural subject. He is compelled by blindness to do what, had he done it when he saw, would have saved him from error: take men at their word. In a sense, therefore, his finding his own truth brings him around to Lear's position; that is the way of paradoxes. But the quality of reaching that point remains radically different; his plus is the product of minuses. There is immediacy in Edgar's summoning up of the cliff; but, as we the spectators know, it is arrived at by squaring mediacy: blindness times lying equals "truth." When the extremes of a paradox meet, a great deal depends on the direction from which the meeting point is approached.

If the metaphor for Gloster's blindness is covering, that for Lear's madness is stripping. Edgar as Tom o' Bedlam is the touchstone. To Gloster his nakedness is an offense:

> If, for my sake,
> Thou wilt o'ertake us hence a mile or twain
> I' th' way toward Dover, do it for ancient love;
> And bring some covering for this naked soul,
> Which I'll entreat to lead me. (IV, i, 43-47)

And his madness is a deficiency of reason, the remaining glimmer of which Gloster looks for: "He has some reason, else he could not beg." Lear, on the other hand, sees in the naked madman the true pattern of man stripped and essential, and so he eagerly sets about becoming like him:

> Ha! here's three on's are sophisticated! Thou art the thing itself; unaccommodated man is no more

> but such a poor, bare, forked animal as thou art.
> Off, off, you lendings! come, unbutton here.
> (III, iv, 110-14)

(The cadence of "Off, you lendings" will shortly recur in "Out, vile jelly!") Lear resists the efforts of Kent and Gloster to separate him from this "philosopher" and guide him to the covering of a house; madness and nakedness have come to mean truth to him.

How has he come to this? The Fool's jest tells us:

> This is nothing, Fool.
> Then 'tis like the breath of an unfeed lawyer; you gave me nothing for it. Can you make no use of nothing, nuncle?
> Why, no, boy; nothing can be made out of nothing.
> (I, iv, 141-46)

But the Fool can make use of it:

> Thou wast a pretty fellow when thou hadst no need to care for her frowning; now thou art an O without a figure. I am better than thou art now; I am a Fool, thou art nothing. (I, iv, 210-14)

Lear discovers that his faith in directness was mistaken because it ultimately did rest on an intervening matter of fact: the sovereign's power to make good his words. The power gone, so is the immediacy; power was the integer before the zero. The formula "Nothing will come of nothing" is now looked at from the other side. In the first scene it had meant for Lear that the sovereign has, and can endow others with, creative power: Say something, and that something will be. Now the axiom has become the formula of impotence, and so the Fool explicates it. The king, who scorned to construe the meaning of words by indirect evidence, is now under the humiliating necessity of interpreting by signs, by "frowns" and "cold looks," of looking for reasons why his orders are disobeyed and his messengers slighted. In the play's most pitiful scene—the bargaining with Goneril and Regan over the number of retainers—he tries to cling to the illusion, to hold on to the shreds of royalty that will cover the nakedness of the zero he has become; and even as we tremble lest he might fail in this attempt, we tremble lest he might succeed. But he fails, is not left even the shreds. The choice is forced upon him between submitting to the subject's lot, learning the arts of indirection in order to have a roof over his head, and going out to confront reality nakedly, with nothing to interpose between himself and the turmoil of unstructured nature. When he discovers that there *is* a gap between sentence and power, he chooses immediacy, nakedness, the truly royal essence of what his still impure image of himself had been. That is why the "foolish, fond old man" of the end is more regal than the king was.

It is common to take Lear's compassionate concern for the Fool and his prayer for the "poor, naked wretches" as evidence of his conversion from a blind pride to an understanding of man's common humanity and of the superficiality of rank and power. And so, of course, they are. But they do *not* constitute a turning point in his fall; they only mark a stage. He is now stripped of the title and additions of a king and so learns what it is to be poor and wretched. But he is not naked yet, nor mad. For a moment it seems as though he might find a halt in his prayer, by identifying himself with the common man, finding consolation and support in a kind of Christian pity and humility; but at that moment Edgar's voice first emerges from the hovel and reads the precise and as yet incomplete measure of Lear's descent:

> Fathom and half, fathom and half! (III, iv, 37)

And Lear's passion for the real and naked immediately instructs him that there are depths yet to be plumbed—those of madness—and a cover yet to be stripped: discourse of reason.

III

Blindness, since Homer, Tiresias and Oedipus, has behind it a long tradition as a noble affliction; it is the mark of the seer and poet, of the superior being who has penetrated behind the veils of appearance that enclose ordinary men. Madness is quite another thing. To be sure, the tradition of divine frenzy, of seizure by a higher power, is also an old one; man has long paid the tribute of awe to this kind of madness. But Lear's madness, as Shakespeare portrays it, is of a different sort. It does not issue in dark oracles or hint at mysteries; it is very much of this earth. Edgar's feigned madness appears (as it *is*) literary next to it; he trades in the standard goods of seizure and possession: "The foul fiend haunts poor Tom in the voice of a nightingale," or: "Frateretto calls me; and tells me Nero is an angler in the lake of darkness." (Later, with the fallen Gloster, he will continue to deal in devils and divinities.) Lear's madness is the real thing, and it would seem that, once he has talked with his "learned Theban," he has intuitively penetrated Edgar's disguise, sensed that his madness is not of his own, royal kind—an utter nakedness of mind—but a "garment":

> You, sir, I entertain for one of my hundred; only I do not like the fashion of your garments. You will say they are Persian, but let them be changed.
> (III, vi, 83-86)

He does not gibber oracularly about foul fiends nor chill our spines with the stock properties of witchcraft; when he sees himself beset, it is not by Obidicut, Hobbibidence, Mahu and Modo, but by dogs:

> The little dogs and all,
> Tray, Blanch, and Sweetheart, see, they bark at me.
> (III, vi, 65-66)

To convince us that this very ordinary madness is the truly regal affliction was a formidable task—the more so because it is counterposed to what Shakespeare makes us accept, against all tradition, as the servile suffering of blindness. It seems almost perverse for him so to have stacked the cards against himself; my guess is that only the necessity of truth could have brought him to undertake the attempt.

For the truth is that what we call reality comes to us prefabricated, cut to orderly measure and built into orderly structure by language; poets, at least Shakespeare, did not have to wait for Whorf to discover this truth for them. Discourse of reason, though it may be employed to correct the falsities of this structuring, cannot but remain their victim; every coherent sentence written against the tyranny of words is ultimately a rattling of chains. That is why truth, which cannot reside outside discourse, cannot reside in it either. It is enacted in a confrontation of the real which is either silent and incommunicable or, if it is uttered, madness.

Lear's raving is, as Edgar says, "matter and impertinency mixed,/Reason in madness." It is natural for the commentator to cling to the reason, to talk about the lines exposing the relativity of justice and the deceptiveness of appearance, and to pass over the "impertinencies." But this is an evasion, not only of the scene's terror but of its truth. Shakespeare makes this point clearly. Directly before the entrance of Cordelia's men, Lear "preaches" to Gloster:

> Thou must be patient; we came crying hither.
> Thou know'st, the first time that we smell the air,
> We wawl and cry. I will preach to thee; mark . . .
> When we are born, we cry that we are come
> To this great stage of fools.—This' a good block.
> It were a delicate stratagem to shoe
> A troop of horse with felt. I'll put 't in proof;
> And when I have stol'n upon these son-in-laws,
> Then kill, kill, kill, kill, kill, kill! (IV, vi, 182-91)

The burden of the "preachment" is the same as Edgar's later words about our going hence and coming hither —which means that we should stop quoting them as though they were the distillate of Shakespeare's tragic wisdom. They may be noble to Gloster's ears (and Gloster is most of us most of the time), but Lear knows them for what they are: eloquent commonplaces from the Stoic's repertory. That is why he breaks off in the middle, weary with the formulable precepts of faith or even disillusionment, and turns his mind, or rather perception, back to realities far grimmer, because without any order. Of Gloster's "block," or hat, he sees not the form or social function to which it has been pressed, but the raw material; and this he presses to the purpose of total destruction. (Here again is the garment metaphor, associated with Gloster, stripped by Lear. For the equation garment equals ordered speech, which I have inferred, there is also direct textual warrant:

> Gloster: Methinks thy voice is altered, and thou speak'st
> In better phrase and matter than thou did'st.

Edgar: You're much deceived. In nothing am I changed
But in my garments.
Gloster: Methinks you're better spoken.)
(IV, vi, 7-10)

This naked directness and substantiality of perception, this apprehension of the "raw material" which makes all wisdom sound brittle, is one mark of Lear's madness. It applies also to words, which for him assume a phonetic corporeality that strips them of meaning and would, if it were consciously done, be called punning: "Peace, peace; this piece of toasted cheese will do 't." The same directness leads Lear's mind along the path of free association, in which ideas and images are not functionally ordered in a reasoned chain but assume a body and life of their own:

> Ha! Goneril with a white beard! They flattered me like a dog, and told me I had the white hairs in my beard ere the black ones were there.
> (IV, vi, 97-99)

The second mark, or theme, of his madness is his royalty; it stands at the beginning, middle and end of this scene:

> No, they cannot touch me for coining; I am the King himself. (83)
> Aye, every inch a king! (109)
> I will be jovial. Come, come; I am a king,
> My masters, know you that? (203-04)

And Cordelia's Gentleman answers for all of us:

> You are a royal one, and we obey you. (205)

Had Lear held on to his discovery of human fellowship, we would have welcomed and pitied him (as we are always ready to do when we see someone brought down to our level); his tragedy would have been one in the medieval sense: a fall from greatness. We might have been awed, but our awe would have been paid to the eternal powers that make the wheel of fortune turn, not to Lear himself. Edgar states, in rhymes a deal too neat, the force of such tragedies:

> When we our betters see bearing our woes,
> We scarcely think our miseries our foes.
> Who alone suffers, suffers most i' th' mind,
> Leaving free things and happy shows behind;
> But then the mind much sufferance doth o'erskip,
> When grief hath mates, and bearing fellowship.
> (III, vi, 109-14)

But Lear is meant, or rather wills, not to o'erskip any sufferance by finding grief-mates; he is the king and has no fellows.

He defines his kingship for us: he cannot be touched for coining. As every coin the king issues is necessarily a true coin, so every word he sovereignly speaks is a true word and every judgment a just judgment. The king can do no wrong—that is what sets him apart from men and forces him, once he understands it, to his fearful directness and confrontation. It is he who justifies:

> None does offend, none, I say, none; I'll able 'em.
> (IV, vi, 172)

But who, then, will "able" *him*? Before he saw Edgar, Lear thought he knew. Though powerless, he could call on the "great gods" to send their "dreadful summoners" and bring criminals before the bar of their "higher" justice. At that point he could still speak of himself as more sinned against than sinning, as having a just claim. Then he knew who was guilty and who was not, because then, for a brief moment, he thought he could find refuge in fellowship and the subject's consoling sense of being *under* the law; he could abdicate and become plaintiff before the court of divine law. Now he knows better. First he summons a court of his own, with the Fool and the Madman as justices, to try his daughters. And finally he summons all mankind, judge and felon, beggar and beadle, into the searing light of his discovery that there is nothing and no one to able him, no "natural law" or "right reason" to mediate between him and chaos. He is the *source* of justice and truth and so can receive none.

It is this knowledge that is his madness—not in the sense that he is mad to think so, but rather that no one who penetrates to this point can stay sane. Here words like truth and justice, the comforting constructs under which sane men seek shelter, cease to have meaning. This is the harvest of Lear's proud faith in the substantiality of his words; nothing now *has* come of nothing, the word as entity has created its meaning and drawn the universe into the chaos of universal negation. The "name" has become absolute: Lear, utterly divested of all that gives "meaning" to the name of king, is now king "in name only" and so, paradoxically, king absolute and quintessential.

This is "the worst," as Edgar has negatively but precisely defined it:

The worst is not
So long as we can say, "This is the worst."
(IV, i, 29-30)

The stress is on the "say." That simplest of sentences implies, in its four ordered words, a whole ordered universe and hierarchy of values. It presupposes a meaningful order. Lear no longer can say it; he has rejected meaning as "mean" in both senses: demeaning and mediate. If in the preceding paragraphs I have been obscure and groping, the obscurity should not cast doubt on my interpretation. For all interpretation is "report," and at this point the interpreter (and the reader) can only say, with Edgar:

> I would not take this from report. It is;
> And my heart breaks at it. (IV, vi, 144-45)

It is—it no longer means. Report and interpretation try to make sense, to clothe the nakedness of being in the decent and orderly garments of rational discourse. They either falsify *Lear* at this point or break at it. It is—the worst.

IV

When Lear awakens from madness and sleep, he no longer is king; all the respectful solicitude of Cordelia and her servants will not persuade him to it. He has earned his release from the frightful office and will not be distracted from the truth he has won—and for which there is no name but Cordelia. His new state is discontinuous with what he was before: he has had "fresh garments" put on him, but "all the skill I have/Remembers not these garments"; he does not know where he "did lodge last night," but sees himself surrounded by spirits and souls in bliss. In short, he is transfigured.

With his fresh garments he has put on a new language—and yet what he speaks is nothing new and dark. It is, rather, wholly private, has the intimate directness of people who believe they stand outside all social orders and need not rely on the mediation of custom and authority to give meaning to what they say. It is as natural as the song of the birds:

We two alone will sing like birds i' th' cage.
When thou doest ask me blessing, I'll kneel down
And ask of thee forgiveness. So we'll live,
And pray, and sing, and tell old tales, and laugh
At gilded butterflies, and hear poor rogues
Talk of court news; and we'll talk with them too,
Who loses and who wins; who's in, who's out;
And take upon's the mystery of things
As if we were God's spies. (v, iii, 9-17)

As natural and as intimate and as remote. Injustice and justice no longer concern him; he does not want to see Goneril and Regan. Cordelia's eight little unstructured words suffice him: " (And so) I am, I am" and "No cause, no cause." The first four lifted him from the depth of nothingness, and the last released him from the chain of cause and effect, the iron and ironic consequences of his unchallengeable "Nothing will come of nothing."

It seems as though irony has been vanquished; in the two scenes in which Lear and Cordelia appear before being led to prison, Shakespeare and Lear almost persuade us, against our better judgment, that the plots and armies swirling around them do not matter, that a realm has been won, even if it is only a bird's cage, where the immediate is possible. But it is not only the soldiers and Edmund who warn us that this idyll cannot last; it is something in Cordelia's way of speaking:

We are not the first
Who with best meaning have incurred the worst.
For thee, oppressed king, I am cast down;
Myself could else outfrown false Fortune's frown.
(v, iii, 3-6)

There is the rhyme, so oddly formal at this point and from this woman; there are the antitheses of reasoned discourse, the coining of epigrammatic wisdom of general currency, the play on words. This might be Edgar speaking to Gloster; it ought not to be Cordelia speaking to the new Lear. If we have understood the play rightly, we will be frightened by these lines more than by Edmund's preceding soliloquy. Lear *is* frightened, as his frantic "No, no, no, no!" shows.

What is he warding off? Ultimately, of course, the loss of his daughter, but more immediately the knowledge that she still belongs to that other realm, still is a queen, cannot extricate herself from the world of war and stratagem. Goneril and Regan are still what she so pointedly calls them: her sisters and Lear's daughters. The almost unspeakable simplicity of directness, purchased by unspeakable suffering, cannot be the last word, or if it is, must literally be the *last* word. For speech remains tied to the social order—and with it truth.

Since almost anything the interpreter can say about the end of *King Lear* is a trivialization, I will risk one that may seem ludicrous: Shakespeare had to write the end because he had to return to living and writing. If the finding of Cordelia had meant the finding, at whatever cost, of a new "style"—the conquest of irony, the beginning of the direct mode—the conclusion could have been triumphant; we might have been dismissed with the lines about the mystery of things. But the end of *Lear* does not yield a new style; it is the absence of all style. Style is the summary term for the way the poet uses "devices"; it is, therefore, the tribute exacted by the "mystery of things." The essence of the experience of direct confrontation—namely its directness—remains incommunicable; every word violates and distorts it. It is the pain of this insight, I think, which Shakespeare embodies in the play's last scene.

When Lear, mad, encounters Gloster and Edgar near

Dover, his second sentence—following the one about coining—is: "Nature's above art in that respect." The meaning of "nature" in the play is, as Empson has shown, vastly complex, but at this point it is reasonably clear. "Art," for Lear, is all that he has stripped away; he is now the natural king, and his coinages are natural. From this point on, in what concerns Lear directly, art is abandoned, Nature speaks. In Shakespeare—in fact in poetic drama—I know of no "naturalism" to equal the end of this play.

Since I have made so much of immediacy, I may seem to be caught here in a discrepancy. We are made to *see,* with cruel directness, the blinding of Gloster; we are not made to see the killing of Cordelia. But here, too, Shakespeare is rigorously exact. In Gloster's sphere, physical fact is primary; hence the blinding is presented as physical fact, to which the words are a feeble accompaniment. But in Lear's sphere words are primary, so that a physical directness, which with Cordelia's murder would silence all, would be false. *Words* must carry the whole burden, as Lear carries his daughter; to manage things otherwise would have been, for Shakespeare, an evasion of his task and—odd as this may sound—of his pain. Far from sparing himself and us a last, insupportable horror, he makes us bear all of it—in words. For the poet there is, or may be, a release in the abdication from speech; Shakespeare does not allow himself that release. He must speak, or—if speech refuses its office—"howl."

Lear's "Howl, howl, howl!" as he enters with Cordelia's body should have been enough to keep any English poet from entitling a poem "Howl." To howl is a privilege so bitterly earned that only experiences like Lear's can ever justify it in poetry. There is a quality in the last scene which anywhere else we should have to call indecent—an insensibility to all but that one dead body which, except here, would be subhuman:

> Kent: Where is your servant Caius?
> Lear: He's a good fellow, I can tell you that;
> He'll strike, and quickly too. He's dead and rotten. (v, iii, 283-85)

That is Lear's acknowledgment of Kent's loyalty, of no more account now than the treacheries of Goneril and Regan:

> Your elder daughters have fordone themselves,
> And desperately are dead.
> Aye, so I think. (291-92)

Lear is not mad, though now we might wish he were. He is totally cut off from everything and everyone, wholly given over to his forlorn hope of a faint breath. It is not even Cordelia as a person that all his senses are fixed on, but only her lips, her breath, her speech:

> Cordelia, Cordelia! stay a little. Ha!
> What is 't thou say'st? Her voice was ever soft,
> Gentle, and low; an excellent thing in woman.
> (270-73)

And his final words are the cry of the man who cares for nothing more except the hope that truth has breath and voice and that from it issue visible realities:

> Do you see this? Look on her, look, her lips,
> Look there, look there! (310-11)

He ends, it might seem, where Gloster, with his "Lets see," began. But he dies believing that he has seen living breath, not letters—words, not signs.

Besides this absorption, all else is what Albany calls Edmund's death: "but a trifle." We are, all of us, dismissed. At best we are, with Edgar, among those who must "speak what we feel, not what we ought to say." There can be honesty in speaking what we feel, but what we ought to say is the naked truth, and it cannot be said. Make "nothing" into a substance, and you get Nothing; take it for a mere sign, and you have "nothing." Be king or subject—nothing will be the sum of your earnings. But the uncompromising logic—the logic of life and language, not of syllogisms—with which we work out or more likely let ourselves be led to this sum is, perhaps, something. Since we are dismissed into the stewardship of Edgar, we may be forgiven for covering the shame of silence with saying: "Ripeness is *all.*"

IX

THE KING'S LANGUAGE: SHAKESPEARE'S DRAMA AS SOCIAL DISCOVERY

My aim in what follows is to interpret seven of Shakespeare's plays in a way that will reveal an inner logic in the development of his dramatic poetry. I do not find this logic in archetypal myths nor in conceptual antinomies such as appearance and reality or will and reason; I find it in what, for the poet, is a stubbornly concrete substance: language. As I read them, the plays testify to Shakespeare's gradual, and painful, discovery of his medium and thereby of his own true function and powers.

I must begin with some cursory remarks about that most slippery of words: truth. The condition a statement has to meet to be called true is commonly conceived to be simple: a true statement is one which corresponds to the matter of fact it purports to describe. But truth is, of course, much more complex than this. There is, for example, the automatically true statement, which institutes or creates the corresponding matter of fact—as when a sovereign declares his country to be at war with another. The trouble with statements of this sort is that, being automatically true, they are not really true at all; where the possibility of error or falsehood is ruled out *a priori,* truth has no meaning. A second kind of statement which shows that truth is no simple one-to-one relation is the equivocation. Iseult's oath of fidelity, made good by God though it was, was not a truth, since it was meant to be misinterpreted by her listeners. (And in the end God sees to it that the balance is righted: though Iseult has, by equivocation, saved her pretty hands from burning, she loses lover and life by the black-for-white lie of her namesake, Iseult of the White Hands.) Truth, then, is at least a three-way relation, a correspondence of fact, statement, and understanding. It takes two to tell the truth as well as to quarrel; truth has a social dimension.

A poet may, of course, claim to speak creatively, to give an airy nothing a local habitation and a name. But since he lacks the authority which alone can give this claim objective force, his airy nothings remain in or, after their brief hour upon the stage, revert to their original state: breath, a slight commotion of the air, is all they are. This is all right as long as the poet is satisfied with being an entertainer; the applause of his audience vindicates his enterprise. But—a good deal of "hard-boiled" Shakespeare criticism notwithstanding—Shakespeare was more ambitious; the man who wrote, "The play's the thing wherein I'll catch the conscience of the King," and who claimed for his magic that it enabled "all of us to find ourselves when no man was his own," had grander designs.

But if the poet ascends, or descends, to the level of ordinary speech and subjects himself to the normal criteria of truth, he encounters other difficulties. Modern criticism has made us wary of considering even a lyric poem the direct, personal utterance of the poet; poems have been described as verbal icons and hypothetical verbal structures; they have even been called "mute," "dumb," and "wordless." A play is clearly no direct utterance; we have no warrant to accept anything said in it as the poet's personal communication to us. It may be considered—as it often has been—a replica of life;

but the imitation theory leads to endless difficulties, especially with Shakespeare; and again there is ample reason to think that Shakespeare himself did not subscribe to it. In what sense, then, can a poem be true? That is to say, what matter of fact does it state in such a way that purport and understanding coincide? I hope to show that for Shakespeare the matter of fact to which poetry must be true, and through which it and the poet remain indissolubly tied to the social order, is language itself.

In every dialogue the social order is a silent but essential partner; the simplest remark presupposes two analogously structured habit systems, and consequently the faith that the social order is coherent and pervasive enough to have instilled the same habits in the listener as in the speaker. In a radical sense, therefore, all speech is question-begging: it presupposes the community which it pretends to establish. One can imagine a social order so fully and rigorously articulated that language atrophies into a mere system of vocal signals (armies tend toward being such orders); on the other hand, where the social order has its boundaries, linguistic boundaries will develop which in time will become barriers, while within the order itself the need for a standard language is felt as strongly as that for a standard currency.

The fact that the social order acts as the ultimate mediator and therefore is directly involved in the speaking of truth (in the tricornered sense I have defined) has grave implications. For there can then be no truth without it, and yet the order itself may be a perversion. Or again, as long as truth and justice simply echo each other, with no possibility of recourse from one to the other, they may become a perfect but empty tautology, compelled to deny legitimate human aspirations because to admit them would endanger the order's stability. Finally, if the order disintegrates, language is likely to disintegrate with it. Shakespeare's plays, in their progress, are explorations of these various possibilities and of their consequences for the poet.

Next to "To be or not to be," the best-known and most-quoted lines from Shakespeare are Juliet's great nominalist protest against the bondage of "names," i.e., of words. Sure of the ability of two true lovers to establish a lasting union, Juliet sees in the social order—or in its precipitate, the linguistic one—only a system of unnatural barriers, imposing a deadening fixity upon experience and feeling; she rebels—as we all do—against the arbitrariness of usage and tradition which forces us into categories when we want to be, and are sure we could be, simply and truly ourselves. The Rousseauistic yearning for a state of nature, from which we could construct a new, better, and more natural order, for the poet assumes a verbal form: if he could be the Baptist, the name-giver, he would at once be free of the falsifying restraints of the existing language and have a clear and splendid function as the man who renders communion possible.

But this, of course, is idle dreaming, and Shakespeare loses no time exposing it:

> What man art thou that thus bescreen'd in night
> So stumblest on my counsels? (II, ii, 52-53)

Juliet cries in fright when Romeo addresses her, and insists on identifying him by the name she has just implored him to doff. Accosted in the dark, she does not find it reassuring that the speaker has hands, feet, and any other part belonging to a man; what she needs to know is the "who" of the matter, and for that words are indispensable. Nor only for that. What is the love of these lovers but a gorgeous outpouring of words, an insatiable delight in the beloved "name"?

> Bondage is hoarse, and may not speak aloud;
> Else would I tear the cave where Echo lies,
> And make her airy tongue more hoarse than mine,
> With repetition of my Romeo's name.
>
> (II, ii, 161-64)

This is confusing: echo is to be made hoarse with repeating the name which Juliet, because of her bondage *to names,* is too hoarse to shout. We begin to suspect that Shakespeare, like Juliet, wants to have it both ways.

Romeo and Juliet is, as Shakespearean tragedies go, a "clean" one (to borrow a term from our atomic weaponeers); it has a symmetry which, even though it is a symmetry of conflict, is comforting. Montagues and Capulets oppose each other, but they are held as in a frame by the larger, overarching order of church and state. The aspirations of the lovers are in full harmony with the interests of this larger order; the disharmony is not intrinsic but accidental. The word is consequently both good and evil; it is, on the one hand, the "airy word" which has bred strife between the families, and, on the other, the "holy word" by which the Friar joins the lovers and hopes to end the discord. So that finally we are left with the sense that the lover's misfortune is a private one, arising not from the order of things, but from a concatenation of private quarrels and ill-starred circumstances. The two are what Capulet calls them, "poor sacrifices"; the closing reconciliation has a certain patness. Shakespeare has raised a problem and then evaded it; the ambiguity of the word "bond" is not fully confronted and so not satisfactorily resolved.

For all its appearance of conventional comedy plotting, *The Merchant of Venice* (written probably within a year of *Romeo and Juliet*) is a far more searching treatment of the problem. That the play ends happily rather than tragically is due to the judgment of Portia; and what renders this judgment noteworthy is that it is not a decree by which authority arbitrarily decides the issue in favor of goodness, nor a victoriously eloquent appeal to human feeling, but rather an interpretation showing that the most literal and rigorous acceptance of the bond will serve the ends of humanity.

This interpretation is not easily come by; in fact, the body of the play is devoted to drawing the saving Portia into the action. In the judgment scene, "bond" becomes so potently the vehicle of Shylock's malice that we are in danger of forgetting how it was this very bond that enabled Bassanio to court Portia and so has brought her to the seat of justice; what threatens to destroy Antonio is also the source of his deliverance. But not only Antonio is delivered; the state likewise is saved from itself. For until Portia's appearance, the state is caught in the fearful dilemma of having to sanction a fiendish injustice in order that justice may be done. The order, for all its good will, is self-defining and circular; justice is what the law says, and the voice of humanity cannot penetrate into this closed system. The fine speeches about the quality of mercy fall upon deaf ears or enter impotent hearts. But the bond has, through the venture of Antonio's love, released the energy which in the end transforms the vicious circle into a ring of love.

Read in this way, the play becomes a paradigm of the poet's ideal relation to the social order. Recognizing that, because his medium is language, he is not nor ever can be a free creator, the poet acknowledges his bondedness, his dependency upon the order for that means of exchange which is peculiarly his to manage and which he makes available so that men may enter into the free and personal communion of love. And it is this love, in turn, which can renew and revitalize the order, preserving it from the deadly rigor of automatic self-definition. Perhaps this interpretation can draw some support from being able to resolve the old critical problem of how we are to take Shylock. Our ambivalent feelings about him are by no means merely anachronistic responses, derived from attitudes toward Jews which were alien to Shakespeare's audience. They rest, on the contrary, firmly on the text, especially on the famous "I am a Jew. Hath not a Jew eyes?" and so forth. The fact is that Antonio has treated Shylock with the haughty, indeed brutal, contempt of one who is beyond all "use and usances," who gives freely of his substance and thus sees himself as standing above that order which the Jew must rely on. The Jew is under the law; but the Christian's notion of being beyond it, far too easy and self-righteous, furnishes Shylock with a very real eloquence.

What Shakespeare discovers in *The Merchant of Venice* is nothing less than a new principle of order. Symmetry, though easiest to come by, is always dangerous, because it is dichotomous. *The Merchant of Venice*, unlike *Romeo and Juliet*, is ordered in ring form; the high-spirited last act, which, after the essential business of the plot seems over and done with, plays jubilantly about the ring, celebrates this discovery. For it is much more than merely an esthetic one. I don't think the suggestion extravagant that through this resolution of the paradox of his "bond," Shakespeare released the joyful creative energy of the great romantic comedies; they are, we might say, Antonio's "argosies." Finding that he is not exempt from "use," he at the same time finds a true social function; his word is now "in circulation."

But *The Merchant of Venice* still rests on faith: faith in the basic justice and stability of the state. At the beginning of what is called Shakespeare's tragic period, this faith is shattered, and the poet begins to explore the desperate consequences of the state's disintegration or corruption.

Julius Caesar presents disintegration as it occurs: the daggers that rend Caesar's body rend the body politic. And language, thus deprived of its support, acts strangely and destructively. Brutus and Antony are not merely opposite characters; they use language differently. Brutus the Stoic relies on a kind of disembodied truth and on men's natural reason; he thinks it a simple matter to bring the two together, and, once they are brought together, he cannot conceive of their being separated. Justice and truth, for him, do not reside in the state and in language, but beyond them, free of contingency and circumstance. He acts and speaks accordingly; with a bloodless and inhuman logic ("And in the spirit of men there is no blood") he dissects the living, integral man and gives each separate part its separate due: "As Caesar loved me, I weep for him; as he was fortunate, I rejoice at it; as he was valiant, I honour him; but, as he was ambitious, I slew him."

Antony's deadliness is of a different sort; it is bloodily corporeal. To him the death of Caesar means no return to a more natural order, but chaos with its horror and its opportunity. He makes himself the very voice of Caesar's gashes:

> Over thy wounds now do I prophesy,
> Which, like dumb mouths, do ope their ruby lips
> To beg the voice and utterance of my tongue....
> Domestic fury and fierce civil strife
> Shall cumber all the parts of Italy. (III, i, 259-64)

Truth and justice have become empty sounds; language, like the money of Caesar's legacy, is now merely a means, to be seized and used by the strongest.

The recoil upon the poet is immediate. Two poets appear in the play, in two brief and seemingly inconsequential scenes. Cinna, who has the ill fortune to be namesake to one of Caesar's murderers, is halted by a mob and lynched. Vainly he protests: "I am Cinna the poet, I am Cinna the poet!" The reply is brutal and to the purpose: "It is no matter, his name's Cinna. Pluck but his name out of his heart, and turn him going." This is not only the bloody stupidity of the rabble but, in the most literal sense, poetic justice. With the social order no longer there to mediate, language deteriorates into the disembodied and the crudely physical: the realm in which words have no substance, so that they readily join in repellent conjunctions ("I, that did love Caesar when I struck him"), and the realm where words are mere physical substance, so that Cinna is Cinna, and there's an end. The poet, who, relying on the stability of the order, has played his games with language, now is killed by a pun.

The other, nameless poet is not killed; he is brushed aside as a futile prattler. He breaks into the tent where Brutus and Cassius have just composed their quarrel and admonishes them, in hackneyed rhymes, to be friends. For Shakespeare, the time is past when poets could claim a public function by rhyming political commonplaces into Mirrors for Magistrates and Schools of Princes; as Brutus says: "I'll know his humour when he knows his time. What should the wars do with these jiggling fools?" Long before this, Shakespeare had discovered a profounder and truer function for poetry; if we recall how Portia became its embodiment in the social order of Venice, we will not miss the more than merely personal weight of Brutus' "Portia's dead." It is a different Portia, to be sure, but so was Cinna a different Cinna and yet was killed. For Shakespeare, it is not in dreams but in names that responsibilities begin.

In *Hamlet* the body politic is corrupted more slowly and insidiously, by poison—administered through the *ear*. What we see in the play is the gradual working of this poison—most directly on Hamlet's mind, but through it on the entire court, innocent and guilty alike, until in the final scene it breaks into open virulence on the point of swords. And the pollution of the order presents itself to Hamlet in the form not merely of murder, but of incest. To apply the terms of my interpretation: in a perverted order the union of language and authority is incestuous, one lying (in the punning senses of the word) with the other in an unholy embrace. The discovery that this is so is both paralyzing and dangerous to the poet.

The paralysis of Hamlet's will is the most famous crux in criticism. A generation ago it led T. S. Eliot to formulate the doctrine of the objective correlative; he saw the crux as evidence of Shakespeare's inability to find an adequate embodiment for Hamlet's (and also his own) emotions. But it strikes me as improbable that a play which has engaged audiences and readers so fully and for so long a time as *Hamlet* has should have, for its mainspring, a flagging of poetic invention. It seems more plausible to think of the paralysis as the consequence of a new awareness; with Eliot, Hamlet might have said: "After such knowledge, what forgiveness?"

I believe we ought to be more puzzled than critics usually have been by Hamlet's failure, or refusal, to see the murder of Claudius as a political act. The question of succession, which is implicitly at issue, is the most important political question in monarchies, and Shakespeare himself had so treated it many times over. Claudius speaks of Hamlet as the heir apparent, as do Laertes and Polonius; but Hamlet fixes with seemingly obstinate blindness upon the purely private aspects of the revenge. In this he stands in sharp contrast to both Laertes and Fortinbras; the former particularly does not hesitate to make his private quarrel a public cause. Not once does Hamlet, in his self-searching and self-admonitions, try to draw resolution from the manifest truth that Denmark is ruled by a criminal usurper, and that he himself is not only a man personally wronged but also the legitimate heir, to whose succession the wronged state has as much right as he himself.

Eliot may well be right in surmising that "Hamlet's bafflement . . . is a prolongation of the bafflement of his creator in the face of his artistic problem." My only *caveat* would be against the word "artistic." The poet has moved close to the center of sovereignty and shrinks back in disgust and fear, because language—by which and through which he must exercise this sovereignty—is incestuously tied to the corrupt order and thus involves him in its corruption. His ideal function—the standing surety to those immediate personal unions through which the order is continually regenerated—is no longer fulfillable; his voice is now necessarily a public one, as Laertes explains to Ophelia:

> He may not, as unvalued persons do,
> Carve for himself, for on his choice depends
> The sanity and health of the whole state;
> And therefore must his choice be circumscrib'd
> Unto the voice and yielding of that body
> Whereof he is the head. Then, if he says he loves you,
> It fits your wisdom so far to believe it

As he in his particular act and place
May give his saying deed; which is no further
Than the main voice of Denmark goes withal.
(I, iii, 19-28)

But the main voice of Denmark being Claudius', speech for Hamlet is almost always divisive; words are beaten into swords. They are hooks to catch the conscience of the king, daggers to enter the queen's ear. They are ineffectual in prayer but of marvellous force in cursing; even in self-communion and toward Ophelia they are all edge: "You are keen, my lord, you are keen." One of the oddest passages in the play is Hamlet's answer to Gertrude's contrite question: "What shall I do" (III, iv)? "Not this, by no means, that I bid you do," he replies and then, in loathsome detail, bids her betray his secret to the king. Why the elaborate double negative? Because language draws its force and urgency from the representation of what is sordid, "rank," "stew'd in corruption"; so that good is a negation of evil, rather than evil a deficiency of good. "Custom" has this potential of negative goodness; though it is "damned" and "monstrous," though it transforms drunkard Danes into beasts and hardens grave-diggers into insensibility (elsewhere in Shakespeare, "customer" means "whore"), yet

That monster, custom, who all sense doth eat
Of habits evil, is angel yet in this,
That to the use of actions fair and good
He likewise gives a frock or livery,
That aptly is put on. (III, iv, 161-65)

Despairing, therefore, of the very possibility of love and truth, Hamlet bids Ophelia go into the nunnery—meaning either a convent or a brothel—into a purity that is merely sterile or into a vile and venal promiscuity. (Isabella, heroine of the later *Measure for Measure,* has followed Hamlet's command; she has opted for untainted sterility, but is forced to expose herself to the threat of having to sell herself. Her dilemma is resolved by the machinations of the absconded sovereign, who works behind the scenes, truly a playwright, to bring about a somewhat *ad hoc* happy ending.) Hamlet's "I say, we will have no more marriages" is programmatic for Shakespeare's tragic period; the true fulfilment of his craft—the "marriage of true minds," which he had celebrated and embodied in the great romantic comedies—will not be granted him and us again until *Antony and Cleopatra.*

I see, then, in *Hamlet,* not so much the bafflement of the poet who cannot find an adequate embodiment for his feelings, but rather the shrinking from the knowledge he has gained. How is he to wrest truth from a medium which has no being apart from the social order and is by this very order corrupted to falsehood? How, in other words, is he to get rid of the third partner to every dialogue, when that partner stands revealed as an ear-poisoner? There are two possible ways, both explored by Shakespeare and both fraught with tragedy: the faith that language, in and by itself, *is* a true medium, at least in the poet's hands; or, conversely, that the poet can speak as an absolute sovereign, who, by virtue of this creative sovereignty, endows speech with the *a priori* truth it must have if he is not to be a liar and accomplice to corruption. *Othello* and *King Lear* explore these alternatives.

The two tragedies move in opposite ways: the action of *Lear* is falling, the unraveling of the consequences of an initial fatal error, while that of *Othello* rises, turn by turn of the screw, to the consummation of a diabolic scheme. And since it is natural to fall but takes doing to rise, there is in the two plays a marked difference in wroughtness, in management. "Nature" is the key word for *Lear,* and its action and language are natural; there are virtually no "set pieces" and at the end language attains the ultimate in colloquial force. *Othello,* conversely, is, through its hero, so grandly eloquent that it has invited criticism; the "being wrought" of Othello's final speech may be taken in two senses, as applying not only to him but to the play that bears his name.

If my provisional interpretation of these tragedies as explorations of absolute trust and absolute sovereignty is valid, we should expect their respective characters to be the reverse of what they are: it should be the play of sovereignty that is wrought, and the play of loving trust that is natural. But Shakespeare is concerned with discovering the consequences of two absolutist stances; and it is in the nature of absolutes that they bring forth their opposites. Lear falls into utter impotence, while Othello is maneuvered into arrogating to himself the sovereignty of the priest-king, of the ultimate judge and bringer of sacrifices. The language of sovereignty turns at last into mad raving and the monosyllabic stammering of the "natural man"; the language of loving trust turns into pathetically futile self-assertion.

The poet of *Othello* is, to use a cliché, a playwright's playwright. I mean the cliché literally: Iago is a sort of built-in playwright, who, presented with a donnée and glorying in his subtlety and skill, sets about shaping a play from it. In counterpoise to his intense artfulness stands the love of Othello and Desdemona—a love pure and spontaneous, defiant of paternal authority and social custom, and quickly removed from the normal social matrix to the isolation of an island. Though the action begins with a marriage, Shakespeare studiously avoids any reference to the ceremony; Iago's question, "Are you fast married?" remains unanswered. We are led to think of the union, not as a socially sanctioned contract, but as a pure love match, to which the order gives a belated and grudging consent.

Why then is it so easily destroyed? For even after we make full allowances for dramaturgical exigencies, Shakespeare leaves no doubt that Othello falls a ready, almost eager, victim to Iago's insinuations. Othello gives the answer:

> Thinkst thou I'd make a life of jealousy?
> . . . No! to be once in doubt
> Is once to be resolv'd. . . .
> I'll see before I doubt; when I doubt, prove;
> And on the proof, there is no more but this—
> Away at once with love or jealousy!
> (III, iii, 177-92)

There is an ominous rigor about this, the absolutist's rigor. Othello's commitment is unreserved—only it is not so much to Desdemona as to her truth. Out of it comes the ghastly command: "Villain, be sure thou prove my love a whore!" For, paradoxically, the absolutist can never be sure enough of his absolute, since it is his sole support, "the fountain from the which my current runs or else dries up," and without which "Othello's occupation's gone!" Perdition is always lurking just beneath:

> Excellent wretch! Perdition catch my soul,
> But I do love thee! and when I love thee not,
> Chaos is come again. (III, iii, 90-92)

Thus Othello is easily wrought; his love lacks body,

has the intense thinness of absolutes. And it lacks irony. Being black, he sees nothing of Desdemona but her whiteness, and nothing is so fragile as whiteness. Truth is her sole dimension:

> Had she been true,
> If heaven would make me such another world
> Of one entire and perfect chrysolite,
> I'd not have sold her for it. (v, ii, 143-46)

What Othello refuses, in fact cannot afford, to acknowledge is the inevitable mediacy, and thus ambiguity, of human communion, the ineradicable irony inherent in language—its way of meaning more, or less, than what it seems to say, the way it has of making us say what we do not want to say or of preventing us from saying what we do want to say. Othello is pitifully inept at steering amid the shoals and reefs of speech:

> Is he not honest?
> Honest, my lord?
> Honest! ay, honest.
> My lord, for aught I know.
> What dost thou think?
> Think, my lord?
> Think, my lord!
> By heaven, he echoes me,
> As if there were some monster in his thought
> Too hideous to be shown. . . . If thou dost love me,
> Show me thy thought. (III, iii, 103-16)

He says "Show me thy thought," as though speech, if it is not mere echo, were the physical precipitate of what goes on in a man's mind. (Desdemona likewise is too pure for her own good; in the very act of refusing to say "whore," she does so twice over: "I cannot say 'whore.' It does abhor me now I speak the word.") It is this ineptness and refusal that leave the stage to the great ironist Iago, who thrives on equivocation and innuendo.

From Hamlet's dilemma, then, there is no refuge in absolute trust. Even if it were objectively justified (as with Desdemona it would have been), it is not sustainable in the infinite ambiguities of communion; it is too easily practiced upon and cannot, in its rigor, withstand the storms of circumstance. Shakespeare here practices upon Shakespeare, the verbal artificer upon the poet who, no longer buttressed by a stable and valid order, has staked all on the objective existence and knowability of Truth. The third term, eliminated by a desperate and wilful blindness, reenters in the form of Iago—"honest Iago"—to expose the fragility and hubris of Othello's faith.

The opening scene of *King Lear* tests the viability of the other direct route to truth: the route of sovereignty. What we witness in this scene is more than the folly of an imperious and rash old man; we see the impossibility of speaking truly—of creating a true communion—where speech is conceived as sovereign. The loyal Kent is unmannerly, but that is not why he is banished; he is banished because he has sought

> To come betwixt our sentence and our power,
> Which nor our nature nor our place can bear.
> (I, i, 173-74)

The full, gapless identity of sentence and power, of word and act, is the essence of Lear's conception of himself and his place. This same identity he imputes to his daughters; they are to create their realms by talking. Lear refuses to consider his daughters' words as words normally must be considered—under the categories of truth and falsehood. Rather, he assigns to them an automatic truth, or better (since truth is impossible under this dispensation), an automatic efficacy: what his daughters say is "operative," validates its meaning in the act of speech itself. From this it follows inevitably that he responds to Cordelia's "Nothing, my lord" with "Nothing will come of nothing." If speech creates what it states, Cordelia receives her precise due.

There is another occasion in the play, counterpointing the first scene, in which speech becomes sovereign and creative. When Edgar leads the blind Gloster to believe that he is standing on the edge of Dover Cliffs, his poetic lie attains the substantiality of fact, because there is, for Gloster, no extra-verbal fact to judge it by. Gloster is the poet's ideal audience, totally delivered over to the creative power of the word. But, unlike Lear, Edgar knows that this sovereign use of words is a pious fraud, justifiable only because it is directed toward a beneficent end; and later he calls his deception a fault. His conscious feigning throws Lear's self-deception into sharper relief, as his feigned madness is a foil to Lear's genuine raving.

And yet self-deceived is not an adequate word for Lear; his fall is into nature, and it derives its terrifying grandeur from being not passive but willed. At no point is Lear less than royal; he insists on it most in his madness, and it is then we most believe him. The reason is that he will not settle for less than his original claim; its impossibility means to him that he must divest himself of everything—of authority, of illusions, of shelter, and of reason, even of clothes: "Off, you lendings!" There is in him a passion for nakedness, a fierce will to strip off all that stands between him and the truth; it is this imperious refusal of the mediate that gives him his dignity. Even at the beginning he is not so much practiced upon as royally disdainful of the very possibility of deceit. How servile, for all his stature, does

Othello appear next to him; how still more servile Gloster. These we see, again and again, led, counseled, deceived, allowing report to stand between themselves and reality. There is something ludicrous about Gloster's fall; Lear, even at his maddest, is never ludicrous. For his fall is not into a fraud but into that marginal condition of man where all that is sophisticate and indirect, all art and all the artful constructs of rational discourse, are stripped away and the bare forked animal alone is left.

"They cannot touch me for coining; I am the king himself. Nature's above art in that respect"—these are the first words of Lear mad. He has yielded nothing; whatever coins the king issues are true coins, as whatever words he sovereignly speaks are true words. But the claim now has a different substance—the substance of nature rather than art. Lear is king now, not by virtue of his "title and additions," but because he is "crown'd with rank fumiter and furrow-weeds." A sphere is here penetrated which is beyond our mind's normal reach and understanding, a sphere where finally majesty and truth will confront each other, bless and forgive, and watch a world that will keep chasing shadows:

> We two alone will sing like birds i' th' cage.
> When thou dost ask me blessing, I'll kneel down
> And ask of thee forgiveness. So we'll live
> And pray, and sing, and tell old tales, and laugh
> At gilded butterflies . . .
> And take upon's the mystery of things
> As if we were God's spies. (v, iii, 9-17)

With this, a point of no return is reached. We can only guess at the experience which lies behind (or better perhaps, in) the end of *Lear*; but it cannot be a sustainable one for the poet. The immediate is not for him; his office, like Edgar's, is to shape through the most mediate of media. If in *Othello* Shakespeare practiced upon himself, in *Lear* he transcends himself, goes beyond the confines of his art into a realm of naked truth so immediate that even lines like:

> Men must endure
> Their going hence even as their coming hither;
> Ripeness is all (v, ii, 9-11)

assume a faintly false, patent-medicine ring, next to Cordelia's "And so I am, I am" and Lear's "Never, never, never, never, never."

With *Antony and Cleopatra* Shakespeare returns, as the form of the title indicates, to the theme of *Romeo and Juliet,* the question of how, in a world of discord, error, and deceit, the primary human union is to be created. But the similarity serves only to point up the difference. Already, in *Troilus and Cressida,* the unifying social structure had disappeared, and the problem had been how, in the clash of armies and the calculations of diplomacy, love could survive. The despairingly cynical answer was the dismissal of the lovers into separate sordid and futile lives, with the epilogue given to the Pander. But now the themes of sovereignty and love, of *Lear* and *Othello,* are joined: the lovers themselves are sovereign. They are neither embedded in a social order nor torn apart by two conflicting ones, but move with imperial freedom in the strange servitude and into the stranger liberation of love.

All that Shakespeare has bitterly discovered since *Romeo and Juliet* makes up the substance of *Antony and Cleopatra.* No longer is the heroine pure and true; she is dark as the dark lady of the sonnets, devious and meretricious, "the whole world's commonplace." No longer is there a benign or even a reluctant social order to bless the union; love defies what order there is, even self-interest and manly virtue. There is, to be sure, a marriage, designed to unite the riven state and applauded by all whose sense of order is architectural rather than musical: the marriage between Antony and Octavia. But it is, as Agrippa says, "a studied, not a present thought, by duty ruminated." The final marriage, on the other hand, is self-blessed and self-celebrated; it is the conclusion and apotheosis of a union, not its beginning, and it sanctifies retroactively all manner of degradation.

Let me, at this point, briefly recapitulate. Shakespeare begins with an implicit trust in the social order as the ultimate guarantor of true human communion—the trust on which all ordinary discourse rests and which, insofar as it is justified, leaves the poet free to move and please us, to be—in however noble a sense—an entertainer. With the growing awareness, first of the order's impotence, then of its instability and corruption, the poet is forced into different roles. The first of these—the poet as surety—being found wanting, he then tests two possibilities of direct truth: trust in the purity of language, and reliance upon the automatic truth of creative speech. Both of these attempts to do without the third, the social term, are bound to end tragically; the nature of his medium forbids directness.

This would seem to exhaust the possibilities, and in a sense it does. But one thing remains: to foreswear the absolutes, to surrender with open eyes to falsehood and thus to gain sovereignty and truth. This, I think, is what happens in *Antony and Cleopatra,* though it sounds unpleasantly paradoxical in so abstract a form.

Neither truth nor sovereignty exists objectively in the play, even at the end: Antony (like Romeo) kills himself upon the feigned news of Cleopatra's death; Cleopatra's gratuitous lying to Caesar about her jewels keeps her to the end in an ambiguous light. Sovereignty is not merely lost; Antony's empty assertions of it betray him into posturing and fustian. And yet the play leaves us, like no other play by Shakespeare, with a sense of triumph that asks for no compensations beyond it. These lovers, though dead, are not "poor sacrifices" but victors; they are not lovers thwarted but lovers united—and united with a legitimacy greater and in a truth more inclusive and rich than any of their forerunners.

All this we know, as it were, despite the facts. The sense of triumph which the play engenders springs from its immense daring, which, if it were not ultimately made good, would be mere defiance. For better than four acts we have observed Antony in his various degradations, Cleopatra in her ambiguous stratagems, both in their debauches. And now, at the very end, Cleopatra, in order to convince Iras of the necessity of suicide, tells her and us of the humiliations that await them if they should be taken back to Rome:

> The quick comedians
> Extemporally will stage us, and present
> Our Alexandrian revels; Antony
> Shall be brought drunken forth, and I shall see
> Some squeaking Cleopatra boy my greatness
> I' th' posture of a whore. (v, ii, 216-21)

This is, even to the boy actor, the precise recapitulation of what we the spectators have just been witnessing—which is to say, it is a dare to us to resist the poet's will and intention, to free ourselves from the power of his immediate word, to find footing somewhere outside it, even if that outside is no more than the scenes he himself has just put before us. What happens here is that we are compelled, against common sense and the everyday certitudes about truth and falsehood, to accept illusion *as* illusion, trickery *as* trickery, and in this acceptance find truth. We are compelled to surrender to the poet's will—knowingly and so unconditionally that *we* will it and triumph in it. In other words, we are made to participate fully in the poet's own mastery and his own acceptance.

There are no villains in *Antony and Cleopatra,* no Iagos and Edmunds; for these are the hypostatizations of an absolutism that insists on pure truth and thus must bring forth pure falsehood. But there is a man who falls disastrously short of what the situation demands of him: Enobarbus, the man of common sense, who sees Antony's folly and Cleopatra's trickery for "what they are." He is, we might say, the man who leaves before the play is over, convinced—as well he might be—that the rest can be nothing but empty mouthings. He dies of self-contempt, enslaved to Antony by his desertion as he never would have been by loyalty. Had he been true, he would have been released to serve Caesar freely, as Dercetas is. And as we are. For it is the peculiarity of this play that it dismisses us into the world of prose and Caesar, not with the sense that too great a price has been paid to restore an order in which mediocre men can live, but with a certain composure, because no more is rendered unto Caesar than is his.

A case could perhaps be made that with the death of the lovers the Roman Empire is united and will now enter upon its Augustan Age—so that Antony and Cleopatra serve, by their death, a restorative purpose not altogether unlike that of Romeo and Juliet. But the argument would be specious. The mighty opposites are not reconciled; they celebrate each its incommensurable victory. In his attempt to separate the lovers, Caesar *is* "an ass unpolicied"; poetry has established its own realm, in which the writ of Caesar does not run. Shakespeare here awakens in safely domesticated prosaists some sense of the capriciousness and infinite variety of this mistress, language, whom most of us tend to think of as a lawfully wedded, rather dull wife. Poetry, properly understood, will undermine our linguistic certitudes, call into question our faith in the verbal order as representing the order of reality, and in the social order as an adequate guarantor of truth. Its immediate impact, therefore, is disruptive. But the poet cannot leave it at that; his ultimate purpose is to establish a more perfect union. This is no easy matter, because, unlike our Founding Fathers, he has no natural law to fall back on; practically his initial discovery was that in language there is only positive law, and no footing is provided outside it. So he takes language unto himself, not for her purity (she has none), nor as her sovereign lord (she must somehow remain tied to truth), but as she is. By doing so, he renders her true to herself, that being the only truth she is capable of. And while we are domestic tyrants or cuckolds to her (mostly both), she becomes a true wife to him.

From this, I confess, unduly metaphorical description, it might seem that poetry is a closed system, without relevance or meaning beyond itself, and that therefore those critics are right who describe poetry as autonomous, even mute. The more perfect union would appear to be merely one between language and the poet, of no use to the rest of us. But I do not think that is so, at least for Shakespeare. For though a language which is true only to itself is not, in any intelligible sense, true at all, still he who has once been drawn into that magic circle will not be the same when he comes out again. When words return to their prosaic functions, they will carry with them some of the magic potency they had inside the circle, and they will impart it to the things they stand for. That is to say, language will be somewhat less a mere system of signs and somewhat more a substance, somewhat less a token currency easily manipulable by the wielders of power, and somewhat more a gold currency, with an inherent value. I do not know whether the history of language bears our Gresham's Law, bad currency driving out good, which becomes the hoarded possession of fewer and fewer people. It does sometimes seem as though today verbal gold were considered altogether too rare for circulation and so were struck only into special medals intended for numismatists. But these are matters beyond my scope. As for Shakespeare, his bounty is like Antony's: there is no winter in it; an autumn it is that grows the more by reaping.

APPENDIX:

NOTES ON THE THEORY OF INTRINSIC INTERPRETATION[1]

I

LET US assume that God created the world, and that he did so in such a way as to instruct and enable man to understand it. The world, then, would be an object of interpretation from which the Creator's design and thus probably also His "meaning" could be known and understood. Our assumption describes the concept of nature held by the West for the greatest part of its history. From the natural philosopher of the Middle Ages to the scientist of the nineteenth century, men have regarded it as their task to interpret the "Book of Nature" and thus to discover and to reveal the meaning of creation. The contrast between medieval natural philosophy and modern natural science, however, is radical—and not just with respect to differences in matters of religious viewpoint. Natural science begins with the assumption that the only reliable method of interpretation for the "Book of Nature" is intrinsic interpretation—i.e., "empiricism." This assumption did, of course, not appear suddenly, nor was it total; science, after all, did not spring full-blown from the head of Bacon. But looking back and simplifying, we may say that in the interpretation of nature, scientific method and intrinsic method belong inseparably together.

[1] "Intrinsic Interpretation" is our term for the original "Werkimmanente Deutung." In Burckhardt's usage the term contains at once elements of such English terms as "explication" (in its recent critical use), "integral," and, as his argument indicates, "empirical." Readers interested in our use of "intrinsic interpretation" and its variants are referred to the German text of the essay.—R.C.E. and R.H.P.

To the medieval mind, it seemed that the Creator had manifested His will in two books: in the "Book of Books" and in the "Book of Nature." Of the two, the first had the unquestioned priority; for God had expressed himself in it directly and with little need of interpretation, whereas, in the second book, it became man's task to try to fathom the "correct"—i.e., God-intended—rules and teachings. To put it differently: the Bible was actually and literally a book, a statement, whereas the "Book of Nature" had to be "read" metaphorically. Consequently, since medieval man was in possession of the direct expression of God's meaning, he found it quite "natural" to interpret the "Book of Nature" as allegorical, illustrative material for the actual text—the Word of God. It would have been meaningless to attempt an intrinsic interpretation of nature.

The case of the Bible itself, however, was less clear. When I said that this book needed little interpretation, that was a questionable simplification, justified only in contrast to the "Book of Nature." The correct method of interpreting the Bible, even in medieval times, was a hotly disputed question, which cannot be discussed here. It was not until the Reformation that the question finally became unanswerable. For until that time, it was still believed that the Bible, although often vague and sometimes even ostensibly inconsistent, nevertheless clearly guided the interpreter, whose divine duty and privilege it was in matters of dispute and doubt to demonstrate the true meaning and the "True Word." For this purpose God himself had instituted the Holy Catholic Church with St. Peter and his successors at the head—as could be proved from the Bible itself. The "Book of Books" was distinguished from other books not because it was clear and unambiguous in every sentence and precluded all dispute, but because it was in itself a source of ultimately valid interpretation. At the time of the Reformation the Bible ceased being in this sense the "Book of Books." The passages upon which Rome had based its claim to being the final and binding court of interpretation were differently interpreted, and thereby the Bible became a book like any other. Worse still, in this respect it proved to be an extraordinarily inconsistent book, inconsistent not only with itself, but also with the "Book of Nature," which now gained undreamed-of significance and authority.

As we have seen, the interpretation of the Bible had in a certain—if very precarious—sense been intrinsic. It was believed possible to deduce from the book itself the authorized agent of interpretation. This intrinsic method was precarious, however, because ultimately it still depended on the principle of authority. It proclaimed: if you, the reader, are in doubt as to the true meaning of a particular passage, then turn to Rome, where it can and will be explained to you *viva voce*. This meant, however, that the voice of God was not limited to the Bible; it continued to speak through the mouth of the Pope and the Councils. And so the burden of infallibility was transferred from the Bible to an outside authority. Yet, if in important cases of dispute the voice of God did not speak from the Bible itself, but from somewhere else, then why must it necessarily speak from Rome—why in fact must the Bible be considered holy and infallible at all?

Since the authority of Rome had been derived from the very book which Rome considered itself authorized to interpret, this medieval version of intrinsic interpretation rested on a grandiose *petitio principii* which did not become more logical by virtue of its extraordinary historical vitality. Rome's claim could be refuted simply by calling it into question. Whoever claimed the right to interpret the Bible thereby also obtained the right to reinterpret those passages upon which Rome had based its privileged position. As soon as the *petitio principii* was no longer accepted on faith, it revealed itself as a pure claim for power.

For the interpretation of the other divine book, on the other hand, a truly intrinsic method was necessary and prescribed. As soon as nature became more than just an illustration for the now ambiguous Word of God, the principle of infallibility—that is of a totally consistent, perfect creation—led to certain inferences, which may confidently be called the foundations of science. In the "Book of Nature" God did not speak directly, but rather exclusively through metaphors of the sensory world. Here, therefore, there could be no assertions which derived their ultimate interpretative authority from a specific institution. It also no longer sufficed to explain individual phenomena as edifying annotations to God's Word. Interpretation now meant proof of a necessary connection and harmony with other phenomena—i.e., the recognition of ever more general laws.

The idea that such laws existed and that mankind could and would discover them—that, to be sure, remained the underlying postulate, without which the whole interpretive enterprise would have been meaningless. Every "law," however, was simply an *attempt* at interpretation—a hypothesis; it had to be verified by proving that apparent discrepancies were consistent after all, and that apparently disparate elements were in fact somehow related and interdependent. An observed discrepancy meant neither an irregularity in creation nor an invitation to turn to authority; it meant a contradiction between an hypothesis and an observable phenomenon. Every hypothesis, then, was subject to the jurisdiction of phenomena. A law in the scientific sense could never be a "prescription" which the phenomena had to "obey"; it could only—more or less adequately—make clear their necessity. Naturally it took a long time before the concept of a law of nature was able to shed the prescriptive character, which in nonscientific language continued to live on. Thus, planets continued to follow their "prescribed" orbits and stones continued to "obey" the law of falling bodies. As long as God was still considered the actual lawgiver, even of natural laws, there was no reason to change such expressions. But the crucial point was that a law, as perceived by man, in the absence of any direct divine pronouncement, could never be anything but a human formulation of a divine meaning; it was a hypothesis which continually had to justify itself in the face of phenomena.

Because it was unthinkable that there should be discrepancies in the design of creation, apparent discrepancies became the most essential element of scientific discovery; stumblingblocks, one might say, were turned into cornerstones. Man has an apparently incurable penchant for wanting to dictate to God what He ought to prescribe for both nature and man. This transpires, to be sure, in the most pious and respectful way—perhaps somewhat as follows: "It is irreconcilable with our image of God's perfection that the orbits of the planets should be other than circular, for the circle is the perfect figure." Our thinking is suffused with such oftentimes hidden assumptions, and it is one of the chief tasks of research to bring these assumptions out into the open in order to test their validity. To do this, "discrepancies"—and with them the postulate of infallibility (of the Creation, not the interpretation)—are indispensable. These two elements, in fact, are so indispensable, that one could almost believe that the Creator, foreseeing human fallibility as well as the conditions of human comprehension, deliberately built them into His creation. It is the "discrepancies" which compel us to account in precise detail for the prescriptions which we all too readily want to make for creation.

A second probably incurable human weakness is mental laziness. Instead of transforming stumbling-blocks into cornerstones, we are tempted to dispose of them by means of an explanation invented solely for this purpose. In order to obviate this weakness, science has subordinated itself to the "principle of economy," which requires that one must economize not with mental effort but with hypotheses. One hypothesis is not only better than two, it is also necessarily truer, according to the principle of infallibility in creation. Otherwise, the interpreter would be free to introduce a new hypothesis for every discrepancy that threatens a faltering hypothesis.

Certainly not the least important reason for the amazing development of the sciences is that they have been able to satisfy the material needs of mankind. Still, it seems clear that a method appropriate to its subject—i.e., an interpretive method—was the *sine qua non* of this progress. And this interpretive method was intrinsic in that it was entirely subservient to the phenomena and at the same time entirely faithful to the belief in their utter lawfulness and consistency. It may be that Einstein was the last great proponent of this belief, the last great representative of classical science, and that now science sees itself compelled to give up the classical principles of interpretation. Be that as it may, no scientist would think of suggesting that it might have been better never to have honored the classical faith at all. Such a suggestion would be absurd, for it is the knowledge achieved through the classical faith which ultimately led to the necessity of questioning the faith.

The scientist has the right—indeed the duty—to point out the inadequacy of the classical method in cases in which it no longer does justice to phenomena. This, however, does not give other interpreters the right to quote such criticism in a gloating way, as though relieved that the weaknesses in their own methods are now justified. The often quoted uncertainty principle, although valid for physics (at least in part), is—as far as we can foresee—not valid for the interpretation of other kinds of "books." The all-too-apparent "uncertainty" in literary interpretation is up to now of a totally different kind than Heisenberg's; it is quite simply uncertainty *tout court*; for interpreters, despite endless debates, are still unclear about the actual foundations of their method. Before we can proclaim uncertainty as a principle, we must first try to reach the limits of that which is certain. Yet we are so far from having reached these limits that, for the time being, all talk of uncertainty must be regarded simply as a lazy way out. For the physicist the classical age may be obsolete; for the literary critic it has barely begun.

II

"Intrinsicality" is even now less a term descriptive of an interpretative method than a banner-cry in literary battles. As in all battles, one states one's case not on its own grounds, but in terms of one's opponent's position. The proponents of intrinsic interpretation point with arrogance to the worst outgrowths of positivism, while their opponents dwell on the most sterile examples of otiose and minute "structural analysis." Each is less than modest in his claims for his own method; the duties and limitations imposed by the method he is less eager to face.

It is not my primary concern here to break a lance

for intrinsic interpretation, but rather to bring into relief its underlying assumptions. It would be pointless to praise one method—whatever it may be—as unconditionally correct. Methods always—and of necessity—have conditions, not only because of their objects but even more because of the postulates on which they are ultimately based. A method is not conditioned, however, by the incompetence of those who use it. Naturally, as in every human undertaking, incompetence is a limiting factor, but it cannot be called an error inherent in the method. Any method aims to exclude, insofar as possible, the sources of error of human perception and interpretation. Yet human frailty, far from disqualifying the method, is its very *raison d'être.*

One can, of course, reject any and all methods for interpreting a particular kind of object. In literary criticism one then speaks of empathy, of the unteachable "art" of hearing the "voice" of the poem, or of direct comprehension and similar talents that resist the straitjacket of any particular method. This is the pure "protestantism" of interpretation—the claim that, through godly grace and immediate infusion, one has grasped the true meaning of the creator and that no further interpretive effort is needed. Let us call the proponents of this view the "pietists," and let us hold them in respect. In fact, let us be clear that such "pietism" represents the basis of all literary scholarship. A person who has never felt himself directly addressed by a piece of creative writing should not undertake the interpretation of such writing. He who regards poems only as objects to be "processed" according to one or another method should admit to himself that the processing of leather into shoes is more useful to mankind than the processing of poems into interpretations. The fact that the profusion of scholarly journals would be reduced to a fraction of their present number would be a most welcome consequence.

At the same time, however, we must realize that, as pietists, we all have the same rights; for the poem's message to me is verified simply by the fact that it has spoken to me. Thus, I may go and found my little church with exactly the same authority as everyone else. If I am eloquent enough, I may succeed in gathering around me a congregation; if not, then I will pray in my closet or under the open skies. What I cannot claim, however, is any official authority. I should like to suggest that one who tries to speak *ex officio* about literature has the right to be a pure pietist. Official position places one under the obligation of speaking with general validity—i.e., in such a way that one's statements are meaningful not only for oneself, but for others as well. This, of course, does not mean that the position itself guarantees this validity, nor that on the strength of one's office (read "professorship") one automatically becomes literary pope. On the contrary, one must continually show his credentials via the object, via the "holy writ" of the poet. It means that one must render an account about the way in which he interprets the "Word." Public office demands a method.

I have tried to show that the method of intrinsic interpretation rests on two axioms: infallibility and economy. This does not mean that I proclaim the infallibility of a given poem as an objective fact, but rather that I subjectively recognize it as an *obligatio*n binding for me and my method. The poet may "in fact" have made some mistakes, but *I* can never defend inconsistencies between the poem and my interpretation of it on the basis of such mistakes. Inconsistencies between poem and interpretation call into question the interpretation, not the poem. If, despite honest effort, I am unable to attain an interpretation that completely "fits," then I must simply say, "I have progressed to this point, but I can go no further."

The concept of "poetic mistake" is not a simple one, and a competent literary critic will seldom be satisfied with blaming the poet for the mistake. Instead, he will try to "explain" the mistake, possibly on the basis of another law outside that of the poem itself. Such, for example, is the law of genetic history. If we know that a poem has undergone distinct stages of development, we like to believe that we can recognize the eggshells clinging to the final form. If we know of no earlier version of the poem, we construct a "development" for the poet, making conjectures as to the poem's earlier form on the basis of what the poet thought or experienced at the probable time of its inception. Moreover, there is the always readily available "Zeitgeist," to which poets—like other mortals—are subject, and which may dictate things to his pen which are difficult or impossible to reconcile with other things in his writings. Or again, the critic may rely on intellectual history, on influences, on psychological complexes or socio-economic circumstances. All of these, it is argued, may guide the poet's pen, according to laws to which he is subconsciously and irremediably subjected, which we, however, because of our superior historical and psychological hindsight can recognize. And in case all of this does not suffice, one can add mistakes in the sense that poets are forgetful, that they must somehow end the poem, or make concessions to public taste, or that they were unaware of something which they should have known. The explanations available for inconsistencies in a poem are endless.

The intrinsic method maintains neither that such explanations are necessarily false, nor that there is no such thing as a poetic mistake; it does maintain that as soon as such explanations enter the picture, interpretation in its true sense—which must regard the poem as an ordered whole—*has stopped.* Whoever explains apparent inconsistencies through laws which are not derived from the poem itself thereby indicates that he considers interpretation beyond this point impossible. Or more correctly, that is what he should say! Unfortunately, however, he is usually unaware of the fact that he is now beginning to write a prescription for the poem. The rules to which he subordinates it seem so obvious and sensible to him that he considers them as given, indeed as fact, without in the least suspecting that he may be tyrannizing over the poem.

Let us be clear about the fact that this type of "explanation" of apparent inconsistencies in a poem does not differ in principle from its "condemnation," from the kind of judgments passed by eighteenth-century critics who proceeded according to "classical" principles. There is little difference between Gottsched's or Voltaire's damnation of Shakespeare and what the highly enlightened critic of today does when he explains a difficult scene in *Tasso* by stating that it must derive from an earlier version of the work. Whether the law which is being cited comes from Aristotle or from another source is of little relevance; the important thing is that it is extrinsic to the poem. For as soon as something is explained according to laws outside itself, it is no longer being interpreted.

Stated differently: the actual object of a genetic interpretation of *Tasso* is no longer *Tasso,* but something else —probably Goethe himself. Now there is not the least objection to Goethe as an object of interpretation—quite the contrary! But there are two things we must not forget: first, that Goethe is a very much more complex and difficult object of interpretation than *Tasso* (which God knows is difficult enough); and, secondly, that it seems hardly permissible to assume a clear understanding of the object "Goethe" as a prerequisite for a discussion of the object *Tasso*. Whoever can claim to have grasped the law according to which Goethe proceeded may well produce this law in explanation of *Tasso*. I doubt, however, that there can be such a person, at least as long as *Tasso* still remains uninterpreted. Whoever wants to construct an *Ur-Tasso* in order to explain inconsistencies in *Tasso* must first be asked to demonstrate validly the law of Goethe's development.

Goethe thought of human beings as *entelechies*, i.e., as beings who obey an internal law. Thus with the generosity of a great man, he attributed to all mankind a characteristic which I believe belongs only to a few, namely the characteristics of inherent lawfulness and autonomy—that is, of interpretability. An interpreter of Goethe must take the poem "Urworte. Orphisch" quite seriously. Goethe seems to me theoretically interpretable; ordinary mortals only "explainable"—that is, their actions and words are understandable according to the general laws of psychology or according to the physiological or social conditions of their existence. Goethe, on the other hand, creates the impression of an autonomous man. One might say that the interpretability of a human being is in direct proportion to his "greatness," to his degree of autonomy. It seems to me that the Goethean concept of the "daemonic" refers specifically to this kind of greatness. In this sense, the "daemonic" is by no means uninterpretable, on the contrary, it is unexplainable, and thereby truly interpretable. For only that which carries its law in itself is fully interpretable. Seen in this light, only the physical universe, a few great human beings, and *some* works of literature are interpretable. Most of what confronts us—including most works of literature—is at best explainable.

It is a fundamental principle of explanation that established knowledge must be used to explain that which is not yet established. Thus the laws which are cited in the explanation of a poem ought to have greater certainty than the law, i.e., the meaning, of the poem itself. This principle clearly gives interpretation priority over explanation. For the laws lying outside the poem—whether they be psychological, sociological, or intellectual—are very much more uncertain than the laws of the poem itself. This must be so because they derive from a much less determinable universe than the poem is. Even as relatively limited a universe as "Goethe"—not to mention "history," "psychology," or "social conditions"—is much less determinable than let us say *Tasso*. When in the course of an explanation one introduces "Goethe," one is not introducing a fact, but an hypothesis—and a very daring hypothesis at that. Without justification, indeed without plausibility, one assumes that the law of "Goethe" is already known and may be used at any time for purposes of explanation. The opposite is much closer to the truth: if we knew the intrinsic laws of all of Goethe's poems (in chronological order), then perhaps we could discover the law of Goethe.

I am aware that I have equated interpretation with the intrinsic method, so that "intrinsic interpretation" is a tautology. I think that the study of literature would be well served if the term "interpretation" were always to be used in this sense and thus sharply differentiated from "explanation." Interpretation, then, would mean the attempt to know the law of a poem *solely from the poem itself*, on the necessary assumption of the infallibility of the poem. Explanation, on the other hand, would mean the attempt to demonstrate how parts of a poem obey an already known, established principle. (The latter could conceivably be the intrinsic law of the work itself, after it had been clearly established.) This kind of terminology, it seems to me, could contribute substantially towards making us aware of our *duties* as interpreters or "explainers."

III

Many literary scholars have declared intrinsic interpretation to be in principle impossible. As a "method" it is a deception that opens the doors to ignorance and mindless speculation. Their basic objection may be formulated as follows: since poems are works of language, and since language by its very nature must address itself to our (historically shaped and limited) understanding, a poem cannot possibly be interpreted simply out of itself. Instead, it is the task of the serious interpreter to increase his historical knowledge to the point of understanding what the "words" (taken in the broadest sense) must have meant in their historical setting. He ought to be in a position to recognize *topoi,* to take into consideration historical literary conventions, to point out contemporaneous allusions, and to understand the ideas and concepts of the poem in their original historical form. A poem, it is maintained, if not a biographical object, is certainly a cultural-historical object, which in order to be interpreted, must be understood within its intellectual-historical context.

These objections rest on a basic misunderstanding of what takes place in a true interpretation. (It must be granted that the blame for the misunderstanding does not lie solely with the opponents of the method; its proponents have often fostered it.) Again, the natural sciences offer an illuminating analogy. Scientific interpretation does not begin from a *tabula rasa*, from a naked assumptionless will to knowledge; on the contrary, it begins with a human being, who both as an individual and as a child of his time has already formed a very specific mental picture of the world. One need only recall Kepler's state of perplexity in order to see how difficult it is even for an extraordinary mind to free itself of its inbred concepts. What takes place in natural science is a continuous, often tedious correcting of such concepts on the basis of observable phenomena and according to the axioms of infallibility and economy.

The reader of a poem quite naturally forms some kind of "impression" as to the meaning of the poem. The deeper his historical knowledge, the richer and more differentiated this impression will be. Let us say that the uneducated reader of a Baroque poem is like a person who, relying solely on his senses, is convinced that the sun revolves around the earth; the educated person, on the other hand, is someone who has already acquired the Copernican world view as part of his mental set. It would be pointless—indeed impossible—to try to eliminate such knowledge from one's mind. Thus, if I have read Curtius, an inseparable part of my perceptive capacities will be to recognize certain *topoi*; they will, so to speak, have become part of my vocabulary.

Now if interpretation involved nothing other than a more or less complete gloss on a given poem, then little would be needed beyond an abundant vocabulary. A gloss is based on the assumption that the reader will be able to understand the poem as soon as its "words" (again taken in the broadest sense) have been explained to him. And, indeed, for many poems glossing is quite sufficient; they do not need interpretation, for (given an understanding of their vocabulary) they are easy to grasp.

Interpretation becomes necessary and should be used only when, for some reason, such immediate comprehension does not suffice. I would find unnecessary an interpretation of "*Ich bin din, du bist min*" (of course I could be mistaken about this), although a glossary for the medieval *topos* "key" would be very valuable. It is equally clear, however, that for Hölderlin's *Der Rhein,* not even the most complete gloss would begin to touch on the essential elements of this poem; here one needs interpretation.

The two cases chosen above are extreme. It is not always easy to say whether or not a poem needs interpretation. The decision as to whether interpretation is necessary depends on the reader and sometimes even on a particular moment of reading. (I may read a poem ten times without realizing that there is "more to it," that it obeys laws other than the obvious ones, but at the eleventh reading suddenly something "bothers me.") The decision as to *how* to interpret, however, does not depend on the reader, but rather is prescribed by the nature of interpretation and of the particular poem.

In order fully to understand intrinsic interpretation, however, we must clear up two sources of misunderstanding. For much which goes under the banner of this method is little more than a demonstration of those technical tricks and stratagems by virtue of which a poetic work of art may be distinguished from a simple declarative statement. Rhythmetic analysis and the tracing of imagery, sound structure, and symbolic themes are not *as such* interpretation. If the critic limits himself to demonstrating the appropriateness of vocabulary and imagery to the thought and emotional content of the poem, he has not yet identified what we have been calling the inner law of this particular poem, although his efforts may naturally contribute to its discovery.

Another misconception about interpretation is that it involves viewing a poem from a specific "approach"—the psychoanalytic, the Marxist, the Christian approach, to cite but a few. A poem may, of course, like other things be cited as "evidence" for such approaches; in fact, it is not impossible that something might be gained for purposes of interpretation from such a reading of the poem. It is equally true that every reader of a poem reads it from *some* point of view, though it may be neither conscious enough nor well enough defined to have a name. Nothing should stop a Marxist from being an interpreter, provided he is willing, while interpreting, to call his Marxism into question. This goes for all viewpoints, particularly the unarticulated ones. Viewpoints are as hard to shed as is knowledge, but they can be corrected. They are a necessary part of our initial comprehension of the poem, of the world view which—at least at the outset—we wish to find corroborated in the poem. Interpretation, where appropriate, will very likely lead to a correction of this world view.

What occurs, then, when I really do interpret? Something which in principle is very simple. I read a poem and the poem "speaks to me." At the same time, however, or perhaps only after several readings, I get the impression that I have not yet grasped its true significance. Something "disturbs" me. What it is that will "disturb" me is never predictable. It may be a "discrepancy" (a contradiction, sometimes purely factual, which seems to reside in the poem itself); it may be an apparent whim of the poet or a seemingly inappropriate word; it may be a configuration whose meaning is obscure; or it may be (as with Hölderlin's late hymns) that the coherence of the whole completely escapes me. Finally, any conception of the poem which contradicts my own may also disturb me in this sense.

I begin to interpret when I tell myself that the "disturbing element" arises from a discrepancy between my conception and *the poem itself*; it begins when I recognize that this conception is an initial and possibly subconscious *hypothesis*, which must be revised in accordance with the text of the poem. (Any understanding of any statement, even in daily life, is in principle only a hypothesis, except that in most cases immediate confirmation makes both explanation and interpretation unnecessary.) The revision of one's hypothesis must proceed in such a way that the disturbing element is finally proved both reasonable and *necessary*—i.e., the new hypothesis must account for the previously disturbing element.

But naturally not *merely* the disturbing element. At this point the principle of economy—that most abused of all principles of interpretation—comes into the picture. Let us once again use an analogy from the natural sciences. The Copernican hypothesis or interpretation of the solar system represented a significant advance over the Ptolemaic. Nevertheless, in order to preserve the earlier notion of circular planetary orbits, it was necessary to set up all kinds of supporting hypotheses which could be used to "explain" the discrepancies between the main hypothesis and observable phenomena. The magnificent discovery by Kepler was a new hypothesis, which made the supporting hypotheses superfluous, and thus pressed through to a totally new law of the system. There is nothing easier than to create a supporting structure for an interpretation. The more all-inclusive one's attempt at interpretation and the smaller the discrepancy, the greater the temptation to explain away the discrepancy. As we have noted, there is never a dearth of such explanations, and one or the other always seems plausible. Nevertheless—or perhaps for this very reason

—they obstruct the path to a better law, much of Copernicus' epicycles for a long time obstructed the way to Kepler's law.

One might object that the method here recommended invites the most uncontrolled speculation, because one simply cannot assume that every "disturbance" encountered by the reader will have some significance. In the first place, it could be that the poet really did make a mistake and yet the interpreter would have to invent some kind of hypothesis that had no real basis. Worse still: *one* reader (in particular an untrained one) could easily be "disturbed" by something which appears completely natural and reasonable to a more highly trained reader. In this way, the wildest of hypotheses might be set up in order to interpret quite imaginary discrepancies. Two points may be made in reply: first, *no* method guarantees correct results; at best it reduces the sources of error. Thus one ought to ask not whether the intrinsic method harbors risks (for we know it does), but rather whether these risks are greater or smaller than those of other possible methods. I am convinced that they are smaller, because (and this leads to our second answer), under the principle of economy, a misleading hypothesis will be quickly revealed as such. Let us assume, for example, that a reader is disturbed by a certain word in a Baroque poem because the word has changed its meaning since the seventeenth century. If instead of consulting Grimm's *Wörterbuch,* he revives his interpretation of the poem *as a whole* in order to do justice to the word which he has misunderstood, then numerous other discrepancies which had not previously existed will with high probability, indeed almost with certainty, begin to appear. The new interpretation, therefore, achieves exactly the opposite of what it was supposed to achieve. If the interpreter does not abandon this particular interpretation, burdened down as it is with discrepancies, then instead of having to construct only one supporting hypothesis (to explain the "disturbing" word), he will have to construct several. (The fact that there are critics who are willing to do this says nothing against the method. No method can compete with an *idée fixe.*)

Let us consider the opposite case: a reader is "disturbed" by a certain word, but knows enough to look it up in Grimm immediately. Here he finds the historically correct meaning, which fits naturally and "undisturbingly" into the system of the poem. Does this prove that he ought not to have felt "disturbed" in the first place? Not at all! It is very possible that the poet intended an ambiguity (as, for example, Shakespeare often did), which is of great importance to the meaning of the whole.

Since the systematic interpreter has usually had scholarly training, the preceding example was probably too simple, and thus not very plausible. The following case will seem more plausible. The reader is disturbed by a seemingly capricious and rather farfetched literary conceit. He thereupon consults his Curtius or a book on Mannerism and discovers that this conceit has been traced back to Petrarch and was also frequently used in the sixteenth century, so that it may be regarded as a *topos*. Presto, the disturbance has been removed! In this case, the danger of misinterpretation seems to me greater than if the reader—unaware that this particular conceit is a *topos*—had regarded it as something invented by the poet specifically for this poem, and then had proceeded to interpret the poem accordingly. In the ideal situation, of course, the reader will be aware of the fact that he is dealing with a *topos*, but will *nevertheless* regard it as significant for the poem and crucial for interpretation. For the choice of a particular conceit, or perhaps the form in which the poet presents it, may be more decisive for the meaning of the whole than the fact that it was also used by other writers.

Yet even this is a largely lexical and hence relatively simple case. It would be easy to climb further up on the scale of complexity (perhaps to the level of consulting source material) and to show how at each step the risk of misinterpretation is shifted more and more to the area of extrinsic interpretation—or rather explanation. The fact is that by means of explanation the "disturbing" elements are indeed removed, but under the assumption that the poet used them without special attention to them, that the thing is quite "natural" etc. This means that the initial interpretation can be more or less unquestioningly accepted, making it unlikely that it can ever be thrown open to question by the poem itself. Worse still: a potentially erroneous explanation (explanations, like interpretations, can be erroneous) is not easily detected as being erroneous, since it refers to only part of the poem, and is of no necessary consequence to the whole. If, for example, I try to attribute a discrepancy to the "forgetfulness" of the poet, then it is unlikely that this explanation will be proved false, for it certainly does not create more discrepancies than it removes. If on the other hand, I try to *interpret* the discrepancy (if, i.e., according to the principle of infallibility, I revise my initial interpretation in such a way that the discrepancy is proved meaningful), then a misguided attempt will have necessary consequences which will reveal that the attempt is misguided.

IV

It is high time that we demonstrate with an actual poem how interpretation actually proceeds. The poem will have to be an unusually simple one, since the interpretation of a complicated work would be too lengthy. The case will therefore not be quite typical; because of its simplicity, the poem will just barely require interpretation. Nevertheless, I hope in what follows to be able to demonstrate the principles of interpretation.

Let us summarize these principles briefly:

(1) Interpretation assumes that its object is an ordered, autonomous whole—a cosmos.

(2) Interpretation focusses on the law which governs this cosmos, on the assumption that this law comes closest to the "meaning" of the creator.

(3) Interpretation is subject to the principles of infallibility and economy.

(4) Interpretation is limited to those poems whose meaning or law is for some reason not directly manifest.

(5) Interpretation is especially concerned with "disturbing" elements in the poem—that is, with elements, which seem to contradict the most satisfactory available hypothesis. For only thereby can the interpreter approach the ideal of a complete interpretation.

(6) A complete interpretation means the comprehension of *the* law which accounts for the necessary existence of every "word" in the poem.

As my example I have chosen Mörike's *September-Morgen*:[2]

Im Nebel ruhet noch die Welt,
Noch träumen Wald und Wiesen:

[2] *September Morning*: "The world is still at rest in the mist; woods and meadows are still dreaming. Soon, when the veil falls, you will see the blue sky unconcealed, the quietened world in its autumnal vigor, awash in warm gold." (*The Penguin Book of German Verse*, ed. Leonard-Foster, p. 351.)

Bald siehst du, wenn der Schleier fällt,
Den blauen Himmel unverstellt,
Herbstkräftig die gedämpfte Welt
In warmem Golde fliessen.

The single most "disturbing" element in this poem—both visually and audially—is the word "*herbstkräftig.*" It seems to have been invented by Mörike solely in order to assemble the large number of consonants r b s t k r. This array of consonants and the rhythm of the word itself makes "*herbstkräftig*" stand out sharply, almost explosively, from the soft lyrical progression of the poem. It is a kind of raw trumpet blast, which suddenly interrupts flowing, dreamy flute tones. Now, it would be easy to explain the word as "appropriate": Mörike no longer wishes to depict autumn as calm and full of presentiment, but wants instead to express its rough, sharply defined character. But having been already "disturbed," I shall let myself be further disturbed—this time by the rhyming word "*Welt*" at the end of the same line. It is worth noting that Mörike here repeats the rhyming word of the first line of the poem, rather than varying it in some appropriate way. One might almost believe that at first he had written "*das gedämpfte Feld,*" only to change it to "*Welt*" rather arbitrarily and in violation of one of the elementary rules of prosody. And here, I should like to maintain, we are faced with a real problem and we may now inquire as to which law inherent in the poem forced the poet to "disturb" us and the rules of prosody in this way?

We are confronted, so it seems, with an identity problem. For, if identical rhymes are prohibited, in what sense is the "*Welt*" of the first line *not* identical with that of the fifth? Or, stated generally, wherein lies the nonidentity of true rhyme? What, in fact, is rhyme?

Since we know that it is a principle of order, what kind of order does it signify? What kind of cosmos are we dealing with, which is—at best in part—governed by the rules of rhyme?

Naturally these questions cannot be answered either from themselves or from the disturbing elements; instead they lead us into the poem. (And if the poem remains silent about these questions, then it is very likely that the questions are incorrectly posed.) The poem answers with the word "*unverstellt,*" with another unexpected ambiguity. Concretely it means that the morning fog no longer veils or obstructs the view towards the sky; at the same time it means that the sky is unmoved, i.e., remains in the same place; and finally it means that the sky discloses itself with great openness and does not hide behind some deceptive garb. The poem, then, would be an unveiling process—in which the new thing we uncover shows itself to be identical with the thing we began with.

The word "*unverstellt*" has now been added to the list of disturbing elements. What would result, if we were to eliminate all the disturbing elements in the poem thus far identified, so that we might read it in an undisturbed way?

> Im Nebel ruhet noch die Welt,
> Noch träumen Wald und Wiesen:
> Bald siehst du, wenn der Schleier fällt,
> den blauen Himmel—und das Feld
> In warmem Golde fliessen.

Now, in a somewhat banal, late romantic way, this is quite pretty. There is only one thing that mars it: the rhyme *fällt* and *Feld*. But why does this mar it? (In a French poem, it would not.) Again we are confronted by a problem of rhyme: the words do not rhyme because they rhyme too completely! Have we hereby grasped the very essence of rhyme (at least of German-English rhyme)? Is not rhyme a principle of order, which, to be complete, must allow room for incompleteness? Does not rhyme protect us from total, completely tautological and therefore meaningless identity in exposing us to an imperfect echo? And does it not at the same time protect us from the completely coincidental and therefore meaningless similarity of a homonym such as *fällt/Feld*?

Since *fällt/Feld* cannot be used, let us try substituting the following:

> Bald siehst du, wenn der Schleier fällt,
> Die Erde unter blauem Zelt (or: unterm
> Himmelzelt)
> In warmem Golde fliessen.

The problem with this version is that it leaves us disturbed in precisely the wrong way. It meanders along effortlessly and then just when a rhyming word is needed, "*Himmelszelt*" happens to appear. All of this is very homey, somewhat in the sense of "Weisst du, wieviel Sternlein stehen/An dem blauen Himmelszelt." In this nursery world there are simple, reassuring answers to all questions. Thus, we read, "Gott der Herr hat sie gezählet/Dass ihm auch nicht eines fehlet." Everything rhymes beautifully, and each word has a prompt and harmonious counterpart. We must simply, in childlike manner, place our trust in God—or in the poet—for he will surely make it all come out all right.

The resulting peace of mind has its price, but this we barely notice. The fact that after the veil ("*Schleier*") has fallen, the heavenly canopy ("*Zelt*") is still there, does slightly disturb the metaphorical logic, but it makes for a reassuring state of affairs. It means that we still have a roof over our heads—a lovely blue one at that, dotted with stars, created and cared for by God himself—under which to dream wonderful dreams. In this way, the rhyme lulls us through "disturbances" which are of its own making. In order to remain tranquil, we need something with *-elt*. "*Welt*" won't do, nor "*Feld*," but "*Zelt*" can get by; it even fits quite nicely. The "rhyming-urge" has been satisfied, and who is really going to notice a slight metaphorical discrepancy?

I do not for a moment wish to assert that these thoughts even so much as crossed Mörike's mind, nor that he ever considered the alternate versions of the poem which we have suggested above. But at this stage of the interpretive process—when one is constructing hypotheses—there is no limit to speculation. The question then remains: how did Mörike arrive at his extraordinary fifth line, why does he use the end-rhyme "*Welt*" twice, and why the ambiguous word "*unverstellt*"? One thing that seems certain is that the poet wanted to arouse us out of our dreams of a childlike, springtime world in which things are always orderly, unambiguous, and neatly rhymed.

But all this raises the question: what, after all, is completeness and orderliness? A rhyme strives for complete identity and thus ought to be complete to the degree to which it achieves this identity. However, since such completeness, even if it were attainable, would not really be so very satisfying, we set up a rule: a rhyme, in order to be perfect, must fall just short of being really perfect. As soon as the paradoxical rule is put into practice, it no longer seems a paradox but something natural; our desire for completeness has been fulfilled by a *rule*. It is the ethic of the nursery, from which we are never quite free, that perfection means adherence to rules. This is the veil, the heavenly canopy of order under which we continue to dream undisturbed.

The veil however, does fall, and must fall if we are ever to see the heavens and the earth "*unverstellt*"—in an unobstructed way. To be more specific, the poem itself tears down the veil. The first tug is the ambiguous word "*unverstellt,*" the second, the harsh "*herbstkräftig*" and, the third and last, the rule-defying use of the word "*Welt.*" I have characterized the poem as an unveiling process, and like all genuine poems it enacts what it describes. Here again we come upon a type of identity, but a strange one; for the enactment of what is being described can hardly be called tautologous. It is the *creation* of an order, of which to be sure there had been some premonition, but which was not yet at hand. A poem is not true simply because it accurately describes some external, independent truth. Similarly, it is not perfect simply because it obeys some external rules. It must *create* its own truth and *establish* its own order. It must do justice to the truth, to the law hidden within itself, and must bring it to fruition and completion. A true poem is something "daemonic"—i.e., something interpretable; it obeys itself.

Now, however, we are confronted with a very pressing question, namely, "What does all this have to do with autumn, with woods, fields and the blue sky?" Does our interpretation discover a law which barely touches on the actual contents of the poem? Interpretation must not fail us at this point, and I do not believe that mine does. *September-Morgen* is a poem about a season, it is a fall poem. The first four lines, however, are not at all specifically autumnal. The veiled world is depicted with the kind of romantic lyricism which can just as well be found in a commonplace pastoral poem about spring.

It has the charm of the potential, but also its vagueness—the soft imprecision of the childlike. At the same time, however, it is somewhat imitative. I would almost lay a wager that if someone were to hear only the first four lines of the poem (excluding "*unverstellt*"), he might well identify it as third-rate Eichendorff. This is no longer true spring, it is a copy of spring. Nothing happens here except that the prerequisites of the morning song are dutifully met. It is this veiled world which is torn asunder by the word "*herbstkräftig*" and the new world is therefore no longer imitative, because it recognizes itself for what it really is—an autumnal world. It discovers its own harsh beauty, which consists of greater clarity of vision, increased distinctness of lines and sounds, and a more masculine self-assured rhythm. (Since Mörike was a Swabian, I dare not put much weight on the progressive sharpening of the rhyme "*Wiesen*"—"*fliessen.*")

A difficult word, however, has remained uninterpreted —"*gedämpft.*" I will leave it uninterpreted for the simple reason that I see no easy way of fitting it into the law which has been set up. A supporting hypothesis could easily be found. What is needed here, however, is not an "explanation" but a *confirmation.* One ought to be able to prove the necessity of "*gedämpft,*" and although it is possible that this word might be in accord with my "unveiling" law after all, I am still unclear as to how this would be the case. Thus, my interpretation has been shown to be provisional—at best incomplete, at worst in need of revision. This much is certain, however, a more correct interpretation will not be able to ignore my own—or rather, the disturbing elements from which my interpretation set out.

I am going to end my methodical excursus with this question mark, for I do wish it to be considered simply an excursus. A method is justified only by its results; it can be proved only by its fruits. The starting point for all interpretation is piety and the best method is the one which most favors it. If I consider the intrinsic method to be the best, this is not because it seems more "scientific" than others, nor because I wish to play the natural scientist. I find science appealing not because it has made possible the atomic bomb, but because it has discovered and recognized some principles of method according to which the interpreter of the "Book of Nature" must subordinate himself to the words of this book, i.e., to phenomena. It is only because such subordination seems to me to be an indispensable prerequisite to all true interpretation that I give preference to the (rightly understood) intrinsic method. After having defended this conviction in what I hope was a "*herbstkräftig*" way, I am now reminded that I must stop sharpening my methodical scythe and return (*gedämpft*) to my actual work: the task of harvesting.

INDEX